With the Compliments
of

[signature]

IN DEFENSE OF THE
UKRAINIAN CAUSE

Books by Roman Rakhmanny

The UPA in Western Europe (1949)
Blood and Ink (1950)
Along the 50th Parallel (1969)
Not by Word Alone (1971)
Fire and Cinders (1974)
Conversations With the Young (1978)
In Defense of the Ukrainian Cause (1979)

IN DEFENSE OF THE UKRAINIAN CAUSE

By

ROMAN RAKHMANNY

Edited by Stephen D. Olynyk

Foreword by John Richmond

THE CHRISTOPHER PUBLISHING HOUSE
NORTH QUINCY, MASSACHUSETTS

*To all the men and women
who have sacrificed their personal liberty and life
in defense of the Ukrainian cause*

FOREWORD

Time present is contained in time past.

Where injustice occurs it is necessary to know not only the nature of the injustices themselves but their genesis. The author of this volume, concerned with the present and its future reverberations, has analyzed the more significant (and little known) aspects of the Ukrainian situation. He has done so not from a parochial point of view but rather as an object lesson. An English poet, Blake, has said that infinity is contained in a grain of sand.

To many the Ukraine, the systematic destruction of its culture, may appear a matter of little moment. But the planned death of a particular way of life, enriched by its past, valid as to its present, and condemned by those who can rein only over areas where the bulldozer has done its work is of consequence to us all. In a world increasingly smoothed out so that it can be controlled by those for whom human nature exists only that it may be conditioned according to non-human specifications, the fate of the Ukraine is an element of vital concern.

It is a microcosm of what the future may hold in store for all who wish to retain their identity as part and parcel of a life lived with a heart and not a mechanical appliance. Death is the great leveller. It is essential that life does not share its same status.

John Richmond,
The Literary Editor
of *The Montreal Star**

*This foreword was written by John Richmond shortly before his death in 1977.

PREFACE

In Defense of the Ukrainian Cause is a collection of political
commentaries and essays by Roman Rakhmanny on the contemporary aspects of the Ukrainian situation. The majority of the
pieces in this collection are recent, those of earlier years having
current relevance for they reflect Roman Rakhmanny's personal
insight and understanding of the problems of the Ukrainian liberation movement in which he was intimately involved both as
an objective journalist and political activist.

Many of Roman Rakhmanny's writings have appeared in
Ukrainian publications, others have also been published in
major newspapers and journals of Western Europe and North
America in a number of languages, among them Dutch, English, French, German, Norwegian. The more pointed of these
contributions have been selected for republication here to making them available in one volume to English speaking readers.

This collection is divided into seven parts within which the articles are arranged chronologically. Brief annotations are provided where it was considered appropriate.

The transliteration from the Cyrillic is based on the Library of
Congress system with some hopefully useful modifications. Some
names of persons and places have been retained in their common
English form. In a few cases the titles of articles (originally in
newspaper headline form) have been modified to suit the book's
format.

Grateful acknowledgement for permission to reprint articles is
made to the following: *The Baltic Review* (Stockholm); *The Brant-*

ford Expositor (Brantford, Ontario); *The Commentator* (Toronto); *The Czechoslovak Society of Arts and Sciences in America* (Washington, D.C.); *The Edmonton Journal; The Gazette* (Montreal); *The Globe and Mail* (Toronto); *International Journal* (Toronto); *The London Free Press* (London, Ontario); *Military Review* (Fort Leavenworth, Kansas); *The Montreal Star; The Mouton Publishers* (The Hague); *The Ottawa Citizen; The Ottawa Journal; The Province* (Vancouver, B.C.); *Saturday Night* (Toronto); *The Southam News Services* (Ottawa); *The Telegram* (Toronto); *Die Weltwoche* (Zürich); *The Windsor Star; The Winnipeg Free Press; The Winnipeg Tribune; World Digest* (London).

Washington, D.C.   S. D. Olynyk
April 1979

CONTENTS

PART I

INSURGENCY IN THE UKRAINE

EDITOR'S NOTE

UPA? What do the initials stand for?

During the Second World War resistance movements in Eastern and Southern Europe were in the main communist and anticommunist or nationalist. In the Ukraine these forms of resistance existed side by side, and, on occasions, against each other. The communist "partisan" movement was strongly supported by the Red Army.

The noncommunist Ukrainian nationalist resistance, represented by the Ukrainian Insurgent Army (UPA), fought against both the Nazi and Soviet rule in the Ukraine in pursuit of the goal of national liberation and the establishment of a Ukrainian independent national state.

Unlike other resistance movements in Europe at that time, the UPA was not supported from outside by anyone, morally or materially. It was an independent force whose power base was its own Ukrainian people. Roman Rakhmanny witnessed this struggle as an active member of the political underground.

1

UKRAINE'S STRUGGLE FOR FREEDOM

One had hoped that with the end of the Second World War the totalitarian police-state would have vanished. But the "armed peace" brought a new dictatorship, with its executions, its special courts — and, in Eastern and Central Europe, its "Neo-Resistance," with thousands of political refugees and the whole world split into two armed camps. So far Russia has been able to determine the battlefields on which the "Cold War" is to be fought; but now the question arises whether a purely negative defense is enough.

George F. Kennan, Russian expert in America's State Department, wrote last year in a memorandum: "There are elements buried within the Soviet Union which in the course of a single night could bring this nation from its present power to a state of extreme weakness."[1] These elements are mostly to be found in the Ukraine, where Russia in the time of Peter the Great seized the strategic gate to Europe in the direction of the Balkans and the Dardanelles. In the Ukraine, in the war against Charles XII of Sweden (1709), the fate of the Baltic States, Poland, Belorussia and the Caucasus was decided. Catherine the Great's most earnest desire was that all these should become Russian. In her

Reprinted with permission from *World Digest* (London), XIX, No. 111 (June, 1948), 63-65. It is a condensed version of the original article first published in *Die Weltwoche* (Zürich), March 25, 1948, where it appeared under another pen-name, *Romain d'Or,* and was entitled, "Ukraine — die vergessene Barrikade" (Ukraine — the Forgotten Barricade).

instructions to the Procurator General, Count Viazemsky, she wrote: "The Ukraine, Finland, and Courland are to be no more than Russian provinces. These provinces, as well as that of Smolensk, are to be Russianized. As soon as the Hetman dies in the Ukraine, everything must be done to stop a successor being chosen, so that the very title of Hetman will disappear."[2]

Yet the national consciousness of the Ukraine has survived for nearly two and a half centuries, and from the beginning of the Bolshevik Revolution down to the present has been a thorn in the flesh of the new regime.

Lenin knew that an independent Ukraine meant the end of the Bolshevik Revolution.

The Allied Powers of the West, which had intervened against Bolshevism, never decided to apply Wilson's Fourteen Points to the Ukraine, but supported the monarchists of Imperial Russia.

Thus the Ukraine found itself crushed between two Russian Empires, the hammer of Red Russia and the White Russian anvil, opposed to one another but both agreed to restore the frontiers of the former empire. In this war on two fronts, and also in consequence of the conflict between its own reactionaries and its peasant-anarchist tendencies, the Ukrainian Republic collapsed. Moscow set up a "Tito Government," which immediately declared its "voluntary accession" to the Russian federation.

It was the seizure of the Ukraine that laid the foundation of Russia's new strength. Expressed in figures, this means today: 40 million inhabitants, an area of 232,000 square miles, half the Soviet mineral wealth, one-third of the steel and coal production, two-fifths of the locomotive output. Recent events in Hungary, Bulgaria, Romania, Poland, Czechoslovakia, and above all in the oppressed states of the Baltic region, are a repetition of all that took place in the Ukraine between the two World Wars.

In the Ukraine, too, the collectivization of agriculture was not introduced until Russian power had been established; and the Ukrainians received a special cultural and economic autonomy. For a time, even an opposition was permitted. This was a clear way of showing who had been the supporters of Ukrainian independence, and made the subsequent liquidation the easier. The opposition of the Ukrainian peasants was crushed by the great famine, which cost the Ukraine more than five million dead and which was ended by compulsory collectivization. The defenders of Ukrainian independence, including hundreds of famous scientists and even those "Red Quislings" who had helped Moscow to sovietize the Ukraine, fell victim in the trials and the purges. In their place non-Ukrainians came forward. Every sign of resistance in the Ukraine — political, economic, religious, and cultural — was compelled to go underground. Only the purges in the Ukraine stand as witness that the battle for the Ukrainian barricades goes on.

In this battle, hope of liberation from without, from the West, played its part. National Socialism seemed to many Ukrainians to be a part of "Western civilization," and Germany the only land in the West to take a keen interest in the Ukrainian question. Long before Hitler had power, there was a Ukrainian Scientific Institute in Berlin, and the German nationalist propaganda was certainly not without its full effect on the Ukrainians in the Soviet Union.

When the Second World War was over, the Ukrainians found themselves disappointed once more. Now there is the first appearance of something of which little is known in Europe.

During the German occupation, Ukrainian partisan groups were established. There were the "Forest Brothers" in Estonia, the Belorussian "Peasants' Army" in the area between Smolensk and Pinsk, the Polish "Armia Krajowa" and WIN (Freedom and Independence). At the end of 1941 the "Ukrainian Insurgent Army" (UPA) was organized under the command of General Taras Chuprynka. Politically, the UPA is under the Supreme Ukrainian Liberation Council (UHVR), the highest organization in the battle for Ukrainian liberty. Since the spring of 1947, UPA units have carried out armed operations in the rear of the Russian armies stationed in Central Europe. Indeed, a Three Power Pact had to be concluded by Russia, Czechoslovakia, and Poland in order to liquidate the UPA bastion in the Carpathians. But some UPA groups fought their way through to Yugoslavia, to the British and American zones of Germany, and to Austria.[3]

It was the peoples of the border states who, between 1917 and 1923, called a halt to the Russian plans for aggressive conquest. The Russian advance then came up against the barricades of the Ukraine, the Caucasus, the Baltic States, Poland. And now?

In 1947, while the thirtieth anniversary of the Bolshevik

regime was being celebrated in Moscow, the MGB, the "Red SS troops," were on the march through the Ukraine and all the satellite states of Moscow. Moreover, for the first time, in place of the former purely selfish resistance, the attempt is being made to co-ordinate the liberation movements into an organization — the ABN, or Anti-Bolshevik Bloc of Nations.[4]

The deadly threat to Russian expansion lies not in the machine-pistols of the UPA and the other underground armies, but in the effect that can be made with the words: "Liberty for all and for each."[5] That which goes without saying in the West is, under the Russian despotism, of explosive power. The aim is to drive the military and police forces of Russia from the Baltic States, from Belorussia, from the Ukraine, Georgia, Armenia, and Azerbaijan to enable the peoples to decide their political lives for themselves.

The West either does not really know about these aims or it underestimates and distorts them. Napoleon in his Moscow campaign achieved no positive solution; Hitler was unable to bring freedom to these peoples.

Today, when the survival of mankind is at stake, it can no longer be reasonably asked whether Russia's expansion can be halted in Greece or Korea, for to ask is to balk at the real problem — the existence of Imperial Russia's need to expand. The barricade of freedom begins not at the farthest limit of Russia's advance, but in the very heart of Russia. There is the secret weakness that is the cause of her aggressive "need for security," and there, too, lies the best hope for the final triumph of the free Western democratic forces in the cold war between the two worlds.

REFERENCE NOTES

[1]Reference is made to a policy memorandum prepared by George F. Kennan, then on the staff of the US Department of State, for James Forrestal, Secretary of the Navy. The text of the memorandum was subsequently published in *Foreign Affairs,* under the title: "The Sources of Soviet Conduct," and signed anonymously with an "X". The so-called X-Article eventually became regarded as the first conceptualization of the American

"policy of containment" with respect to the Communist Bloc. See, *Foreign Affairs,* XXV, No. 4 (July, 1947), 566-82.

[2]Quoted in S.M. Soloviev, *Istoria Rossii s drevneishykh vremen* (History of Russia from Ancient Times), (Moscow: 1965), Book XIII, p. 340.

[3]In April 1947, the Soviet Union, Poland and Czechoslovakia signed a tripartite agreement to coordinate their anti-guerrilla operations against the Ukrainian Insurgent Army (UPA) along their contiguous borders. See *The New York Times,* May 13, 1947.

[4]The idea for ABN—Anti-Bolshevik Bloc of Nations—originated during a conference of representatives of Captive Peoples of Eastern Europe and Asia in November 1943 in the forests of Western Ukraine. The ABN as a political action organization was formally established in West Germany in 1946, where it still maintains its headquarters today. Its members are representatives of the various captive nations (Ukraine, Belorussia, Bulgaria, Hungary, *et.al.*).

[5]"Liberty for All and for Each" (or in another version, "Liberty to Peoples and the Individual") was a political slogan adopted by the Ukrainian Liberation Movement during and after World War II.

2

THE INCLINED PLANE

Some Observations on Russian Expansion

It has happened. The last country in Europe with a Slav population, hitherto posing as a mediator between East and West, has been occupied by Russia; Czechoslovakia has become a "Protektorat" once more. This has come as a surprise to many people. However, events in Czechoslovakia have laid bare the inclined plane on which the states in the Soviet orbit repose and which inevitably leads to occupation by the USSR. A brief survey of some almost unknown occurrences which took place in Czechoslovakia and her neighbor states in 1947 may shed some light on this problem.

The Triangle of Death

The Second World War restored bi-national Czechoslovakia's sovereignty. Her immediate neighbor is the Ukraine, a country occupied and exploited by Russia since 1920. Between 1941 and 1945, a vigorous political and military liberation movement has operated in the Ukraine. Both the UHVR—the Supreme Ukrainian Liberation Council—and the UPA—the Ukrainian Insurgent Army—have been extremely active against the Russians as well as the Germans.

Reprinted with permission from *The Baltic Review*, II, No. 2 (June, 1948), 48-51.

In the Carpathian Mountains on both sides of the "Curzon Line" (the Polish-Ukrainian frontier) heavy battles were fought in 1946 and 1947. Communications were cut, Russian and Red Polish garrisons were disarmed, the kolkhoz system was obliterated, the Soviet commissars and NKVD officials were liquidated — though not on any larger scale than elsewhere in the Ukraine. Nevertheless, the combat in this district became increasingly irritating to the Russian aggressors: the thunder of the guns was audible in Western Europe and foreign correspondents (e.g., the correspondent of *The Times*) could state on personal evidence that a struggle for elementary human rights was going on there.[1] When, moreover, General Swierczewski, Stalin's "Plenipotentiary for Poland," fell in a battle against UPA on March 28, 1947, Moscow decided to crush this hornet's nest.[2] Accordingly, a "Treaty of Three" for the coordinated combating of the UPA was signed by the USSR, Poland and Czechoslovakia in April, 1947.[3] Under this treaty Czechoslovakia agreed to put up a brigade of mountain troops, her police and constabulary at the disposal of the Russians to cut the westward retreat of the UPA detachments and to liquidate them in this "triangle of death."

Cutting Across Czechoslovakia

General Taras Chuprynka, the Commander-in-Chief of the UPA, whose headquarters are in Central Ukraine, gave his menaced troops very explicit orders: (1) The troops are to use the tactics of evasion and avoid decisive battles and possible annihilation at any cost; (2) A large group is to break through to the Prypet marshes (operational section of the UPA-North) and another to Odessa (operational section of the UPA-South); (3) Three smaller groups are to attempt a raid through Czechoslovakia and contact the Yugoslav (anti-Tito) resistance movement.

It should be evident from this why the great Russo-Polish-Czech annihilation offensive proved a washout. When the Czech mountaineers had linked up with the Polish infantry and a Russian armored corps and were celebrating their "victory" over UPA, "small mobile detachments of the UPA were swarming all over Slovakia and Central Czechia," to quote the Czech press. Some of them crossed the Danube south of Lake Balaton in Hungary and reached Yugoslavian territory, others reached the American or British zones of Germany or Austria and were disarmed there.[4]

The UPA command has explained the objectives of its operations on the Czechoslovak territory in numerous pamphlets and at no less numerous meetings: its aim was to establish and organize cooperation between the Soviet-oppressed nations with a view to throwing off the Russian yoke. The UHVR appealed to the Czechs and Slovaks to resist the Russians immediately with all their might and, above all, to give up their Russian orientation and their illusions about Russia.

This appeal did not go unheeded. The Czech troops hardly fought the UPA units and the Slovak troops did not do this at all. Heavy fighting took place only near Svaty Martin and Ruzomberk, where the cadets of a military college were sent against the UPA. The Slovak population fed and housed the UPA soldiers and gave them useful information.

For Russia—Against the Fighters for Freedom

It may sound incredible, but the leaders of the Czech nation, who have idolized Panslavism for centuries, have actually taken up arms against other Slav nations for the sole reason that these nations have fought Russia. For centuries they have identified Slavdom and the Slav cause with Russia, in spite of the fact that the Russians have oppressed other Slav peoples in the most barbaric way.

The activities of the Prague Government have caused the UPA and the Slovak underground some appreciable losses. Thus, e.g., Burlaka, the commander of an UPA group, was captured thanks to their efforts. Imitating the methods of the NKVD, the Czech police have addressed an appeal "to the members of the UPA on Czechoslovak territory" in the name of Burlaka. Another appeal, signed by the Minister for Internal Affairs, contained the following injunction: "Kill your commanders, throw away your weapons and report to the NB (the Czech security police);" and again: "Surrender! You will live and work! The Slav Truth will win!"

The UPA soldiers who for five years have read similar appeals by SS-Obergruppenfuehrer von dem Bach (the Nazi plenipotentiary for combating the insurgents in the Ukraine in 1943) and by Russian commissars, would not let themselves be taken in by the "Slav Truth."

Then General Svoboda,[5] also a trustee of Moscow, organized a volunteers' division consisting of "Red guerrillas." It is a well-known fact that these Red guerrillas had never fought the Germans but that they were the mainstay of the Communist Party in Czechoslovakia. In consequence of its very low fighting value this division proved extremely ineffective in the field and its positions were easily overrun by the UPA. Nevertheless, the "neutral" General Svoboda had thousands of armed communists at his disposal during the recent crisis in Prague, when they demonstrated for Gottwald[6] as . . . "armed workers."

Meanwhile the Prague Government thought fit to announce that it considered the "military and police action against UPA," which had only compromised it, as having ended. In spite of this official position, appeals by the Ministry for Internal Affairs to the UPA were posted "unofficially" in the towns and villages of Czechoslovakia as late as January, 1948. In February of this year [1948] UPA Commander Burlaka succeeded in escaping from a Czech concentration camp in Kosice and the majority of the UPA detachments have transferred their activities back to the Ukrainian territory.[7] The Czechs, who were recently repatriated from the Ukraine, state that the UPA troops in the district in question seem to be endeavoring to break through to the north and the east. This information is corroborated by recent Russian measures in the Ukraine: garrisons have been increased and railway stations fenced in with barbed wire and provided with machine gun posts.

The Great Dilemma

Although the UPA raid across Czechoslovakia was not of long duration, it has been of great importance to the struggle for independence of nations united in the ABN. Western Europe has seen that mighty national liberation movements are afoot against the Russian dictatorship and the underground movements in Czechoslovakia, Hungary, Romania, Yugoslavia and Poland have received a new impetus, these nations having in fact joined the ABN.

In order to prevent this "new European resistance" from developing and growing and at the same time to bring down the iron curtain more securely, Moscow has decided to annihilate what was left of Czechoslovakia's independence. Under the pretext of economic and cultural collaboration and of a united front against UPA, Russia managed to put its agents in key positions in the secret police, the constabulary, and the judiciary, in addition to "neutral" high commissioners in the army and the Ministry for Foreign Affairs. The above-mentioned "Red division" was the foundation of Gottwald's "action committees." The Czech leaders had nothing with which to oppose this Russian attack. They had relinquished their only weapon when they sanctioned the sending of thousands of Czechs and Slovaks into battle against the Ukrainian and Slovak fighters for freedom. Now Prague sees whose abject tool it has been. It had neither the courage nor the determination to put its trust in the West, to proclaim an uncompromising adherence to Western ideals and to combat Russian aggression together with the other oppressed nations.

Meanwhile in the Ukraine, the Baltic area, Belorussia and the Caucasus the struggle has not abated. "Deep raids by the UPA—in the vicinity of Kiev, west of Kharkov, north of Odessa—gave the impression of a general insurrection in the Ukraine," says a Reuter message from Shanghai. Actually UPA can work so successfully in the Ukraine only because it enjoys the support of the whole population. A general revolt must and will take place not only in the Ukraine but simultaneously in all the countries under Russian occupation. It is, therefore, essential that all nations envisage the fact that they will slip down an inclined plane if they collaborate with Russia and lay themselves open to peaceful penetration. The Czech nation, too, will have to undergo a spiritual revolution and to dig up the weapons buried in Jan Huss' time, and use them in regaining its independence.

Today, right now, every nation is facing a great dilemma: it must either acknowledge every other nation's right to freedom and independence and fight with the struggling nations for a new and free world, or resign itself to slipping, slowly and inevitably, down the inclined plane that leads to the Russian yoke.

REFERENCE NOTES

[1]Reference is made to two correspondents for *The Times of London*—John Curtiss and Derek Robinson—who covered the UPA operations and Communist Polish Government's counterinsurgency efforts during 1946-47.

[2]General Karol Swierczewski fought in the Spanish Civil War on the Republican side under the name of "General Walter." During World War II he commanded the Second Polish Army on the Soviet side against Nazi Germany. After the war he was appointed Deputy Minister of Defense in the communist-dominated Polish Government. During one of his inspections of the Polish army counterguerrilla operations in the Ukrainian ethnic region of Eastern Poland he was killed in an ambush set up by an UPA unit. See article No. 3 below for an eyewitness account of the ambush.

[3]See note 3 to article No. 1 in this collection.

[4]See, *The New York Times*, September 19, 1947.

[5]General Ludvig Svoboda commanded Czech communist units on the Eastern Front during World War II. After the war he became Minister of Defense (1945-1950) and President of Czechoslovakia (1968-1975).

[6]Klement Gottwald, Czech communist leader, Premier of Czechoslovakia under the Beneš regime (1946-1948), and President after the communist take-over of the country (1948-1953).

[7]Contrary to reports circulating at the time about his alleged escape, Commander Burlaka was extradited by the Czechoslovak authorities to Poland where he was sentenced to death. See, for example, M. Kvapil, "The Night on Mt. Lupča,"*Čéskoslovenský Vojak*, XVI, no. 19 (1967), 4-7.

3

THE UNKNOWN FRONT

September 1947: A fair-sized group of soldiers belonging to the Ukrainian Insurgent Army (UPA) broke its way out of encirclement in the Ukraine reaching the West via Czechoslovakia.[1]

I interviewed members of these detachments—remarkable for having achieved this feat of determined valor.

Among them I met a guerrilla fighter who took part in the so-called attempted assassination of Poland's Vice Minister of Defense, General Karol Swierczewski.

The General was killed in the encounter with an UPA detachment.[2]

"This was no terrorist attempt on his life," objected Mykola Prykui, a burly 30 year old UPA non-commissioned officer.

He added: "We are, in principle, opposed to individual terrorism and we regard ourselves soldiers of a regular Ukrainian army fighting Moscow and its janissaries. General Swierczewski, one such representative of Russian imperialism, was a legitimate target in justifiable military combat."

"It was, indeed, a typical guerrilla action," confirmed his comrade-in-arms B. Sokolenko.

Prykui continued:

"In the winter months of 1946–47, the Polish communist authorities made another in a series of attempts to resettle the

This is an English rendering of the article which had originally appeared in the Swiss weekly *Die Weltwoche* (Zürich), November 12, 1948, and is reprinted here with the permission of its editors.

Ukrainian population, forcing people from their homeland along the new Polish-Soviet border. At the same time they were anxious to clear the same districts of our UPA units, as was then demanded from the Warsaw authorities by Moscow.

"The winter was harsh with high snowdrifts hampering our movements. The Polish and Soviet army units pressed us ever closer to the Sian River and the high ridges of the Carpathian Mountains. Incidentally, quite a few enemy troops were regular Soviet soldiers. When we took prisoners they admitted having been given Polish uniforms thus buttressing the Polish Communist Army.

"Nevertheless, our two most experienced commanders, Burlaka and Khrin, continued to weaken the blockading units of the Warsaw regime's army.

"It is not surprising, then, that the commander of the Polish garrison in the provincial capital city of Peremyshl, General Wieckowski, encouraged his troops in the following way: He promised extra clothing and footwear to every soldier of the detachment which brought in Burlaka or Khrin, dead or alive.

A Hospital Destroyed

"Early in March of 1947, when the snow on the slopes began melting, our military sector suffered a terrible setback. A well-camouflaged underground hospital, situated close to a small creek in the Sianik district, was discovered and destroyed by the enemy.

"It happened in this way. A UPA convalescent was spotted by a Polish patrol as he fetched water from a creek. The soldiers tracked him to the hidden area. Two companies of regular army and police, supported by a detachment of the MO (*Milicja Obywatelska* — Civil Guard) encircled the fortified hospital.

"There were then four medics, four nurses, five seriously wounded and four convalescent UPA soldiers.

"The attack on the hospital continued for over 26 hours. With no one left to put up active resistance, the survivors finished themselves off with handgranades, refusing to be taken alive.

"Once the details became known, every detachment, naturally, was eager for revenge. At that time, our unit operated in the vicinity of Balyhorod and Tisna — a triangular region formed by the borders of Czechoslovakia, Poland and the Soviet Ukraine.

"At dawn on March 28, 1947, our leader, Commander Khrin (a very genial fellow despite serious bullet wounds suffered in both arms) put our company on the alert.

"Our reconnaissance learned that some high ranking officers from Warsaw were due for a tour of inspection of the Polish troops in the region. Thus, the hour for vengeance had struck," he said.

"The objective of the announced movement order was a section of the road between the towns of Balyhorod and Tisna. It was a pleasant morning. No snow. No footprints. The sight of the budding green filled us with assurance that hunger and severe cold were no longer going to be the allies of our enemies.

"Having reached our objective, we received additional information from our reconnaissance: four armored vehicles and four army trucks were coming our way. They were full of Polish soldiers.

"The lead column passed by without noticing anything unusual although enemy soldiers were keeping both sides of the mountain road under observation. The stillness reassured them.

A Regular Battle

"Our commander ordered us to take up assigned positions along the road. I was to cover the road with my machine-gun from the edge of the woods. The commander himself stood just a few paces behind my post. Our three squads were taking cover in the brushwood to the right of me. Then I spotted through my binoculars a staff car and a truck with about a score of soldiers in it rapidly advancing towards us. I still remember seeing three officers in the car, with their caps off and their bald heads reflecting the sunshine.

"Soon, the action started without warning. As our units were still taking up their positions, the staff car reached the point of no return.

"It was within my line of fire. A sudden burst of fire from the machine-gun and other weapons immobilized the car almost at once. A somewhat heavy-set officer jumped out of the vehicle and frantically tried to organize the surprised soldiers into battle order. Courageous but altogether futile. Moments later he fell and I still believe I heard him say: 'Colonel, I am done for. . . .' "But Colonel Gerhard (we learned his name later) was helplessly wounded. The same Colonel Gerhard who had ordered his soldiers to destroy a Ukrainian Catholic church in the town of Lisko barely three months earlier.[3]

"I cannot say with any certainty whether General Karol Swierczewski fell hit by my machine-gun bullets or someone else's. There was no time to confirm such detail entangled as I was in the exchange of fire with enemy shooting at us from behind the truck. What I do know, however, is that not far from my own position Lieutenant Hran', former Soviet soldier and a veteran of the Soviet-Finnish War of 1940, occupied a commanding position. A sniper, he could have hit the prized target General Swierczewski in the confusion of such a surprise attack.

"The whole encounter lasted about 15 minutes. Balyhorod signalled that a relief force was being rushed to the scene. Our orders were to break contact. To withdraw into the depth of the forest.

"No point in risking a protracted battle with a better armed and larger enemy force. We had accomplished our task.

"Late on the same night, a peasant travelling along the road from Sianik told our people that five killed and six wounded had been brought into his town. Among the dead was General Swierczewski, Polish Vice-Minister of Defense, or 'General Walter' as he had been known during the Spanish Civil War.

"Next morning, we crossed the border and entered Czechoslovakia."

The Road of Vengeance

"The road between Balyhorod and Tisna, however, witnessed yet another encounter of a similar kind. A UPA detachment operating there under orders of Commander Bir avenged our friends murdered in the underground hospital in the early spring.

"It happened on April 2, 1947.

"A group of officers and men from the Polish units stationed in and around Tisna were travelling to Balyhorod. It was pay day. . . . As they neared the point where General Swierczewski was killed in March, they got off their truck and guardedly followed the vehicle, weapons at the ready. Before long, their commanding officer, having taken another quick look around, reassured his subordinates: 'Well, boys, all clear! Board the truck!'

"But before they could speed off, they were enveloped in concentrated fire from UPA automatic weapons. . . . At least five officers, eleven non-commissioned officers and five men (including the commandant of the local police) were later reported to be among the killed or seriously wounded.

"Our intelligence learned afterwards that most of those under that attack had taken active part in the destruction of the underground hospital," said M. Prykui.

"Both events—the destruction of the hospital and the act of vengeance—took place in the same district, close to the same mountain creek," added another UPA soldier, one of the members of the group that broke through to West Germany, across Czechoslovakia, from the Ukraine in September 1947.

"The democracy of our dead had not registered their hopes in vain."

REFERENCE NOTES

[1]See, *The New York Times*, September 19, 1947.

[2]See note 2 to article No. 2 in this collection.

[3]For an eyewitness account of this battle from the Polish side and Colonel Gerhard's role in the counterguerrilla operations against the UPA, see his memoiristic work *Luny w Bieszczadach* (Fires in the Beskids), (Warsaw: MON, 1958), pp. 586-604.

4

UKRAINE ADVISES

HOW TO ROCK KREMLIN

Recently, Mr. Edward W. Barrett, United States Assistant Secretary of State for Public Affairs, was greatly surprised to receive a letter from the Ukrainian Underground in the Soviet Ukraine. This letter was written by Major P. Poltava,[1] a leading member of the Ukrainian Insurgent Army (UPA), and sent to Washington. There, Mr. M. Lebed, Foreign Secretary of the Supreme Ukrainian Liberation Council, made a literal translation of the letter for the State Department.[2]

The conditions under which that letter, written in some hiding-place in the Ukraine—which with its forty million population, is dominated by the Soviets—was then passed through underground lines of communication, made it a sensational event when it finally reached Washington. This was the first time in history of the "Iron Curtain" and the "Cold War" between the West and East, that a letter had come from the depth of the Russian secret empire, written by an underground leader and addressed to the State Department, specifically to its branch the "Voice of America."

Reprinted with permission from *The Globe and Mail* (Toronto), April 14, 1951.

"Frog in Its Throat"

This letter points out just how successfully the "Voice of America" has done its work and how it might be more successful in this same work if it employed suitable approaches toward the nationalities of the Soviet Union.

For, to them, the "Voice of America" has been giving its "true information" for almost two years in the Russian language, and over a year in the Ukrainian. The State Department has received many criticisms from the Ukrainian emigres. In the current debate on the effectiveness of the "Voice of America" between Senator Benton of Connecticut and the State Department, the former has charged that "the Voice of America has a frog in its throat" and that it is not what it is supposed to be: "the voice of peace and freedom for the free world."

Now, one of the many listeners in the Soviet Union gives his views on this subject.

He says, "My fellow-countrymen and I are constantly surprised by the fact that, while the Kremlin's propaganda never neglects to take advantage of even the smallest discontent of some labor organization in the USA nor does it fail to make use of forms of anti-regime opposition such as in the Philippines, yet at the same time American propaganda does not take advantage of the fight of the Ukrainian people against Bolshevism inside the USSR."

35,000 Destroyed

This observation is more understandable when it is realized that Soviet inhabitants live in a paralyzing fear of the MVD (Ministry of Internal Affairs) and the police system of the Soviet empire. The success of the Kremlin in stifling opposition inside the Soviet Union forced these people to believe that all such effort is useless. The Kremlin itself seeks to promote this belief by saying that it knows everything and that all conspiracies will be found out.

To illustrate this, the MVD creates fake conspiracies, which it supposedly uncovers, and the mass arrests begin. The Kremlin would rather have ninety-nine innocent people die than to have one "counter-revolutionary" escape.

The Ukrainian Liberation Movement and the Ukrainian Insurgent Army exposed the myth of the invincible power of the Kremlin in the Ukraine. This underground has been active for six years, during which time, according to the latest report of the headquarters of the Ukrainian Insurgent Army, 35,000 MVD troops have been destroyed in the Ukraine.

Indeed, broadcasting these tremendous results of the Ukrainian resistance over all the Soviet Republics would contribute greatly to releasing the Soviet citizens from their hypnotic fear and would also encourage them to a passive opposition to the Kremlin, and perhaps to an active one.

The Ukrainian underground cannot be simply relying only on its own means and strength to carry on this work effectively over such vast territory stretching from the Baltic to Korea. But the "Voice of America" can do this, for it has at its disposal innumerable means which are out of the reach of the Ukrainian or any other underground in the world.

However, in order that the people in the Soviet Union react favorably to the information that is broadcast to them from the United States "psychology must be taken into account, the trend of thought, the disposition and outlook of the people under the Soviet regime have to be taken into consideration as well," Major Poltava says in his letter.

Appeal to Nationalities

He adds, that for want of this the program does not have the desired effect in the Soviet Ukraine. In his opinion the American radio should appeal to the non-Russian nationalities of the USSR who are enslaved by Moscow. Their national oppression by czarist and then by communist Moscow should be shown, and their national sentiments should be encouraged. The arguments that these nationalities have against Bolshevism, based on their culture and historical backgrounds should be utilized.

For instance, during its broadcast in the Ukrainian language the people of the Soviet Ukraine were not told that Mr. Harold Stassen, president of the University of Pennsylvania, demanded that the USA should strive "for the reestablishment of separate national sovereignty and true independence of the Ukraine,

Estonia, Lithuania, Latvia, Poland, Hungary and Romania."[3]

On the other hand, criticism of Bolshevism should be carried on from the point of view of the Soviet people, but not with the purpose of restoring the conditions prior to 1917. For "the Soviet people hate Kremlin's socialism, but in the prevailing majority they are also against restoration of capitalism in their countries," said Major Poltava.

It is evident that neither Major Poltava himself, nor the Ukrainian Insurgent Army, the Supreme Ukrainian Liberation Council, and the Ukrainian anti-communists generally, in whose name he speaks, are against the economic policy of "free enterprise." However, he realizes that the people in the Soviet Republics grew up in the fight against private capitalism — magnates of czarist Russia — and today remain in the struggle against state capitalism. The American broadcasts should also take this into consideration, he argues.

Of course, it is possible to disagree with his opinions and demands. Nevertheless we cannot overlook them. His voice is the voice of many millions behind the Iron Curtain, which really begins on the western border of the Soviet Ukraine. Indeed Major Poltava stresses the possibilities of their being allies of the West. He is saying, that, as an active member of the struggle for liberation from Bolshevism in the Ukraine he feels himself in unison with the free world in its struggle against Bolshevik aggression and tyranny. He is convinced that "the people of the United States of America and the Ukraine are striving for the same common aim: victory over communism."

REFERENCE NOTES

[1]Major Petro Poltava was a leading ideologist of the Ukrainian National Liberation Movement during 1940's under the Soviet occupation of Western Ukraine. He was killed by Soviet security police in an encounter with the UPA in 1951.

[2]For the full text of the letter, see *The Ukrainian Insurgent Army in Fight for Freedom* (New York: 1954), pp. 178-88.

[3]Reference is made to "Victory Without War," an address by Harold E. Stassen, *Round the World Report,* The American Broadcasting Company, January 15, 1951, Washington, D.C.

H.E. Stassen was an American statesman, Governor of Minnesota, President of the University of Pennsylvania, and twice candidate for the presidency of the United States.

5

THE ROOTS OF INSURGENCY
IN THE UKRAINE

The Nationalities Question in the Soviet Union

As I have done before in talks addressed to your predecessors in this illustrious military college, I shall discuss one of the most basic, and perhaps the most crucial, of the USSR's covert problems — its nationalities question.

I am aware that at least some of you, like, I suppose, some of your predecessors, may take a dim view of the topic and think: Now, here comes another civilian to lecture us on how to win a war, if and when it comes.

Well, I have no objections to so open an appraisal. Nowadays far too many civilians are inclined to believe that "war is much too serious a matter to be left to the generals." Recently, indeed, a certain major retired from the Canadian Army perhaps because he believed that as a civilian he would be in a better position to criticize the generals.

And I also will readily agree with you that the subject being discussed today is, in fact, closely related to that of another war, or that of lasting peace.

A satisfactory answer to the question of how to approach the

A lecture delivered to student officers at the Royal Canadian Air Force Staff College in Toronto, Ontario, on January 18, 1960.

conglomerate of nationalities in the Soviet Union might prove an inestimable addition to our studies regarding both defensive and offensive encounters with Soviet Russia. But, at the same time, an effective approach to the nationalities situation of the Soviet Union might develop into a powerful means for preventing the outbreak of another world war.

This may sound depressingly theoretical, on the surface at least. In practice, however, the issue is very explosive. You may be aware that the Kremlin leaders heartily dislike anybody who, raising this issue, tries to tamper with the delicate and very sensitive structure of the so-called Union of sovereign Soviet republics. When, last July, the United States Congress approved a resolution inviting the American people to study the plight of Soviet-dominated nations,[1] it aroused the wrath of the Kremlin rulers. Comrade Khrushchev himself intervened in that well-known publication *Foreign Affairs*.[2] In a special, signed article in the October issue of the American quarterly, he said:

> The authors of the resolution call for the 'liberation' of the Ukraine, Belorussia, Lithuania, Latvia, Estonia, Armenia, Azerbaidjan, Georgia, Kazakhstan, Turkmenistan, and even a certain 'Ural area.'

In his opinion "this ill-starred resolution was regarded by the Soviet people as an act of provocation." Why? Because, as Mr. Khrushchev saw the implication,

> It would be interesting to see, incidentally, how the authors of this resolution would have reacted if the parliament of Mexico, for instance, had passed a resolution demanding that Texas, Arizona, and California be 'liberated' from American 'slavery.' Apparently they have never pondered such a question, which is very regrettable. Sometimes comparisons help us to understand the essence of a matter.

This excerpt from Mr. Khrushchev's article represents the gist of the whole problem about which I intend to speak and about which I would like to hear your comments.

One might scrutinize the problem starting from the point of view taken by many Western writers, and some statesmen, namely: the Soviet Union is a monolithic nation—Russia; her so-called Soviet republics are Russia's administrative provinces; the numerous nationalities of the Soviet Union are Russian subjects "satisfied with their system of government and economy."*

Even though this viewpoint is now current in the official circles of the West, historical facts and the policies of Soviet leaders concerning the question of their nationalities do not justify the conclusion I have just mentioned.

Soviet newspapers and publications never fail to stress the fact that such republics as the Ukraine, Belorussia, and Georgia are established sovereign nations. During the current session of the General Assembly of the United Nations, the delegates of the Ukrainian Soviet Republic mounted the rostrum to accuse Great Britain and France of nineteenth-century colonialism in the Cameroons. At the same time, the Ukrainian delegates pointed out that the Ukrainian people—"free and sovereign"—sympathize with the plight of all African colonial peoples. They stressed the fact that the Ukraine also contributes fair aid to the underdeveloped peoples.

Now, it becomes more and more evident that the Ukraine serves the Kremlin leaders as a show-window for the Afro-Asian peoples' inspection.

Since Stalin's death in 1953, the Ukraine's capital Kiev has witnessed a procession of visiting leaders and representatives of nations of many colors—Chinese, Indian, Egyptian, Sudanese—in addition to those from European satellite countries.

The stress of Soviet propaganda in these cases is always on the productivity of the highly-industrialized Ukraine—remarkable even by North American standards. The argument follows a well set and richly embroidered pattern: the Ukraine, in the past one of the most oppressed nations, attained her sovereignty and was able to develop her industrial power *only* under Leninist socialism, and *only* thanks to the friendly help of the Russian people.

One suspects in these tactics a shrewd propaganda maneuver designed for and created by external purposes only. Nevertheless, there are indications that this policy pursued by the Kremlin rulers is also the result of certain internal pressures.

---

*"Text of the Governor's Report on the Soviet Visit," *The New York Times,* August 1, 1959.

When a resolution was put forward by Representative Smith of Wisconsin in the United States House of Representatives, in July 1953, calling for the establishment of direct diplomatic relations with the governments of the Ukraine and Belorussia, the Kremlin jugglers reacted immediately, and vehemently.[3]

The following January, on the occasion of the anniversary of the union between czarist Russia (or rather Muscovy, as it was known then) and the Ukraine in 1654, the Presidium of the Soviet Union, formally and with the accompaniment of powerful state propaganda, handed over the Crimea to the Ukraine.[4]

The Crimean Peninsula had until then belonged to the Russian Soviet Federative Socialist Republic. Lenin and Stalin regarded the Crimea as a Russian Gibraltar controlling the Ukraine and the southern approaches to the Soviet Union. The Ukrainians seemingly did not have any rightful claims to the Crimea before 1953. But after the Russians felt themselves outmaneuvered by a group of American politicians, they acted swiftly and without paying much attention to previous considerations. According to the Soviet press which reflected the official line of thinking, the Ukraine had the fullest claims to the peninsula: historical, economic, cutural, strategic, etc.

The Soviet mass media as a whole did not fail to stress the magnanimity of the Russian nation inspired by Marxism-Leninism. The transfer of the Crimea was "a gift" from the Russians to the Ukrainians—an example of friendship in deed as well as in word.

In my opinion, this proves that the nationality question remains the most vulnerable chink in the Soviet Russian armor. And it has been so from the inception of the Soviet Union; or even earlier—since the revolution in czarist Russia. The Soviets have since been trying to solve that problem. As in other instances, they claim they have succeeded.

Facts tell a different story.

Let's review briefly the historical events leading to the present situation in Eastern Europe.

In February 1917, revolution swept Russia, ending bloodily the Romanov dynasty and opening up new vistas for the hitherto submerged non-Russian peoples. These non-Russian peoples stood thus on the threshold of national emancipation. Heavily burdened by a centuries-old colonial past, they found the road to nationhood not an easy one. Almost without exception, each went about establishing its national statehood in stages marked by hesitant gradualism, hoping at the same time that the former Empire would be transformed into a federation of national republics.

Like their neighbors, the Ukrainians first demanded only regional autonomy, but soon moved towards the establishment of a republic in the face of vacillations and protestations on the part of the newly formed Russian "liberal" government. Once the Bolsheviks seized power in Petrograd, however, the Ukrainians, like other nationalities, committed themselves irrevocably to separate statehood. Following the example of Finland and Latvia, the Ukraine proclaimed independence from Russia on January 22, 1918. Soon to be followed by Lithuania, Estonia, Georgia, Armenia, and Azerbaijan.

No sooner were these declarations made than the young states became victims of outright aggression.

The Ukraine was attacked from every direction: from the west by Poland and Romania; from the south by the White Guard Russians of General Denikin, supported by the French and British; from the north by the Red Army of Lenin and Trotsky. In the more than two-year-long turmoil, Lenin succeeded in setting up a Soviet Ukrainian government in Kiev even as he came to terms with the Poles who had taken Western Ukraine with the city of Lviv.

At the same time, Belorussian and three Trans-Caucasian Soviet republics were set up.

Until 1922 all these republics, the Ukraine included, existed as autonomous states. Lenin, as we know from recent research, prevented Stalin and his Russian centralist supporters from annexing these republics into the Russian Federative Soviet Republic. Moreover, in his now famous "testament" Lenin also warned his Kremlin colleagues against the coming rise of Stalin to power, and against the dangers arising from the Russian centralist:

> It is quite natural that in such circumstances the 'freedom to secede from the union' by which we justify ourselves will be a mere scrap of paper, unable to defend the non-Russians from the onslaught of that really Russian man, the Great Russian chauvinist, in substance a rascal and a tyrant, such as the typical Russian bureaucrat is.[5]

His forebodings were soon justified. During Stalin's long reign, the Soviet Union took on a purely Russian character. The Ukrainians, Belorussians, Georgians, and other nationalities were often accused of bourgeois-nationalist deviations. The Russian language and culture were presented as the only worthwhile expressions of the proletariat. The Ukrainian Communist Party itself was purged almost regularly, and during the all-union monster purges of 1928, 1933, and 1937 — the Ukraine's government and the party's leadership were liquidated almost to a man. Two of the chief human instruments in the bloody purge of 1937 in the Ukraine survived Stalin's regime and are today the men at the top in the Soviet Union — Nikita Khrushchev, Secretary of the Ukrainian Communist Party in 1938, and his assistant at that time, General Ivan Serov who later helped the former to liquidate Beria.[6]

Ukrainian resistance to Moscow's encroachment was broken in 1933, chiefly by mass-famine. Over five million people died of hunger, the result of forced collectivization and the requisitioning of foodstuffs by the Soviet government.

Later, the Second World War seemed to the majority of the non-Russian nationalities in the Soviet Union the lesser of two evils. They expected *the West* to liberate them from the clutches of Stalin's centralized communist empire. This is one of the reasons why the hard-driving Germans scored such great victories during the first months of the campaign against the Soviet Union in 1941. Hundreds of thousands of Ukrainians, Belorussians, Georgians, Uzbeks, Azerbaijanians, and Russians themselves surrendered to the Germans in the belief that they would be set free — or even that they might be able to fight against their Russian overlords. Some of them dreamed of setting up independent national states based on economic free enterprise.

The Germans frowned upon such ideas. They maltreated prisoners of war, and put Hitlerite colonialism into practice in the Ukraine and Belorussia — the two original republics of the Soviet Union entirely occupied by the Germans. Thus they roused against themselves well-nigh all the Ukrainians and Belorussians, who then had to fight against the Germans for their own survival, either in the ranks of the Red Army, or as insurgents in occupied territory.

I had ample opportunity to observe these developments at close quarters. During the summer and autumn of 1941, I took part in the movement of those allegedly "crazy" Ukrainians who attempted, in the midst of the war, to bake the Ukrainian nationalist cake, and eat it too.

Some of the leading members of our underground organization — OUN (Organization of Ukrainian Nationalists) — proclaimed an independent government of the Ukraine, with Iaroslav Stetsko as Prime Minister, as soon as the German armies entered the city of Lviv, on June 30, 1941. Others followed the fast-moving German columns, sometimes actually outrunning them in their advance eastward. The idea was to set up Ukrainian local administration in the liberated territories and, in this way, to compel the Germans to accept Ukrainian independence as a fact. This was planned in spite of Hitlerist racist policy. We were also busy setting up our underground network encompassing for the first time all Ukrainian ethnographic territory.

To illustrate the idea underlying our moves of the period, I'll use our own group of Ukrainian revolutionaries as an example. There were eleven men in the group whose final destination was Sevastopol in the Crimea. We travelled sometimes by the horse-drawn carts used in the Ukrainian steppes, sometimes on bicycles, occasionally on foot, but always independently of the Germans. For the latter approach we had a good reason. Special units of Himmler's police, the dreaded *Einsatzkommando,* attached loosely to the regular army groups, were busy searching out our men and either liquidating them on the spot or delivering them to prisons and concentration camps. According to the Nuremberg Trial documents, Himmler's directive for the three *Einsatzgruppen* concerned the Ukrainian nationalists as much as it did the Soviet commissars. The instruction read in part:

To weed out professional revolutionaries, officials of the Comintern, people's commissars . . . and all Jews.[7]

The Nazis were unable to catch up with our unit only because we stayed too close to the frontline. On the river Inhulets we even lost track of the German front troops. What happened was that we had simply outrun them. We had entered the gap between two German pincers — one aimed at Dnipropetrovsk, the other having as its objective the towns of Kakhivka and Kherson on the lower Dnieper, the gates to the Crimea.

But soon we roamed in Dnipropetrovsk-Mariupol-Kherson no-man's-land region setting up nationalist city and village administration, and hoisting everywhere the Ukrainian blue-and-yellow flags. In a number of places, the German troops would arrive in a town only to be met by a new local Ukrainian administration which expressed its allegiance to the reconstituted Ukrainian sovereign state and its government. The German commanders did not like it but, for the time being, they had to lump it. They did not bother the representatives of the nationalist self-government for about two months. Only after the frontline had moved on far beyond the Dnieper, towards the Donets River, did civilian German administrators gradually begin replacing our local men with their own hirelings. Often these were the communist agents whom the party apparatus had left behind for some specific purposes. In combatting Ukrainian patriots the communists were equal to the example set by the Nazis.

Meantime, our nationalist unit — all the time posing as "local activists" — had reached the shores of the Sea of Azov. The entrance to the Crimea was still barred by the frontline fighting. We had to wait for the inevitable breakthrough which we would again utilize for our own Ukrainian designs as we had done before in other regions.

Unfortunately, we were detained by the terrible *Einsatzgruppe D* that prided itself later on in having killed 91,678 persons in the area assigned to it. It was only thanks to some misunderstanding at the headquarters of General (later Field Marshal) von Mannstein, the commander of the 11th Army to which the *Einsatzgruppe* was attached, that we survived the ordeal. It was decided to send us back to Lviv and hand us over to the Gestapo there. It meant — concentration camp at Auschwitz or Buchenwald.

On our way back, we succeeded in "detaching ourselves" from the convoy. Some of my friends entered the Crimea early the following year, as we all were supposed to do. Some of them were caught again by the *Eisatzgruppe* at Dzhankoi, Crimea, and shot. Others spent over three years in the Buchenwald concentration camp. Myself and two other friends, having escaped the clutches of the Nazi network, continued our underground activities.

By that time, members of our revolutionary government set up at Lviv were already behind bars in German prisons, along with the top cadres of our underground organization. The few leaders who had eluded the Gestapo in September–October 1941 rebuilt the underground network and, through their activities in the wooded regions of the northwestern Ukraine, laid the foundation for the now-famous Ukrainian Insurgent Army (UPA).

The UPA consisted of small mobile groups — in time combined into battalion-strength units — that fought German administration and its police, and Red partisans as well.

German allies — Hungarian and Romanian troops — soon came to respect the fighting abilities of the UPA units, willingly supplying them with arms and ammunition, sometimes in exchange for foodstuffs, sometimes to be left unmolested.

In July 1944, the Supreme Ukrainian Liberation Council was set up to co-ordinate the activities of the underground organization and of the underground army (UPA) under the leadership of General Roman Shukhevych-Chuprynka. These three underground formations were composed of men and women from various districts of the Ukraine, from all walks of life. They represented many social and political views — from radical rightists, to moderate to leftists, and even some former national-communists of the later Tito-type.

This represents an indication of the mood of the Ukrainian people at the time of the German occupation, at a time when Ukrainians were in a good position to express their attitude actively. This they did by supporting our nationalist underground with men, clothes, food, and medical supplies. There were districts where the Germans were unable to control anything but the main supply routes to the eastern front. Their routes were not attacked because our leadership unknowingly agreed with Mr. Truman's suggestion: Let the Germans and the Soviets fight each other until both are weakened by the bloodletting. . . .[8] But actually the ultimate objective of the Ukrainian underground during the German occupation was to prepare itself for the return of the weakened Soviets into the Ukraine.

Stalin, that great juggler of nationalities in the Soviet Union, was aware of the true mood of the Ukrainians and that of his other subjects. And he knew that the same process had been going on during the German occupation of Belorussia, Lithuania, Estonia, and Latvia, with a difference: the Ukrainians were able to organize their freedom movement on a larger scale and with somewhat greater efficiency due to their past experience and the greater human resources for such activities against the Russians.

That is why Stalin insisted, during his negotiations with Roosevelt and Churchill at Yalta in 1944, on the recognition by their governments of the annexations of the Western Ukrainian territories (formerly Polish and Romanian) concluded by the Soviets in 1939–1940. He literally said that the Ukrainians would be angered if he did not defend that point at Yalta. Besides, Stalin demanded, and was granted, the admission of the Ukraine and Belorussia to the United Nations as members. This was supposed to compensate these republics for their horrendous losses during the war, and for their contributions to the allied victory over Germany.

That it was not solely a sly diplomatic move to gain two additional votes in the General Assembly is borne out by quotations from Soviet papers. After the Second World War, the Soviet press played more than ever on the theme of the nationalities question: "Only in the Soviet Union, thanks to Marx, Lenin, and Stalin, the nationalities problem has been solved...." The Ukrainians were often held up as the perfect model—a people who had attained their independence and sovereignty against the greatest odds ever encountered by any nation.

Pravda, on August 1, 1950, enlightened its readers thus:

> The Ukrainian people were able to build their own independent state only because Lenin and Stalin stood at the cradle of Ukrainian statehood.... Only because the Ukrainian people were helped by the Russian people, were they able to defeat all foreign imperialists: Polish, German, French, British, American....

And three years ago, when Nikita Khrushchev denounced Stalin's mistakes and crimes at the 20th Congress of the Communist Party of the Soviet Union [1956], he added another page to the story of the nationalities question. He said that after the Second World War Stalin had intended to deport all the Ukrainians from their lands as punishment for their unfaithfulness to

Russia and to communist ideology. The Ukrainians avoided meeting the fate of the Karachai Republic, the Crimean Tartars, the Volga Germans, and the Chechens, "only because there were too many of them and there was no place to which to deport them," said Khrushchev.[9] And, of course, he must have had his information from the prime source.

Thus the main problem of the Soviet Union has been stressed once again: the non-Russian nationalities are too numerous and their vitality too great to allow the Russians to shake them down. That is why the Kremlin rulers are compelled to balance these nationalities against each other, and to woo them constantly toward the Soviet nesting ground. The perfect example of such wooing was the mentioned Crimean gift to the Ukrainians.

There are other examples, too.

Belorussia has been introduced, along with the Ukraine, as a member-state in the United Nations. Lithuania, Latvia, and Estonia have national anthems and national flags of their own. Unlike the Ukraine and Belorussia, though, they are not deemed worthy to have representatives at the United Nations.

Lately the Soviets have begun to pay more attention even to the problem of the Cossacks. There are three different Cossack groupings, besides the Ukrainians who traditionally call themselves the "descendants of the Cossacks of Zaporozhe." The other three groups are: the Don Cossacks, Terek Cossacks, and Kuban Cossacks. (The latter are the descendants of the Ukrainians who settled in the region of the Kuban River in the 18th century.)

In 1917 the Cossacks proclaimed their republics but were overrun by the Red Army which was, by default, unwittingly helped by the army of General Denikin and his Great Russian chauvinist policy. As usual, Soviet republics were proclaimed for the Cossack regions, but soon they were liquidated and the Cossacks incorporated into the Soviet Russian Republic.

During the Second World War, the Cossacks were given more freedom by the Germans than any other nationality under their rule in Eastern Europe. They were allowed to preserve their military formations and traditions, and carry weapons. The reoccupation of the Cossack lands by the Soviets was a most tragic event in the history of the Cossack population. Today their case is being revived in a slightly more liberal way. In 1952, *Pravda* broke the silence on this subject and, since then, scores of books have been devoted to it. Every effort is being made to convince the Cossacks that only the Soviet Union can bring them happiness in the future. Recently, at the Soviet exhibition in New York, a map was displayed of the Soviet Union's territory as it was in 1917; and it showed the territories of the Don, Kuban, and Terek Cossack republics.

On the other hand the Kremlin rulers still keep a close watch on the nationalities of the USSR lest they get too many ideas into their heads, and start a search for their own roads to socialism and sovereignty. The journal *Voprosy filosofii* recently printed an article in which the writer complains that some officials have incorrectly understood the extension of rights of Union Republics. Consequently, there is a tendency in some Republics to give precedence to local personnel over those belonging to other nationalities.[10]

And *Pravda*, August 13, 1959, reported that in Uzbekistan "nationalist survivals make themselves felt here and there in various forms."

Various examples can be given from every Soviet non-Russian republic indicating the silent struggle of these peoples for the preservation of their national, spiritual, and political identity in the face of Russification. To counteract the undiminishing waves of resurging nationalism in the Soviet Union, the Kremlin leaders use the well-tried method of pushing overboard the unwanted elements so as to make republics like the Ukraine, Lithuania, Belorussia, or Georgia more easily steerable.

The campaign for volunteers to settle permanently on the "virgin lands" of Kazakhstan is still in full swing in these republics. The results of that campaign of persuasion and pressure from officials of the Party and government are these:

The population of the Kazakh Republic increased, according to the 1959 census, to 9 million from 6 million in 1939. In the same 20-year period, the Ukraine's population grew barely a million-and-a-half from its more than 40 million in 1939. In the same way, the population of West Siberia increased by 24 percent, and that of Lithuania decreased.

An analysis of the newspapers published in the USSR (according to languages) shows an increase of Russian and Ukrainian newspapers in the regions of Asia. In the Uzbek SSR, Russian and Ukrainian newspapers constitute 20 percent of all newspapers published there. In the Kazakh Republic the increase is even greater; there, 55 percent of the newspapers are in Russian and Ukrainian.

There are also some indications that the Soviet leaders are quite concerned about this region that faces, generally speaking, the Chinese Province of Sinkiang. Reportedly, Sinkiang has recently displayed tremendous economic development and might perhaps become the base for Chinese expansion in the direction of the weakest side of the Soviet Union.

As you must have noticed, I have talked particularly of the Ukraine. I did this not for any sentimental reasons but practical ones. The Ukraine is the second largest republic in the Soviet Union, and the largest among the non-Russian nations within the Soviet Russian orbit of domination.

In terms of population, the Ukraine ranks approximately with England, France, and Italy. According to the 1959 census, roughly 42 million persons lived in the Ukraine. Her territory is somewhat larger than that of France: 232,000 square miles.

But the Ukraine's potential in raw materials, food, and industrial production is much greater than any of these countries. In 1958 the Ukraine provided 43 percent of the coal in the Soviet Union, 56 percent of the iron ore, 51 percent of the pig iron, 40 percent of the steel, and 41 percent of the rolling-mill products.

Now the Ukraine produces as much pig iron as West Germany; in the production of the rolling-mills she has caught up and surpassed France and Belgium together. The coal industry of the Ukraine occupies third place in Europe, and fourth place in the world. "Except for platinum, gold, and copper, we have actually every necessity for our industry," Anatoly Baranovsky, First Deputy Premier for State Planning in the Ukraine, explained to Western newspapermen last year (1959).

Today, many Ukrainians—civilians, bureaucrats, administrators, managers, technicians, scientists, and military commanders as well, occupy important positions in the Soviet empire.

This is not only a tribute to their personal astuteness as communists, but a sure sign of the importance the Kremlin leaders attach nowadays to the Ukrainian problem. The policy of "sharing the rule of Soviet empire with the Ukainian younger brothers" emerged soon after the death of Stalin in 1953. Since then Ukrainian names have begun to chime all over the Soviet Union.

The active resistance of Ukrainian nationalists during the war and in the first years of the post-war period was also instrumental in forming the current policy of the Kremlin toward the Ukraine and other Soviet nationalities. The extent and the intensity of the activities of the Ukrainian Insurgent Army is illustrated best by the following statistics: in the period 1944–50 about 35,000 officers and soldiers of the special Soviet police force died in combat against the Ukrainian insurgents. In 1947 and 1948 a number of detachments of the UPA broke out from the Ukraine through Poland, Czechoslovakia, and Austria, and reached the American zone of Germany.[11] That unusual feat of arms was achieved by the Ukrainian insurgents by order of the Supreme Ukrainian Liberation Council, which decided it was necessary to attract the attention of Western democracies to the plight of the Ukraine, and to demonstrate her desire for freedom.

If that romantic approach to diplomacy went more or less unheeded by the leaders of the West, it was taken into account by the Kremlin leaders who began after that to stress Ukrainian independence and statehood in their propaganda.

Of course, military and organized political resistance cannot be continued indefinitely. Year by year both types of resistance wear out, until there are more nationalist fighters in the concentration camps than in the woods.

It is to be stressed, however, that various appeals addressed by Soviet authorities to the Ukrainian insurgents during Stalin's reign were unsuccessful. Furthermore, Ukrainians captured by the Soviet forces brought their idea of active resistance to their new homes: to concentration camps in Asia, to the places of their compulsory settlement in Western Siberia, and in the Arctic area of European Russia. We have a number of authors (such as Dr. Sholmer, Mr. Noble, Dr. Varkonyi) who, while telling of their experiences in Soviet concentration camps, stress in their books the role of the Ukrainians as organizers of resistance in those camps.[12]

Soon after the death of Stalin, the Ukrainian inmates of Soviet concentration camps in Vorkuta, Norilsk, and Karaganda organized a mass-strike of slave-laborers there. Their demands concerned better living conditions in the camps and review of sentences—or, if I may use Khrushchev's term, "the application of socialist justice" not only to the communists mistreated by Stalin, but also to the average Soviet citizen. As you have probably read, Soviet security forces have broken these strikes only with the help of armored columns.

In 1956, when the word spread in the West that Soviet authorities had disbanded all the concentration camps and liquidated every trace of slave labor introduced by "the worst enemy of the Soviet people—Lavrenti Beria," Mr. Wadsworth, the American representative to the United Nations, received a unique document. It was a letter from Ukrainian inmates of the Soviet concentration camps located in the Mordovian Autonomous Republic, that is on the territory of the Russian Soviet Federated Socialist Republic. This letter, written on a piece of prison shirt-cloth, made an eight-month trip through Ukrainian underground channels to reach the representative of the Supreme Ukrainian Liberation Council, Mr. Lebed, in New York. He handed this document to the United Nations Commission on Human Rights—as it was so addressed.[13]

In their letter the Ukrainian prisoners testified that Khrushchev's collective leadership was still carrying out widespread genocide in the Soviet Union. "Yezhov, Beria, Abakumov and others, whose executions were ordered by the security organs in order to deceive people at home and abroad, cannot be made to hold full responsibility for everything because crimes against the enslaved nations are still being perpetrated."

By way of inference I would stress one detail. It is perhaps of no great consequence how many Soviet Russians have been killed in their encounters with Ukrainians or other insurgents in the Soviet Union. It is perhaps not of much importance whether the Ukrainian struggle gained any recognition in the West for the Ukrainian cause. Of great importance, however, is the fact that the citizens of the multinational empire called the Soviet Union received proof that the police forces of the totalitarian Russian system *were not invincible.* For decades the Kremlin leaders endeavored to convince their citizens that it was useless to resist them because every conspiracy would be immediately discovered by the NKVD;[14] that no nationality has any chance against the combined forces of communism and the Russian nation—at least inside the USSR.

The struggle of the Ukraine put that contention to severe test and proved it false. Without any foreign assistance, the Ukrainian resistance lasted for more than a decade; and then it developed into dynamic "passive resistance" on an all-Union scale.

Thus, if we combine this internal situation which faced the post-Stalin Kremlin leadership with the fact of the staggering losses the Soviet Union suffered during the Second World War, we are able to explain the frantic moves toward peace by Mr. Khrushchev. The Soviets lost about 17 million men in the war. In the decade we are entering, the Soviet Union is going to feel the results of those losses. There is, and there will continue to be, an acute shortage of laborers and soldiers as well. At the same time, the non-Russian nationalities can be less relied on than ever in the history of the Soviet Union. Consequently, the Kremlin rulers have to put their big house in order first, before entering the warpath against the Western democracies.

One of the most urgent items on the agenda of the Soviet Union is, of course, the nationalities question. The Soviets try to solve it, or rather to adjust it to the views of Lenin and to the current needs of their global policies. We should not be surprised if, in the near future, we might be faced by some startling new moves in that field.

What does the West have to offer in that respect? This is the question that occupies many minds inside the Soviet Union.

But this is the question which has to be answered, first of all, by the military men of the West, by themselves and for themselves. I say this not because I am advocating another war of intervention. I am very much aware of the destructive force of modern warfare. But we must always take into account the possibility of another war. And, for such eventuality, I do not see any reason why we should not study, and exploit the right approach to our enemy's underbelly. After all, why should military men always try to attain their objectives the hard way?

REFERENCE NOTES

[1]See *Congressional Record,* vol. 105, No. 124 (July 23, 1959), pp. 12929–12930.

[2]N.S. Khrushchev, "On Peaceful Coexistence," *Foreign Affairs,* XXXVIII, No. 1 (October 1959), 1–18.

[3]See note 1, article No. 6 in this collection.

[4]See *Vedomosti Verkhovnogo Soveta SSSR,* No. 4 (March 9, 1954), pp. 170–76.

[5]V.I. Lenin, *Collected Works* (4th ed.; Moscow: 1971), vol. 36, p. 606.

[6]On the role of Ivan Serov in the Soviet purges, see Boris Levytsky, *The Uses of Terror: The Soviet Secret Police 1917–1970* (New York: Coward, McCann & Geoghegan, 1972).

[7]The so-called Heydrich's Order No. 8, July 17, 1941. Quoted in the *Trials of War Criminals Before the Nuremberg Military Tribunals,* vol. IV, pp. 123–24, Document No. 3414. Documents referring to the Einsatzgruppe D, and specifically to the Einsatzkommando 10A, are published in the same volume, pp. 16–21.

[8]*The New York Times,* June 24, 1941. See article No. 2 in this collection.

[9]"The Crimes of the Stalin Era," *Special Report to the 20th Congress of the CPSU by N.S. Khrushchev* (New York: The New Leader, 1956), p. 44.

[10]I.P. Tsamerian, "The Development of National Relations in the Period of All-round Construction of Communism," *Voprosy filosofii,* XIII, No. 7 (July 1959), 45.

[11]*The New York Times,* September 19, 1947.

[12]Joseph Sholmer, *Vorkuta* (New York: Holt, 1955), 304 pp. John H. Noble, *I was a Slave in Russia: An American Tells His Story* (New York: Devin-Adir, 1958), 182 pp. Cf. Michael Solomon, *Magadan* (Montreal: Chateau Books, 1971), 243 pp. Aleksandr I. Solzhenitsyn, *The GULAG Archipelago, 1918–1956: An Experiment in Literary Investigation,* 3 vols., (New York: Harper & Row, 1973–76), Part V.

[13]See article No. 7 in this collection.

[14]NKVD—People's Commissariat for Internal Affairs (after 1946, Ministry for Internal Affairs—MVD); the most feared and repressive Soviet institution in charge of militia, secret police, internal security forces, and concentration camps.

PART II
UKRAINIAN NATIONALISM AND
SOVIET-WEST RELATIONS

EDITOR'S NOTE

After the defeat of overt armed insurgency in the Ukraine, the national resistance movement transfered its activities into the political sphere.

Inevitably, it became interwoven with the broader issues of the evolving cold war between East and West.

Roman Rakhmanny comments.

6

THE KREMLIN WOOS THE UKRAINIANS

There have been many editorial comments in the American and Canadian press on the big "celebrations" being held in the USSR to mark 300 years of "fraternal association between the Ukraine and Russia." These comments are friendly to the Ukraine and well-intentioned; most of them assume that nobody back home in the Ukraine or anywhere else is being fooled by Soviet hypocrisy. The Ukraine is confidently presented as a thorn in the side of the Russians.

Most of these commentators presume too much on the very slight effort the West has made to encourage Ukrainian resistance. It is true that Ukrainians carried on a never-ceasing resistance to Russian rule during the war and for several years afterwards, and that even today the underground struggle goes on. But how little the West has ever done to help! During the war their politicians and diplomats were much too tactful to embarrass their Soviet ally by any suggestion of support for Ukrainian independence. The dreadful scenes in Germany in which Ukrainian patriots — so-called "DPs" — were handed over at bayonet point to the Russians, immediately after the war in accordance with the Yalta Agreement, can never be forgotten.

It was not until 1949 that the "Voice of America," and not until 1952 that the "Voice of Canada," began broadcasting in the Ukrainian language. But *never* is anything said over these pro-

Reprinted with permission from *Saturday Night* (Toronto), LXVI, No. 40 (July 10, 1954), 11.

grams committing the Western nations to the cause of Ukrainian liberation. On the contrary, when official spokesmen enumerate the peoples now living in Soviet slavery they don't even mention the 42 million Ukrainians, though they never forget to include the one million Albanians.

Perhaps the most significant move made in any Western country is the resolution put forward by Representative Smith of Wisconsin in the U.S. House of Representatives some time ago, calling for direct diplomatic relations with the government of the Ukrainian Soviet Socialist Republic, and with the Belorussian government, too.[1] The idea behind this was that the Soviets, in trying to gain favor with the Ukrainians and Belorussians by giving them a facade of independence through their membership in the United Nations, had laid themselves open to exploitation by our diplomacy, if only we were bold enough to see the opportunity. Let us not only recognize, but proclaim Ukrainian and Belorussian independence. This idea, up to now, has been too radical for Western diplomatic minds.

But the West has done just enough to spur the Russians to make a real effort on their side. There was first of all the separate flag and national anthem "granted" to the Ukraine in 1950. Since then, more Ukrainians, or at least people with Ukrainian names, have appeared in high civilian and military posts in the Ukraine than ever before in the Soviet era. A General Halytsky now holds the command of the Odessa Military District formerly held by Marshal Zhukov, and Vice-Admiral Parkhomenko commands the Black Sea Fleet. There was even a moment, after the death of Stalin, when "Russification policies" in the Ukraine were publicly denounced. But the celebration of the so-called Treaty of Pereiaslav of 1654 has topped anything to date.

This began in spectacular fashion in January of this year, when the Presidium of the USSR Supreme Soviet formally handed over the Crimea to the Ukraine. There is a long history behind this. During the 16th and 17th centuries the Turks had controlled large reaches of the Ukraine through their Tartar vassals in the Crimea. In 1918 the Germans had categorically refused the Ukrainian claim to the Crimea in the treaty they wrote at Brest-Litovsk with the Ukrainian National Republic. This gave rise to skirmishes between the Germans and the Ukrainians, who had freed the Crimea from the Bolsheviks. The following year the Crimean port of Sevastopol was used, along with Odessa, as a base for British and French support for the White Guard offensive of Denikin and Wrangel against the Ukrainian National Republic.

The Soviet Russia of Lenin, Trotsky and Stalin regarded the Crimea as a Gibraltar controlling the approaches to the Ukraine. It therefore attached this peninsula — just as has been done more lately with strategic East Prussia — *to the Russian SFSR,* though there was no geographical connection, and all ethnic, historical and economic factors were against it. Suddenly, at a word of command, the Soviet press cites all these reasons why the Crimea should now belong to the Ukraine.

The Kremlin, it seems, is prepared to take some slight risk with its "aircraft carrier in the Black Sea" if it can lure the Ukrainians from the "deceitful propaganda of the Ukrainian nationalists and the capitalists of Wall Street." In reality this is a premium paid on an insurance policy intended to avert, in any future war, a repetition of the mass desertions of Ukrainian and other non-Russian peoples from the Red Army such as occurred in 1941.

I have been moved to this warning by the news that my old friend V. Okhrymovych, allegedly parachuted into the Ukraine by "American counter-espionage," has been caught and put to death. I knew Okhrymovych before the war, and I met him several times during the war in the Ukraine.

After the war I shared a room with him in a West European city, until the day he decided to return to the Ukraine. Why did he go back? The place for those who directed the Ukrainian underground, he believed, was home in the Ukraine and not abroad. Officially, he was "requested" to go back by the Supreme Ukrainian Liberation Council, the political body which directs the activities of the UPA, the Ukrainian Insurgent Army.

The Kremlin, of course, calls Okhrymovych an "American spy." It depicts him and his fellow Ukrainian nationalists as nothing more than collaborators of the United States. And it doesn't fail to point out that the United States, to quote from its recent Ambassador to Moscow, George Kennan, looks upon the Ukraine as just as much a part of Russia as Pennsylvania is of the United States."[2] If this, or the concept of the reactionary Russian emigres of the American Committee for Liberation from Bolshevism of a "democratic federation" of the Ukraine and Russia, is all that U.S. policy can put forward, we cannot be confident that we are winning the struggle for the soul of the Ukrainian people.

REFERENCE NOTES

[1]See, U.S. Congress, House, Subcommittee of the Committee on Foreign Affairs, *Hearings, on H.C. Res. 58, Favoring Extension of Diplomatic Relations with the Republics of Ukraine and Belorussia,* 83rd Cong., 1st Sess., 1953, 112 p.

[2]See, George F. Kennan, *American Diplomacy, 1900–1950* (Chicago: University of Chicago Press, 1951), p. 135.

7

MESSAGE ON PRISON CLOTH:
A PLEA FOR FREEDOM

A Special News Dispatch

One of the first documents ever smuggled out of the Soviet concentration camp was handed over to the U.N. Secretariat, declared Mykola Lebed, Secretary-General for Foreign Affairs of the Supreme Ukrainian Liberation Council, at a press conference held today in New York City.

Written on a piece of prison cloth and signed by Ukrainian inmates of a Mordovian slave labor camp, the document is a 2,400-word appeal for human rights. [1]

The prisoners' appeal, printed in Ukrainian Cyrillic letters, was translated into English here by the staff of the Foreign Representation of the Supreme Ukrainian Liberation Council.

The appeal asks the United Nations Commission on Human Rights to investigate genocide in Soviet concentration camps, both during and after Stalin's rule.

The Ukrainian prisoners charge that Khrushchev's collective leadership is still carrying out widespread genocide in the Ukraine.

Reprinted with permission from *The Telegram* (Toronto), July 23, 1956, where it appeared under the headline title "Message Smuggled From Red Slave Camp on Shirtcloth, Pleads for Freedom."

"Does the civilized world know that over the mass burial sites of the prison camps, new camps and cities are built, canals dug, and stadiums erected in order to obliterate the traces of these crimes?" the authors of the appeal ask.

They state that "in the Abez (Komi ASSR), Camps No. 1, 4, and 5 stand on prisoners' mass graves. At Zavod No. 5 in Leplia (Mordovian ASSR), the 1st and 2nd polishing shops, technical laboratory, and the forge were erected on human bones. . . ."

The prisoners' document throws some new light on Nikita Khrushchev's campaign for developing the virgin lands of the USSR by volunteers and members of the *Komsomol.*

It states that hundreds of thousands of Ukrainians "are exiled to the virgin territory of Kazakhstan, Krasnoiarsk and the Far North" while Khrushchev proclaims that only volunteers and members of the Komsomol go out to these areas.

The Ukrainian prisoners in Mordovia voice a demand which might be the truest expression of the beliefs of millions of Soviet citizens.

They say: "Whereas every criminal act against the enslaved nation is perpetrated with the knowledge of the Politburo and of the Central Committee of the Communist Party of the Soviet Union, we demand that the entire ruling class of the Soviet Union be brought before international justice."

Crimes Continue

"Yezhov, Beria, Abakumov and others whose executions were ordered by the security organs in order to deceive people at home and abroad, cannot be made to hold full responsibility for everything, because crimes against enslaved nations are still being perpetrated."

The document took eight months to reach representatives of the Ukrainian Liberation Movement in the West.

The Supreme Ukrainian Liberation Council, an underground committee, was established in the Ukraine twelve years ago for the purpose of directing all Ukrainian anti-Nazi and anti-communist activities.

Its charges are substantiated by recent Soviet and Western reports of the blowing up of a Soviet military train by a group of

Ukrainian Insurgent Army soldiers, and the subsequent mopping up in the forest region of Shepetivka (west of Kiev) by MVD security troops.

Former soldiers of the Ukrainian Insurgent Army and of the Ukrainian civilian underground network make up a considerable percentage of the population of the Soviet concentration camps.

And it was they who initiated the first prisoners' strike in the Karaganda camp system in 1952 while Stalin was still alive. Because of that strike, over 300 were transferred to the ill-famed camps of Vorkuta and Norilsk where they started another three-month strike in 1953.

According to the testimony of a Hungarian physician, Dr. F. Varkonyi, who was released from the Vorkuta camp, these and subsequent strikes, supported by prisoners of all nationalities including Russian, turned into minor rebellions and were only put down with the aid of tanks and aircraft.[2]

REFERENCE NOTES

[1]For a complete text of the document, see "They Speak for the Silent; an Open Letter," *National Review* (New York), II, No. 5 (August 1, 1956), 13–16.

[2]On the prisoner strikes in Soviet concentration camps following Stalin's death and the role of former Ukrainian freedom fighters in these strikes, see references cited in note 12 to article 5 above. Also, see Volodymyr Kosyk, *Concentration Camps in the USSR* (London: Ukrainian Publishers, Ltd, 1962), 108 pp.

8

UKRAINIAN NATIONALISM

*Unwilling Collaborators Cause
Concern to Soviet Rulers*

Despite appearances the nationality problem is still much alive in the Soviet Union, and it is being nourished with the news from Africa. This is the conclusion of this writer after having interviewed a score of Western visitors to Soviet Russia and Soviet Ukraine, and talked to a number of Soviet visitors to Canada and the United States during the past year. The conclusion is also supported by the writer's daily explorations in the dull grey waters of the Soviet press and radio reports.

To be sure, the restlessness of Soviet Ukrainians or Soviet Estonians falls somewhat short of the expectations cherished by their nationalistically minded countrymen and former revolutionaries who, like the writer, have settled in Canada for good. Yet, the dissatisfaction of Ukrainians, Belorussians, Baltic peoples and Georgians with the management of Soviet affairs by their big Russian brother is widespread, and deep enough to cause some uneasiness among the Kremlin rulers.

This internal situation explains to a degree the violent reaction of Mr. Khrushchev and his Soviet colleagues to a very general remark made recently by Mr. Diefenbaker at the United

Reprinted with permission from *Canadian Commentator* (Toronto), V, No. 2 (February, 1961), 20-21.

Nations.[1] The angry reply to a few words concerning the inability of Baltic peoples and of "freedom-loving Ukrainians, and other peoples of Eastern Europe" to elect freely the government of their choosing, contained a significant claim. Mr. Khrushchev's lieutenant in the Ukraine, M. V. Pidhorny, boasted his country was industrially more powerful, economically better developed, and possessed a higher proportion of university-trained young people than Canada, or, for that matter, France or Great Britain.[2]

But it is exactly this industrialization of their country that changes the Ukrainians' position in the Soviet Union; they cannot be bullied as much today as they could in Stalin's time. Even Stalin, if we believe Khrushchev's words, found the limit when he conceded that it was impossible to deport all the Ukrainians "because there were too many of them."[3] So much less so today when the Ukraine's industrial and agricultural power has surpassed that of France, and the Ukraine's productivity constitutes the backbone of the Soviet Union's foreign trade and the aid to the underdeveloped countries of Asia and Africa. This industrial and economic power gives more weight to the Ukraine's political position in the Soviet camp, a position resembling that of Communist China: it is an unwilling collaborator of Soviet Russia.

Unwilling, but not unaware of her own situation. More and more Soviet Ukrainians are awake to the fact that their wealth and industry are being used to further Soviet Russia's political ambitions both in Africa and in Asia. "We work and suffer many privations only to provide food and clothes for Mr. Lumumba,"[4] was the wry comment of a collective-farm manager in the region of Kiev, Soviet Ukraine's capital.

There are also many signs to show that Soviet Ukraine's economy, and its agriculture in particular, are beginning to feel the drag of the many Soviet commitments abroad, and the weight of the bribes offered the Afro-Asian countries. There is a far greater shortage of food in the Ukrainian villages than a year ago; and court proceedings against the collective farm workers who have dared to appropriate a little grain from the *kolkhoz* fields are more numerous in the district towns than ever before in Khrushchev's period.

At the same time a growing number of Soviet Ukrainians are marvelling at the strange fortunes of the newly established inde-

pendent African nations. They are being helped by West and East
alike, they are treated as full-grown states by all the established
powers, big, medium and small; and they enjoy the right of
managing their own internal affairs without interference from
any white "big brother," be it capitalist or communist.

"Our foreign trade is entirely in the hands of the Russians at
Moscow, and our limited autonomy in economic planning (so-
called decentralization) is now withering away. Our country is
not even represented in the capitals of such Socialist countries as
Hungary and China." These are the complaints of a Ukrainian
student in Lviv, Western Ukraine. On the other hand, a Russian
student of Moscow University, recently on leave from the Red
Navy, had another reason to complain: "But you Ukrainians
aspire only to be officers, generals and marshals. . . .". This was in
reference to the growing number of Ukrainians in high military
and technical posts in the Soviet Union.

The hard-driving Ukrainians apparently do not confine their
aspirations to military matters, however. From the Olympic
Games in Rome this year, Ukrainian athletes took home 13 gold
medals, 9 silver and 5 bronze, thus qualifying their country for
the third place in the unofficial Olympic score. "Yet our sovereign republic is not allowed to be represented by a separate
Ukrainian team of athletes," a Ukrainian sport fan remarked
heatedly to a Canadian visitor in Kiev. But he would not comment on the incident of July 19 this year in the Moscow stadium,
when Russian players and a yelling crowd verbally and physically
abused the Ukrainian soccer team from Kiev.

These and other similar points of contact and complaints
compelled Mr. Khrushchev to stage a more forceful show for the
Soviet Ukrainian delegation at the United Nations. Its head delegate, M. V. Pidhorny, expounded his views and his scorn for the
West in the Ukrainian language, just to show how independent
his country is.[5] His line of defense against the "interference of
Mr. Diefenbaker in the internal affairs of the Ukrainian people"
is being followed faithfully by the Soviet press and radio, both in
Ukrainian and Russian. Articles are being published, letters
from the readers are being arranged to voice the "indignation of
the Ukrainian people" against the "ridiculous remarks" of the
Canadian leader.

It seems that Canada's Prime Minister has found the soft spot in the Soviet armored mask. With a few words concerning Soviet Russian colonialism in Eastern Europe, Canada's leader struck at the Red sea of propaganda and exposed, just for a wink, the hidden iceberg beneath its surface: the nationality problem that looms larger and colder for the Kremlin rulers now when exposed to the rays of the African sun of independence.

REFERENCE NOTES

[1]See, U.N. General Assembly, *Official Records,* Fifteenth Session, Plenary, Part One, Vol. I, pp. 108-12 (September 26, 1960).

[2]*Ibid.,* pp. 373-80 (October 4, 1960). The name *M. V. Pidhorny* is the Ukrainian version of *N. V. Podgorny,* former First Secretary of the Communist Party of Ukraine, and the Chairman of the Presidium of the USSR Supreme Soviet, i.e. Soviet Union's president.

[3]See note 9 to article No. 5 in this collection.

[4]Patrice Lumumba, Prime Minister of the Republic of Congo; dismissed and arrested, he was killed in prison in 1961. Communist bloc propaganda exploited his name during the 'sixties; a Moscow university for foreign students was renamed "Lumumba University."

[5]See note 2 above.

9

THE EMERGENCE OF A SUBMERGED
NATION IN THE SOVIET UNION*

Most Western analysts of Soviet affairs have failed to note the changed position of the Ukrainian SSR within the communist camp. During Stalin's long reign the Ukraine became so submerged in the Russian superstate that even many Western statesmen and scholars still regard the country as an integral part of Russia. The partial decentralization of the economy and administration of the Soviet Union in 1957 has given the Ukraine a new role. In contrast to the late 'thirties when the republic had jurisdiction over only 14 secondary ministries, the Ukraine now has jurisdiction in 29 departments, including defense, foreign affairs and agriculture. After thirty years of virtual isolation, its people are making political, cultural and economic contacts with the outside world. In this respect, the foreign contacts the Ukrainian SSR has established during the last three years of peaceful coexistence both with the People's Democracies and the "capitalist" countries have a certain meaning that sheds some light on the internal development of the whole Soviet Union.

Reprinted with permission from *International Journal* (Toronto), XVII, No. 1 (Winter, 1961-62), 30-33.

*This *Note* is based on the paper, entitled "Three Years of Peaceful Coexistence in the Life of a Soviet Republic," presented at the annual meeting of the Canadian Political Science Association in Montreal, June 8, 1961.

Since the herding of the Soviet Republics into the Soviet Union in 1923, the Ukraine had enjoyed only a paper independence. In 1944, however, the Ukraine was permitted, along with Belorussia, to form some of its own ministries and to sign some international treaties and conventions. But the Ukraine still has no diplomatic representatives abroad, and no foreign country is directly represented in Kiev. Though a charter member of the United Nations the Republic had no permanent delegate until P. P. Udovychenko was appointed in 1958. In the same year the Ukraine was admitted to several of the United Nations specialized agencies.

All of this meant little to the Ukrainian public. The changes began to affect everyday life only when in 1958 it became possible to subscribe to some foreign newspapers and magazines, and when visitors from abroad began to appear in Kiev. The Czechoslovak foreign minister arrived to open a consulate; President Gamal Abdel Nasser of the United Arab Republic paid a courtesy call; Wladyslaw Gomulka of Poland came to help the citizens of Kiev celebrate Ukrainian-Polish friendship, and assured them that "the Polish people recognized unequivocally the unification" of the former Polish eastern provinces with the Ukraine "as an act of historical justice." The astute Mr. Harold Macmillan was one of the few Westerners to recognize the new importance of the Ukraine, and he received an unexpectedly enthusiastic welcome when he visited Kiev in 1959.

Friendly relations with European neighbors and with other People's Republics have been particularly encouraged since 1958 through the activities of Ukrainian branches of the mutual friendship "societies" — Soviet-Polish, Soviet-Hungarian, Soviet-Romanian, Soviet-Chinese, Soviet-Albanian, Soviet-Czechoslovak and, later on, Soviet-Korean, and Soviet-French. Each branch has a chairman and five directors who are responsible for the various portfolios of cultural *rapprochement* — science, culture and art, youth organizations, foreign contacts, sports and tourism. The public activities of the societies usually include ten-day festivals to celebrate the culture of the designated country. Festivals of Ukrainian culture were, in turn, arranged in Poland, Romania, Bulgaria, Hungary, Albania, Mongolia and Czechoslovakia.

The Ukrainian Academy of Sciences in Kiev, besides receiving many delegations of foreign scholars, is reported to be conducting "a systematic book exchange" with several hundred institutions in communist countries. Less systematic exchanges were also carried on with some non-communist countries, but these seem to have been somewhat hampered by Soviet red tape. Even so, the contacts between Ukrainian scholars and the world continued to grow.

In the three-year period, the Ukrainian press constantly carried reports of contacts of many other kinds: groups of foreign experts, artists and sportsmen visited the Ukraine; Chinese technicians were being trained in the Ukraine, while Ukrainian scientists were teaching at Shanghai, Harbin and Peking; Ukrainian industry was providing technical and material assistance to India, as well as China and other People's Republics; the Ukraine has established trade relations with 59 countries. Taken together, all these reports help to trace the threads of the intricate web of new responsibilities that tend to reorient the Ukraine out of its pre-war isolation and concentration within the Soviet Union.

But the new outlook must have brought Ukrainians to realize even more sharply than ever their dependent status in foreign relations. Moscow still carefully regulates foreign contacts of the Ukraine and more often than not tends to present the Ukrainian achievements as an integral part of Russia's activities. Ukrainian scholars, scientists, writers and artists are able to visit the "capitalist" countries—and particularly those of North America—mostly as members of all-union delegations. Only under the pressure both from within the Ukraine and from abroad (the emigre criticism showing the colonial dependency of the Ukraine from Russia) did Moscow agree reluctantly to allow the Ukrainian SSR to have its own exhibition at the 1958–59 trade fair in Marseilles.

The Soviet Ukrainians are increasingly annoyed by the preference Russian culture receives in the Soviet performances abroad. When the programme of a group of Ukrainian artists visiting Warsaw turned out to be two-thirds Russian, a Kiev monthly *Vitchyzna* charged that the "concert could not have been called a show of Ukrainian musicianship. . . nor did it represent the whole of the Soviet Union." On the other hand, the Soviet Ukrainians are annoyed, as was a representative of the

Ukraine at the UNESCO conference on adult education at Montreal in August, 1960, when they are referred to by Western speakers and by the press as "Russians."

The Soviet Ukrainian press makes a supreme effort to cover up these deficiencies in the foreign contacts of the Ukraine. It displays an evident anxiety to make the most of every possible aspect of the changed position of the Ukrainian SSR since some decentralization has been effected in the USSR. At the same time it urges citizens to be vigilant in uncovering anti-Soviet influences creeping in with foreign tourists, through radio broadcasts, films or publications. Admittedly, young Ukrainian technocrats and intellectuals, however carefully indoctrinated by the party, are still capable of developing some affinities for "rotten bourgeois" culture and aesthetic tastes; some have evidently even ventured to doubt the wisdom of the Soviet way of life, and to criticize Soviet achievements.

This illustrates the kind of problems Moscow has to face when it feels compelled to let her submerged non-Russian nations emerge even partially. That is why the official Ukraine and its press reacted so violently when Mr. Diefenbaker, at the Fifteenth Session of the United Nations General Assembly, hinted that the Ukrainian people and other Eastern European nationalities were deprived of their freedom to "establish orders in their countries of their own will and choice." For the first time the chief Ukrainian delegate, Mr. Pidhorny, was allowed to make his counterspeech before the United Nations Assembly in the Ukrainian language.[1] The Soviet Ukrainian press and the speakers at the public "indignation" meetings all over the Ukraine echoed his protest against the alleged interference in "the domestic affairs" of the "sovereign" Ukrainian Soviet Republic. Yet tourists who visited the Ukraine after this particular three-month campaign found no evidence of any increased enmity toward Canada among the Ukrainians they met.

Thus from 1958 till 1961, the Ukraine was evidently being allowed a limited opportunity to play the role of model communist state, the perfect demonstration of the communist solution to the national aspirations of the Afro-Asian peoples. The increased economic and cultural exchanges between the Ukraine and the People's Democracies undoubtedly has the object of forging closer integration of the Soviet commonwealth through increased interdependence. Continued on a still larger scale, these new friendly relations between neighboring countries might eventually lead to a permanent pacification of Eastern Europe. The cultural intercourse of the Ukraine with non-communist states has been kept within the narrow bounds of circumscribed book exchanges, limited tourism and restricted participation by Ukrainian scholars in international conferences. The Ukrainian SSR has not been given such free a hand in this respect as, let us say, Poland. Nevertheless the effect of even these limited interchanges must be disproportionately greater than their number or scope might suggest, since they come at the end of thirty years of virtual isolation for the Ukraine.

In the political and diplomatic field the enlarged role of the Ukrainian SSR in the period 1958-1960 represented a partial return to the status enjoyed by the Ukraine before she was compelled to join the Soviet confederation in 1923. The caution with which the Soviet leaders proceed in opening up the Soviet non-Russian nations to the advantages of foreign political contacts shows how keenly aware they are of the dangers the nationality question presents to the unity of the communist "family of nations." The economic and cultural potentialities of such non-Russian Soviet Republics as the Ukraine lend themselves to the Kremlin leaders as useful means to their avowed peaceful conquest of the non-communist world. In this respect, the Western powers, with the exception of the British who made the attempt in 1947,[2] have played into the Soviet hand by neglecting to establish direct diplomatic relations with the government of the Ukrainian SSR in Kiev.

REFERENCE NOTES

[1]See note 2 to article No. 8 in this collection.
[2]See, Great Britain, *Parliamentary Debates*, Commons, Vol. 472, No. 9 (March 13, 1950), p. 28.

10

COMRADE ENKO — THE
WARHORSE OF RUSSIA

Today, as in the past, the lonely Russian people are in search of loyal friends. Through the 14th and 15th centuries the Russians were able to withstand Mongol domination. They confounded Napoleon and twice repulsed the German *Drang nach Osten*. They have built a mighty new empire and have begun to conquer outer space. But neither the pan-Slavism of the czars, nor the internationalism of the Soviet leaders of this century, has succeeded in placating their neighbors or providing Russia with friends or reliable allies. The present ideological conflict with China brings this ancient truth once more into focus.

The centuries-long bloody feud between France and Germany seems at last to be dying out. Presumably, the belief is growing on each side that mutual destruction is the only alternative to peaceful coexistence. The parallel feud between the Soviet Union and Poland has also subsided into "peaceful coexistence," but it is a peace in which Poland has no choice. The October rising of 1956 demonstrated quite clearly that Wladyslaw Gomulka's communists have not yet given their hearts to their Russian brothers.

Moscow is well aware of the unreliable quality of the Polish

Reprinted with permission from *Military Review*, XLIV, No. 6 (June, 1964), 75-79, where it appeared under the author's real name, Roman Olynyk.

friendship. And more or less the same can be said of other neighbors and unwilling comrades in Romania, Hungary, Czechoslovakia, and Bulgaria. The great Yugoslav-Soviet friendship of the war period ended in a bitter feud that is slow to heal even now, eleven years after Joseph Stalin's death.

We must even doubt the sincerity of the devotion to the Soviet cause of those people who come within the inner circle of Russian influence — Ukrainians, Belorussians, and the Baltic and Caucasian nationalities.

Conflicts of Inner Circle

For 300 years the Ukrainians have been exposed to the "fraternization" efforts of the Russians. Catherine the Great, while imposing a barbarously harsh regime, urged the Ukrainians not to regard her Russian subjects as "wolves of the forest." Stalin invented an official vocabulary of jargon for upholding "the Russian people" as the beneficent source of material and spiritual gifts to the Ukraine.

In spite of all these efforts, the average citizen of the Ukraine today knows that only cunning and force brought the Ukraine into the Russian orbit. In the middle of the 17th century the Russians watched while the Ukrainian nation was bled white in struggles with the Poles and the Tartars. Then, as insurance against Ukrainian resurgence, they shared the territory with the Polish feudal republic. Again, in 1923, the four-year-old Ukrainian Socialist Republic, established on the basis of Vladimir Lenin's promise of complete and unrestricted independence for Ukrainians, was cajoled into union with the Russian Soviet Federated Socialist Republic and then deprived of her sovereignty by the USSR Constitution.

Thanks only to their numbers, the Ukrainians survived Stalin's extermination policy. Premier Nikita Khrushchev stated as much publicly in 1956, testifying again to the fact that the Russians cannot trust even their closest neighbors, who are also relatives of sorts. For over three centuries this web of mistrust and suspicion, of hatred and contempt, has been woven between the two nationalities which, perhaps more than any others in Eastern Europe, have common interests and must learn to coexist and cooperate if they are to survive in the nuclear age.

Not by Whip Alone

Perhaps awakening at last, Soviet Russian leadership seems to be evolving new tactics to try to win more willing Ukrainian support. Some long-overdue benefits are being offered. The appearance of Ukrainian sovereignty has been improved by the membership of the Ukrainian Soviet Socialist Republic in the United Nations and by increased responsibilities for her delegations in various UN agencies and institutions. Ukrainians are beginning to take on a role in the Soviet Union that reminds one of the Scotsmen who "ran the British Empire." The sturdy Ukrainian Enko—as he is popularly dubbed from the typical ending of Ukrainian surnames—seems to be making his influence felt throughout the Soviet empire.

This influence cannot be entirely explained on the basis of Ukrainian population density and economic development. Russia is no longer dependent on the resources of the borderlands. She now has developed rich resources of her own and has built a mighty industrial network in Europe and beyond the Urals. The Ukraine, as a separate republic, is useful as a link between Russia and the newer satellites, Czechoslovakia, Hungary, and Romania. But, most important of all, the Ukraine is vital to Russia as a reservoir of trained and trainable manpower.

The Ukrainians are, in fact, the traditional empire builders of Eastern Europe—the first Eastern European empire to extend from the Black Sea to the shores of Finland had its center at Kiev, the capital of the Ukraine today. The Polish feudal state of the 16th century reached its greatest power after it had integrated into the ranks of its nobility the best educated and wealthiest families of the Ukraine and Belorussia. The Ukrainians also played a leading role in the Europeanization of czarist Russia in the 18th and 19th centuries.

The Ukrainian contribution to the growing military power of Russia has been overlooked by many Western Soviet specialists. In the 18th century the Russians succeeded in pushing the Turks from the north shore of the Black Sea only after securing the cooperation of the Ukraine's Cossack regiments. In 1877 the Russian breakthrough into the Balkans was led by the Ukrainian General I. V. Hurko. General R. S. Kondratenko organized the successful defense of Port Arthur in the Russo-Japanese War of

1904–05, although he was later killed and the inept commander of the fortress surrendered it to the Japanese.

The only really imaginative action of that war was carried out by General A. V. Mishchenko who led 6,000 Cossacks 160 kilometers into Japanese territory to destroy communications. The last Russian offensive of World War I was possible at all only because the Ukrainian regiments, little affected by communist propaganda, had preserved their discipline.

On the other hand, Ukrainians made important contributions to the revolutionary movement. Zheliabov, the successful organizer of the attempt against Czar Alexander II, and a number of other prominent social revolutionaries were Ukrainians disenchanted with the "organic approach" of the liberals to the liberation of the Ukrainian people.

The 1905 revolt on the battleship *Prince Potemkin* of the Black Sea Fleet was organized by Oleksander M. Kovalenko. (He died last year in Geneva where he once served as a member of the diplomatic mission of the Ukrainian National Republic.) The first commander in chief of Lenin's army, before Leon Trotsky took over, was M. V. Krylenko, without whose cooperation the marines of the Baltic Fleet and the soldiers of the southwestern front would hardly have supported the October Revolution.

Warhorse of Russia

There were other Ukrainian Soviet commanders of the revolutionary and interwar periods, including such names as Kliment E. Voroshilov and Semen K. Timoshenko, indicative of the fact that Comrade Enko is still the warhorse of the Russian empire.

In the first month of the German advance in 1941, the Ukrainians with other nationalities of the USSR—including many Russians—staged mass surrenders in protest against the miseries of Soviet life and the burden of Russian centralism. To them the Germans had long been thought of as representing the enlightenment and freedom of Western Europe. They soon realized, however, that they could not reach out to the Western World through Hitler's Germany.

Groundwork Laid

The German Field Marshal von Paulus learned how well they could fight when he reached Stalingrad. The Ukrainian Soviet General A. I. Ieremenko commanded the Stalingrad front in 1942–43. Ukrainians were also in command on the Don River in 1942 when the Germans and their allies were dealt crushing blows. When the great German strategist, Field Marshal Erich von Manstein, took charge of the effort to relieve von Paulus' 6th Army, he was thwarted by Lieutenant General Rodion I. Malynovsky (now Marshall and Minister of Defense for the USSR). The groundwork for the destruction of the German forces at Stalingrad was thus laid.

Behind the German lines Soviet guerrilla operations were largely led and sustained by Ukrainians. The deep raid from the Pripet River into the Carpathians in 1943 was the work of the Ukrainian partisan, S. Kovpak. The Ukrainian Insurgent Army (UPA), a nationalist Ukrainian force, opposed both the Germans and the communists until 1944, and withstood Stalinist onslaughts up to 1953. They achieved tactical retreats by Soviet authorities in various sectors of Soviet life, to the advantage of the Ukrainians.

When Ukrainians like Malynovsky, the Soviet Minister of Defense, and Kirill Moskalenko, the Soviet rocket chief, rise to commanding positions in the USSR, they represent the natural pressure of the Ukrainians for acknowledgment of their share in the empire. This also reflects the dependence of the empire on the Ukrainian reservoir of specialized manpower. Ukrainians are winning similarly influential posts in other fields than the military. It has been estimated that Ukrainians make up at least one-third of the skilled personnel in Soviet technology, research, and scholarship.

The Russians are also largely relying on the Ukrainians to build Kazakhstan into a bulwark against the Red Chinese in Sinkiang. The more restless elements of the Ukraine are being drawn off to continue development of the immense, empty "virgin lands."

Historically, the European facing the Russian enigma has been as prone to miscalculations as we are today. Napoleon failed to grasp the advantages of his Istanbul Ambassador's plan for supporting the Ukrainian case against the Russians. When Adolf Hitler refused to give consideration to the Ukrainians' political aspirations, he pushed them into the camp of their oppressors.

The Russians cannot leave the Ukrainians out of their calculations. Comrade Enko has become indispensable, even though from time to time he may still be out of favor and regarded with suspicion as he was in Stalin's day.

In our studies of Soviet activities, probably we should not leave Comrade Enko out of our calculations either. When "Russian" teams negotiate at the United Nations, or at Warsaw Pact conferences; when Soviet engineers and technicians appear on building sites in India, in Cuba, in Egypt; when missions are sent to put gentle pressure on Romania, Hungary, or Czechoslovakia, might it not be useful to calculate how many among them are Ukrainian? And to what extent Ukrainian nationalism is being satisfied and integrated into the empire building of the "elder brother?"

Whoever can locate accurately, and interpret in modern terms, the age-old aspirations of Comrade Enko will discover a valuable key to the Pandora's box of Russian weaknesses.

PART III
MAN, SOCIETY AND RELIGION
IN THE USSR

EDITOR'S NOTE

The unbelievable became feasible, and the wishful acquired real forms. Former members of the Ukrainian Insurgent Army impressed their own brand of human dignity and their will to resist on many minds of the multi-national population in Soviet prisons.

By shedding the scales of fear, the theoretical "Soviet man" turned out to be a real human being of a given nationality. The lonely Soviet crowd found alternatives to both the official state ideology and the state protected Church structure.

Thus, in the atmosphere of a growing new humanism the concepts of both nationality and religion have regained their values.

11

WHY RUSSIA NEEDS TIME AND PEACE

What the Soviet leaders do not like to admit is that their major moves on the chessboard of internal or external policy are usually a response to necessity. And the staunchest anti-communists in this country hardly ever grant such a possibility. No matter how strange this sounds, Soviet spokesmen and their doctrinaire anti-communist opponents agree in stressing the ideological aspect of every Soviet-Russian decision.

Thus the latest Soviet peace drive, ably steered by Premier Khrushchev to the very gates of Washington, has been represented by the official Soviet outlets as an essential, integral part of communism, Leninist "socialism" and, for that matter, a basic trend of the Soviet way of life as well. The anti-communists, on the other hand, view it as just another devilish stratagem of Bolshevism devised for lulling the free world and for getting a foothold on its shores.

Such views might be quite helpful in raising the morale of the Soviet ruling class and of the *Komsomol*. The same way of thinking might also keep up the fighting spirit of those in this country who suffered at the hands of the Soviets, and for that reason oppose them. Yet, it does not change the basic fact of life, that necessity governs the country of socialism as much as it does the countries of capitalism.

Reprinted with permission from *The Globe and Mail* (Toronto), September 23, 1959.

So, the Soviet decision to increase the volume of their trade with Great Britain was not meant to embarrass the Conservative Government of Mr. Macmillan, but was a sound manifestation of the Soviet need to acquire sterling for their purchases from the sterling trading area.

Similarly, Mr. Khrushchev's noisy campaign calling for the Summit meeting and for establishing a term of peaceful coexistence was dictated, not so much by the ideological requirements of his communist faith, as by the sheer necessities of his empire, strained by internal and semi-external pressures.

The latest data of the recent census in the Soviet Union must have stirred into a sense of reality the Kremlin rulers who are the administrators of the empire first and communists second. For the Soviet Union lost, during the Second World War, roughly 10 million men in uniform and about 7 million civilians. The full weight of these staggering losses is beginning to tell: for the next decade the labor population of the USSR will be increasing by only a few hundred thousands yearly as compared with one to two million annual increase during the previous decade. At the same time, the crude birthrate is going to fall to 20 per 1,000 from the 1938 peak of 38 per 1,000.

This is more than enough to justify the cutting of the number of Soviet armed forces carried out within the last two years. At the present time in Kiev and Kharkiv, details of the Soviet Army are being used as a special labor force to spur civilian construction.

The shortage of labor in the USSR manifested itself also in the decree of the Soviet government compelling all students of Soviet secondary schools "to engage in socially productive activities," that is, to work in industry or on the collective farms. There is some substance in the claims that the Soviet government was moved to release thousands of political prisoners, not by any higher sense of "Socialist justice," freely abused in Stalin's time, but by an acute shortage of labor.

Another kind of pressure on the Kremlin is being exerted by the non-Russian nationalities. The Ukraine, the second largest and industrially most advanced of Soviet Republics, is more restless than ever. The people are eager for more economic freedom, more cultural independence from Russia, and local bureaucrats covet a larger share of power and economic planning.

Perhaps no other people in the world is more aware of the real price of war than the Ukrainians. The Second World War was, as Edgar Snow put it, "the Ukrainian War," having resulted in the virtual ruin of the country. Therefore it was a masterstroke on Mr. Macmillan's part, when he went to Kiev and its districts last May, to carry his message of peace to the Ukrainians. Their warm response proved they understood his message.

To disregard these feelings of 41 million Ukrainians, and not to recognize their lack of enthusiasm for a war against the "capitalists," would be great folly on the part of the Kremlin rulers. It might invite, in case of such a war, the disaster Stalin had suffered in the early campaign of 1941; then, over a million, mostly non-Russian Red Army soldiers, surrendered to the advancing Germans.

Nor are the Ukrainians or, for that matter, the Belorussians and the Baltic peoples, unaware of the Kremlin's attempts to reduce their potential by the "volunteer" deportation of their youth to the "virgin lands" of Kazakh Soviet Republic beyond the Caspian Sea. They see, as any student of Soviet affairs can't fail to notice, the Kremlin rulers' eagerness to kill two birds with one stone.

While unloading some unwanted ballast from the Ukraine, Belorussia, Georgia, and the Baltic States so as to make them more steerable, Soviet leaders endeavor to thicken the thin crust of population over Kazakhstan, and, generally speaking, the whole region that faces China's Province of Sinkiang. Reportedly that Province of China, more densely populated than its Soviet counterpart, recently underwent a tremendous economic development. By its sheer population and economic weight it threatens as a dagger at the soft underbelly of the Soviet Union.

Driven by the necessity to avert all possible surprises in that area, Soviet leaders have had to bypass the commandments of their communist creed, and put an all-out effort into the settling of Kazakhstan by so-called "volunteers" from the European Soviet Republics. Small wonder then, that the population of the Kazakh Republic increased according to the 1959 census to nine million—from six million in 1939. In the same 20-year period, the "blossoming" Ukraine grew by barely a million and a half from its 40 million of 1939. In the same way the population of

West Siberia (part of the Russian Soviet Republic) increased by 24 percent, and that of Lithuania decreased.

So time and peace are the essential prerequisites for putting in order the big house called the Soviet Union. And its leaders are responding to the need in a most appropriate way. They call for coexistence — not by virtue of their communist creed, but for the sake of their own survival.

12

THE LONELY SOVIET MAN

The Communist Party of the Soviet Union (CPSU) is in control of a super-state, and in that sense is by far the most powerful of all Communist parties. But in revolutionary spirit, it may well be the weakest. Revolution has ceased to be the motivating force within the party and in the Soviet Union. A sincere believer in Marxism-Leninism is a lonely man there; the modern Soviet way of life must almost literally bore him, if it does not distract him, to death.

This loss of spirit is what lies behind the tragic self-destruction by fire of a Soviet Ukrainian in the central district of Moscow last April. Mykola Didyk's suicide, "because he was not allowed to join the war in Viet Nam," (according to Soviet official version) has dramatized a process that started decades ago. The erosion of Russian communism began with the establishment of the centralized Soviet Union and the final merger of the national Communist parties into a monolithic party under Stalin.

The old Bolshevik party of 1917-21 carried in itself the seeds of a revolutionary movement bent on changing the face of Eastern Europe. It promised social justice to all the under-privileged classes, and unqualified emancipation for the peoples under the oppressive czarist regime of Russia. Inspired by the idea of social

Reprinted with permission from *Commentator* (Toronto) X, No. 6 (June, 1966), 15-17.

justice and national self-determination, Russian communists with the help of their fellow travellers from other nationalities all over the disintegrated Russian empire, swept away their opponents: the Russian "whites," helped by the Western Powers, and the National Democrats in the non-Russian borderlands.

But with the stabilization of the Soviet regime, the spirit of the old Russia reasserted itself in the CPSU once it was in power. As Mykola Khvylovy (a Ukrainian Djilas of the 1920s) wrote at the time, the party had developed into a new class of Russian empire-builders. By committing suicide in May 1933, he registered his protest against the strangling of true internationalism in the community of Soviet nations. His death was preceded by the suicide of the Russian communist poet Vladimir Maiakovsky in 1930. Both writers refused to countenance the transformation of the international movement into a new Russian *petit bourgeois* class.

In the 1930's, the Spanish Civil War revived the hopes of Marxist idealists in the Soviet Union. Like many Canadian, British, French, and American leftists, they saw in the war a basic confrontation between the forces of "true democracy" and the forces of "totalitarian racism." To them it seemed worthwhile to share the burden of fighting with volunteers from many countries, and even to die for the cause of Republican Spain.

Stalin, however, having finished both his personal and state business in Spain, made short shrift of these dedicated men. All the Soviet participants in the Spanish war eventually came under a cloud of suspicion. Most of them perished in the purges of 1937-1939; the remainder survived in the Siberian concentration camps only to see the "patriotic" war of 1941-1945.

Even regular party-men entered the Russo-German war with the feeling of impending doom. At the front, hundreds of thousands of troops surrendered to the Germans; the party apparatus seemed about to disintegrate; and the long-planned guerrilla activity bogged down. Only the stupid barbarism of the Germans, who treated all Eastern Europeans like cattle, enabled Stalin to make a telling appeal to the national spirit of the Soviet peoples.

Thus the national traditions of Russian and Ukrainian peoples were revived and acknowledged by the party, and the German tide was stopped; a powerful guerrilla force appeared behind the German lines in Belorussia and the Ukraine. Significantly, in this crisis, the party had to turn for inspiration to such old-fashioned heroes as the Russian Mikhail Kutuzov[1] and the Ukrainian Bohdan Khmelnytsky.[2] Marx and Lenin as hero-figures failed to rally the people; the gods of communism were dead, and with them had gone the original revolutionary spirit of the CPSU. All that was left was a bureaucratic machine.

In the early post-war years, the magnitude of the task of reconstruction overshadowed gnawing doubts in the Soviet republics. Then Stalin's death seemed to give the party a new lease on life and the people new hope. Although dazed by the revelations of Stalin's "mistakes" after the 20th Congress, the younger generation dreamed of restoring revolutionary "socialist justice," so brutally violated by Stalin, and of pioneering a wondrous new life in the "virgin lands" in Kazakhstan.

But the frontier ventures failed economically and, what was more important, psychologically as well. The young pioneers, recruited largely from the Ukraine and the Baltic countries, saw for themselves that the party had failed to organize the venture efficiently. It was even plain to see that the party cared little what happened to the drive or to the settlers. They were simply left in the desert to fail without the necessary equipment. The upper echelons of the party were obviously more interested in the European power struggle than in the venture that seemed so promising to the young communist settlers.

Hopes of restoring "revolutionary legality" foundered as well. This failure has been crowned by the ridiculous trial and barbaric sentencing of the Moscow critics, Siniavsky and Daniel.[3] Recently, two Ukrainian critics were dealt with equally harshly. Ivan Svitlychny[4] was secretly sentenced by a Kiev court to hard labor in Siberia for allegedly helping to smuggle out of the Ukraine a diary and some not-so-Soviet poems by Vasyl Symonenko.[5] Ivan Dzyuba[6] received a suspended sentence only because he had incurable tuberculosis.[7] (About 30 young Ukrainian communists, mostly men of letters, were arrested in March and April.)[8] Svitlychny was born in 1929, and Dzyuba in 1931. They both grew up under communism and can hardly be labelled "remnants of the old order."

Their only crime was that they believed, as Symonenko put it, that there was "nothing more terrible than unlimited power in the hands of a limited man"; but "too many of our people—have saved their lives at the cost of their dignity, and have turned into animals. . . ."

The war in Viet Nam, illuminated by the best Soviet propaganda (which heavily relies on reports of protests by American students), might have appeared to many young communists as a new escape from the stale, grey frustration of Soviet reality. Under the daily pressure of the high-sounding slogans blared out at home, at school, at work, and at play, they long to join the fight for the cause they believe in—in order to be truly alive among the truly living people. Again, the vested interests of the super-state cut off these idealistic hopes and dreams. The battle-fields of Viet Nam are closed to them by the unwillingness of Soviet authorities to get involved in the war. Meanwhile, Chinese accusations levelled at the Soviet Union for having betrayed the revolutionary cause strike deep into the hearts of young communists in the USSR.

They are a frustrated generation. They see their own party growing fat and stodgy, their society dominated by a new class not unlike the czarist nobility. And they feel themselves being cast into the role of the "superfluous men" of nineteenth century Russia, the role they despise. They cannot easily turn to religion for comfort even though Christianity in the Soviet Union has in some ways grown lean and ascetic, and is gaining ground in its struggle with communism.

The Russian Orthodox Church, having established a *modus vivendi* with the party in the fateful days of June-July 1941, has developed into an established church not unlike the one that served the czarist regime. It rejects scornfully any suggestion of decentralization, or hierarchical autonomy for Belorussian and Ukrainian believers. In return for support of its position, the Church cooperates with the Soviet government more than is good for religion. This, and a flourishing sectarianism among Christians in the USSR, repels young people seeking inspiration and direction for their lives.

Nationalism combined with utopian ideals has always had a strong appeal for East Europeans. But the idea of nationalism is disparaged by the Soviet mass media in campaigns that go on literally day and night. Moreover, to become an effective motivating force in the Soviet Union, nationalism has to get rid of all fascist connotations, both real and imaginary ones.

In the meantime, young people in the Soviet Union seek ways to become involved in the world's problems without submitting to the pressures of the mighty: "Be silent, America and Russia, while I am speaking with my Mother-Ukraine," wrote Symonenko. Thus aroused, some of them protest against the party's policy of Russification in their own republics. Some of them attempt to defend the persecuted writers and artists, Russian, Ukrainian and Jewish alike; some shout in public: "Give us something to believe in."

The authorities are aware of the problem. Like true bureaucrats, they blame its existence on "lack of ideological watchfulness" on the part of intellectuals, and "bourgeois nationalist ideas" disseminated by foreign powers. "Our enemies have cast many rusty nationalist fishhooks bated with rotten worms into the airwaves: some fool may come along and swallow one." Such was the colorful warning of Ukrainian writer Oleksander Korniichuk, (a member of the CPSU Central Committee) at the Party Congress in Kiev last March. He went on: "We still have some young people whose ears are swollen from nightly listening to the sly and deceitful anti-Soviet radio propaganda." He urged the erring ones to come to their senses, "because if you have to face the people, they might take away your Soviet passport and say: Leave our sacred land."

The despair of these lonely seekers who have lost faith in the Soviet way of life has, over the years, led many to the extreme form of protest — suicide. The public self-immolation of Mykola Didyk indicates that rank-and-file young communists find as much to protest about as (to say the least) young idealists in the capitalist countries. The lonely despair of frustrated youth in the Soviet Union has been aptly described by the controversial Ukrainian, Symonenko:

> *Often I am as lonely as*
> *Robinson Crusoe,*
> *Scanning the skyline for a*
> *sail. . .*
> *Dressed in the skins of*
> *slaughtered hopes,*

*I probe in the sky with keen
    eyes...
Send me, O God, at least an
    enemy,
If you don't wish to send me
    a friend.*

REFERENCE NOTES

[1]Mikhail I. Kutuzov, Russian field marshal and commander-in-chief of the Russian armies in the war against Napoleon, 1812-1813.

[2]Bohdan Khmelnytsky, Ukrainian Cossack Hetman, led a successful revolt of the Ukrainian Cossacks against Poland in 1648 and served as head of the Ukrainian Cossack State, 1648-1657.

[3]A.D. Siniavsky (pseud. Abram Tertz) and Iu.M. Daniel (pseud. Nikolai Arzhak), two Soviet writers and literary critics; after having their works published abroad under assumed names, they were arrested and tried in a well publicized Moscow trial in 1965; sentenced to 7 and 5 years of hard labor respectively. Both since released and permitted to leave the Soviet Union; they now reside in Western Europe.

[4]Ivan Svitlychny (b. 1929), a Ukrainian literary critic. Arrested in January 1972, he was sentenced in March 1973 to seven years in severe regime labor camp and five years in exile.

[5]Vasyl Symonenko, a young Soviet Ukrainian poet, died at an early age of 29 (1963). In his writings, he was critical of the Soviet life and official policies. Most of his poems and his diary were never published in the Soviet Union, but they came out in their original Ukrainian version in a book, V. Symonenko, *Bereh chekan'*, (The Shore of Expectations), New York: Prolog, Inc., 1965. His diary was also published in English in *The Yale Review*, LVIII, No. 4 (June, 1969), 563-71.

[6]Ivan Dzyuba (b. 1931), a Ukrainian literary critic and a leading representative of the young Ukrainian dissident movement during 1960s. He is best known for his major work *Internationalism or Russification?*, dealing with the Soviet nationality policies in the Ukraine. R. Rakhmanny reviews this work in article No. 23 in this collection. Beginning in 1965, Dzyuba was

under progressively heavier official attacks and ceased to be published in the Soviet Union for a number of years. In 1972 he was arrested, released and expelled from the Writers Union of Ukraine. The following year, he was arrested again, interrogated at length, and released upon the issuance of a full retracting confession of his "errors" and a promise to write a refutation of his ideas as expounded in his book *Internationalism or Russification?* Such an officially blessed "refutation" appeared in his book, *Hrani kryshtala* (The Facets of Crystal), (Kiev: "Ukraina," 1976), 126 pp.; 2nd and enlarged edition appeared in 1979.

[7]As subsequent information confirmed, of the two men only I. Svitlychny was arrested and interrogated for over six months. I. Dzyuba was only interrogated by Party and KGB officials.

[8]On political mass arrests in the Ukraine during 1965–66, see Part V of this collection.

13

CHURCH-STATE RELATIONS:
LIVE ISSUE IN KREMLIN

Religion may have become irrelevant to the policies of Western leaders, but to the Kremlin religion and church-state relations are live issues that still influence the course of Soviet internal and foreign relations. Recent repressions against some minor religious groups in the Soviet Union reflect the pragmatic approach of the Soviet leaders to the subject, which may be defined as "strike at any living religious institution and favor those which show a weakening of the spirit."

A few days ago, the Soviet government's chief overseer of religious affairs made one of the toughest attacks on the Baptists who broke away from the officially recognized Evangelical Christian Baptist Church because of the latter's subservience to the regime. It is evident from Vladimir Kuroiedov's article in *Izvestia*, that the government felt hurt by the critical views of the break-away group.

Neither did they like the criticism of the Russian Orthodox Church levelled at it by some Orthodox dissenters, such as Anatoly Levitin; he was arrested eventually in September. Earlier this year, the remnants of the Ukrainian Catholic Church were put behind the barbed wire.

All this took place at the time when the Kremlin has been busy

Reprinted with permission from *The Ottawa Journal*, November 1, 1969.

encouraging the dialogue of the Moscow Patriarchate with the ever-ready-to-talk Vatican.

The repressions are explained by Soviet insiders as being caused both by internal pressures and external expediency. The Soviet leaders became worried by the growing numbers of Soviet people believing in God and practicing religion. Neither the party nor the youth organization *Komsomol* is immune to the infectious "prejudices." Then, the Chinese stung the Kremlin leadership with a charge that under the "revisionists of Moscow" there has been a brisk revival of religious feeling among the Soviet people.

The charge, hard enough because religion is not supposed to have any place in a communist society, was the more painful as it was made on the eve of the World Communist Conference in Moscow, last June. The participants, prodded by the Soviet hosts, were about to endorse a resolution calling for a new co-existence between Communist parties and the Christians in the capitalist countries.

The resolution advised the communist followers all over the world that "the mass of religious people can become an active force in the anti-imperialist struggle and in carrying out far-reaching social changes...." Apparently, "conditions have arisen in many capitalist nations for an anti-monopoly and anti-imperialist alliance of the revolutionary working-class movement and broad masses of religious people."

Voting for the resolution, the delegates at the World Communist Conference in Moscow must have been impressed by the successful handling of the Russian Orthodox Church, demonstrated by the Kremlin rulers during the last 50 years. The spokesmen of the church claim to have about 50 million active believers, which is a feat in itself if one recalls the blows the church had been receiving at the hands of such less than subtle anti-religious campaigners as Stalin's secret police chiefs Iagoda, Iezhov and Beria.

But the Russian Orthodox Church's survival has been as much due to the tenacity of its believers as to the accommodation its hierarchy has been able to secure for itself with the Kremlin rulers. During the Second World War, the church supported the Kremlin policies for patriotic reasons at least; the fate of the people themselves was in balance at the time of Nazi-Germany's onslaught. But in peace time, the Patriarch of Moscow, Alexei, and his chief adviser, Metropolitan Nikodim of Leningrad, were loath to abandon the hard won status of the established church in the Soviet Union. Thus, a strange symbiosis of the God-fearing with the godless continued; for a price of course.

Gained a Foothold

By accepting governmental supervision and embracing long-range Kremlin policies the Russian Orthodox Church has gained a foothold in the outside world; it was allowed to make direct contacts with other Christian churches, the Roman Catholics and the Vatican included. Within the Soviet Union, it became again (as it was in the days of the czars) the chief spokesman of the Christians there. Moreover, the Kremlin has legitimized the ageless aspiration of the Russian Orthodox Church to unite, and assimilate within its framework 10 million Belorussians and 45 million Ukrainians.

This is why the two nationalities, while recognized as sovereign political entities in the USSR and in the United Nations, are not allowed to form autonomous church structures under their own orthodox hierarchs.

Since the aims of the Moscow Patriarchy coincided with the official thesis on the "merging of all nationalities," events took a tragic turn especially for the Ukrainians. In the 1920s, the Ukrainian Orthodox Church was completely destroyed by harsh police and administrative measures. In 1946, the communist regime helped the Moscow Patriarchy to liquidate the Ukrainian Catholic Church. Of the six hierarchs deported to Russia only the Metropolitan Josyf Slipyj has survived the 18-year long ordeal.[1] The believers were integrated by force into the ranks of the Russian Orthodox Church.

It is to the credit of the Russian people that this tendency of the church-state collaboration would not go unchallenged. Even the Soviet authorities had to admit that there are "quite a few elements within the church and around the church" who are trying "to overcome this crisis of Orthodoxy by means of a political protest."

Indeed, many a believer was shocked by the price their church had to pay for the protection of the Kremlin. The price was revealed, without blushing, by the editors of *The Journal of Moscow Patriarchate:* "The cause of the revolution is the cause of the Orthodox Church."

And at the conference of all state-controlled religious groups held in Zagorsk July last, Metropolitan Nikodim publicly endorsed the resolutions of the World Communist Conference. Yet, he must have been aware of the Soviet regime's unyielding determination to uproot any religion in the USSR. He had been informed, by means of numerous appeals and "open protest letters" from his believers, priests and some bishops, about the continuous attempts of secret police at infiltrating the local church councils with the purpose of disrupting their work; how the authorities are seizing church property; that a number of churches and monasteries, both in Russia and Ukraine, were burned by some unidentified villains. And he knew that, as of January 1969, there were over 200 Baptists in Soviet jails.

Gave Explanation

This lack of any serious concern with the real condition of Christians in the USSR on the part of the church leaders is explained aptly by the dissenter-priest Anatoly Levitin (Krasnov)[2] in his public indictment of the Patriarchate's policies: "There are bishops in the church who resemble branches of a dead fig tree....Therefore the Russian Church is very ill.... The most serious ailment is the age-old one, that of Caesaro-Papism."

Recently, this voice of the Russian Christian conscience has been stifled, temporarily at least, by Soviet police. And so much poorer has become the average Soviet man. The Marxist-Leninist creed has failed him in his aspirations. Now, the Russian Orthodox Church, having become an established Soviet institution, has abandoned him in the face of an evermore complicated world.

REFERENCE NOTES

[1]See article No. 44 in this collection.

[2]Anatoly Levitin (Krasnow) (b. 1915), a religious writer, former Russian Orthodox priest; sent to a concentration camp for seven years, released in 1956. Represented the so-called "Christian-Socialist" point of view in the Russian dissident movement; former member of the Initiative Group for the Defense of Human Rights in the USSR; in 1974, permitted to emigrate to Switzerland. For a selection of his writings, see documents No. 50 and 51, in *Problems of Communism,* XVII, No. 4 (July–August, 1968), 104–109; also, *Stromaty* (Frankfurt am Main: "Posev," 1972), 155 pp.

14

THE REVOLUTION AND
THE BUREAUCRAT

"Bureaucrats of All Communist Countries Unite!"

Here is, perhaps, the best fitting substitute for the dated and worn out slogan "Proletarians of All Countries Unite!" that once used to stir deeply millions of underprivileged people all over the world.

To begin with, this modernized slogan would more closely represent the essential change that occurred in both the working class and the Communist parties now in power in a dozen countries. As of now, there is little of the social stratum once called proletariat, if one applies to it a strict Marxist-Leninist ruler. And hardly anyone wants to be a proletarian.

In the underdeveloped countries that are still with us, the real poor people do not possess either the qualifications or the consciousness of a proletariat, usually attributed to the alienated and exploited agricultural laborers who, given some capital and a plot, and perhaps some export possibilities for their produce, would easily overtake the long suffering *kolkhoz* laborers of the USSR.

Reprinted with permission from *The Ottawa Journal,* December 2, 1969, where it appeared under the title "Life Has Changed for the Soviet Worker."

More Benefits

And wherever there is any significant industrial development, the workers "in the clutches of capitalists" get more in benefits than the workers in the countries under communist blessing.

All this is a well-known creed to the workers of the Soviet Union and of the so-called People's Democracies of Eastern Europe. They, like their comrades in the West, are motivated today by the profit incentive and desire to live better and happier rather than by some lofty ideology.

To be sure, the Marxist-Leninist jargon still remains much in use there but it is somewhat like sand in a city surrounded by desert; it is there and it must be borne with patience but it is alien to human beings.

Meanwhile, every citizen of a communist country is really interested in reaching the standard of living which would put him on par with a white collar employee in the West, not to "overtake America" but to be able to enjoy life in the prosperity and cultural amenities of the atomic age.

Hence, the massive exodus to schools that has been a headache to the Soviet authorities since 1945 because literally no one there wants to remain voluntarily on a collective farm, in factories or in mines.

Social Conflict

Herein lies a deeply buried social conflict that one day might turn the "socialist" countries upside down. The people want to live a human life both in the material and the spiritual meaning of the word. They want to have freedom of expression and the freedom of sharing their experiences with other nations of the world, for a simple reason not to be left forever on the fringes of forward moving mankind.

But this desire, natural and understandable for once in the Russians as well as in other peoples of the Soviet empire, runs counter to the interests of the ruling circles.

And the situation is hardly different in other communist countries. Once real proletarians, real revolutionaries used to lead the masses; men who had worked from the underground or who had suffered in prison for their beliefs and activities. Their words usually matched their deeds and they were able to rely on some personal and popular support.

Great Disappointment

Nowadays, the leadership of the Communist parties in power consists of bureaucrats who occupy comfortable chairs in their mahogany offices and who send to prisons and concentration camps their own people for some flimsy transgressions.

To a sincere communist, this is the greatest disappointment of his life, that his mighty ones are not ideologists of Lenin's stature, or military geniuses like Trotsky or even masters of mass terror like Stalin was, but that they are just mediocre bureaucrats.

Indeed, there is little difference between the reportedly severe Brezhnev and mild Gomulka, enlightened Tito and conservative Ulbricht. To stay in power, they all have built up for themselves their own pyramids of self-supporting bureaucracies that must prop up one another so as not to be swept away by the restless people once supposed to be proletarians at heart and still urged by the bureaucrats to act as if they were.

No wonder then it was a relatively easy task for East Germany's Ulbricht to promote to Brezhnev the idea of a move into Czechoslovakia and to enlist the support of Poland's Gomulka, Hungary's Kadar and Bulgaria's Zhivkov for the deplorable venture. All of them, including Husak and General Svoboda of Czechoslovakia, came to see that to allow the people a real freedom of thought and of choice would speedily end their own power in their respective countries.

The same fear of losing their foothold in their own societies has prodded the bureaucrats to suppress the dissident intellectuals in Russia and Czechoslovakia, in the Ukraine, the Caucasus, and the Baltic countries.

Alexander Solzhenitsyn, the Russian author of remarkable novels dealing with human beings in communist concentration camps under Stalin, was recently expelled from the Soviet Writers' Union because his writings and his stand against censorship had admittedly made the ruling circles tremble again.

And he is not alone in danger of losing his already limited basis of subsistence in the Soviet regimented society. His Ukrainian colleague, Ivan Dzyuba, has been expelled from the Kiev Regional Writers' Organization for writing a treatise on the anti-Leninist policy of Russification in the Ukraine.[1] Dzyuba has made himself known also as a courageous advocate of Ukrainian-Jewish co-operation for the purpose of defending the two peoples against growing discrimination.

Like Solzhenitsyn before him, Dzyuba is now being reviled by his colleagues — writers and journalists alike — for allegedly giving food for thought to "bourgeois nationalist writers abroad" and "slandering their holy Fatherland."

To these official critics it does not really matter that Dzyuba's book, published only abroad, was not brought to the Fatherland's public opinion; Solzhenitsyn's accusers admitted not having read his suppressed novel.

It was enough for them to be notified that the establishment regarded the book as "alien" to the interests of the ruling circles; meaning, it might stir the people to do their own thinking and, perhaps, to forming their own ideas about the subject.

To prevent the revolt of the as yet-inert masses from occuring in their lifetime at least, these ruling circles in every communist country would do anything to prevent free-thinkers from crystallizing an independent public opinion. They are doing this by forming a united anti-people front of their own.

Indeed, their slogan must be "Bureaucrats of All Communist Countries Unite!"

REFERENCE NOTES

[1] I. Dzyuba's membership in the Kiev Regional Writers' Organization was reinstated on December 26, 1969, after a closed hearing on his case by the Presidium of the Writers' Union of Ukraine, at which he was forced to issue a public statement disassociating himself from the Ukrainian emigres and disavowing "nationalist ideology." See, *Literaturna Ukraina* (Kiev), January 6, 1970. On subsequent developments with respect to I. Dzyuba, see note No.6 to article No. 12, and articles in Part V of this collection.

15

THE GREAT WITNESS

If the ability to see one's own mistake and to admit it publicly while being at the apogee of power is a true measure of human greatness, then Lenin certainly deserves that appellation.

The year 1970 has been proclaimed Lenin's Year in all the countries that are goose-stepping in the wake of the Soviet Union.

And in its 15 republics the official public adulation has already over-reached humanly reasonable proportions. Lenin himself would be shocked to see the Byzantine icon he has been transformed into by this sterile propaganda campaign.

True enough, he is called "great" there but not for the right reasons. As seen through the goggles of Soviet ideologists, officials, scholars and writers, the founder of the first communist state in the world emerges as nothing bigger than a superficially benevolent Russian czar who had succeeded in preserving Moscow's grip on the 14 non-Russian nationalities.

But if one forgets for a while all the ideological trappings as well as the differences in political and economic systems between their federation and ours, then one might discover a trace of a genuine greatness in the man, however buried under the avalanche of slogans.

Reprinted with permission from *The Ottawa Journal,* April 21, 1970, where it appeared under the title "Propaganda, Slogans Hide Lenin's Real Greatness."

First "Protester"

About fifty-six years ago, when Russia's citizens of every walk of life were ardently dying for the czar on the battlegrounds of Europe against the Germans, Austrians and Turks, Lenin single-handedly was trying to stem the tide of the misplaced enthusiasm of the Russian masses.

He became the first "protester" of the century in the name of a principle: the world war had been unleashed by the power-seeking cliques and the duty of every honest man, and above all of a Social Democrat, was to undermine that anti-peoples war.

All the socialists, the Russians and the West Europeans alike, abandoned this principle agreed upon in theory long before the outbreak of the carnage. When it came, only Lenin with his small faction stood by and for the principle.

Czarist propaganda eagerly took advantage of the situation, and Lenin's group was accused by indignant Russian loyalists of being unpatriotic and serving the interests of the enemy. Against this grave accusation which, if sunk into the minds of the people-turned-soldiers, would have destroyed any prospects of the Bolsheviks in Russia, Lenin came out with a forceful and dignified argument.

"Scoundrels"

He wrote that in the name of the Russian national pride "all sorts of scoundrels shouted for the victory in the war" in order to keep Russia "a prison of nations," and to "crush the freedom of Hungary, Poland, Persia and China."

"Only slaves could obey the call of those who were campaigning for the oppression of other nations while covering up their designs by means of patriotic phrases."

In Lenin's opinion, a slave who "justifies and embellishes his slavery (i.e. calls the throttling of Poland, Ukraine, etc., 'defense of the fatherland of the Great Russians') is a menial and a cad, who inspires legitimate anger, contempt and disgust."[1]

To raise one's voice aloud in protest against these abuses, even in time of war, is the patriotic duty of every good Russian, Lenin argued.

Admittedly, Lenin did not weaken the Russian front line, nor did he gain in stature in the eyes of the German or French socialists who shared as much enthusiasm for the war as the Russian socialists, and who were equally devoted to their national cause.

But Lenin's stand, taken in December, 1914, came in most happily for the Bolsheviks in the turbulent year of 1917. Then the war-weary peasant-worker-soldiers regarded Lenin's party as the only true anti-war group whose prediction turned out to be right; the war did bring the end of czardom.

Catchy Slogan

Moreover, Lenin's stand gained for the Bolsheviks an unassailable plank for their agitation among the non-Russians who woke up to demand self-determination for their countries. Lenin was able to coin a catchy slogan of "self-determination up to separation" for all the peoples of the Russian empire as long as they would embrace his economic and political order.

Under the fluid conditions of 1917-19 in the Ukraine, the Caucasus and Central Asia the Bolsheviks would make a lot of hay with this approach. The nationalist movements there would be eventually defeated and the formation of the Soviet Union conceived.

But on the eve of its proclamation (December 1922) Lenin was already on his deathbed and all the power in the newly re-established empire was again in the hands of the traditional Russian bureaucracy. The ruling party of Bolsheviks, under a deft handling of Joseph Stalin, would make a misalliance with that vital force and soon the non-Russian nationalities would feel the familiar noose tightening again around their necks.

Built a Monster

It takes a truly great man to have noticed the trend and admit to have built a monster in spite of himself. But Lenin did more than that. He tried to prevent the inevitable from happening right before his own eyes.

Being partly paralyzed, he dictated a letter to the Central

Committee and warned them against such men as Stalin and his like because they were adherents of too harsh measures.

At the same time, in an article "On the National Question" he implored his followers not to repeat the mistake of the Russian bourgeois bureaucracy—never try to Russify the minorities of the confederation presently being formed.[2]

Lenin's article was published only in 1956, after de-Stalinization took some root in the USSR. Together with other documents and revelations, it prompted many a Russian and Ukrainian to start thinking on their own. Hence the movement of dissenters came into being.

These men and women, having failed to move the authorities through official channels, began turning out their appeals, protest letters, essays and suppressed information by means of the so-called *Samizdat,* i.e. self-publishing.[3] And one of their basic calls in these publications has been for the return to Lenin's ideal of international co-operation.

But in the Year of Lenin, their word is being more than ever suppressed by the authorities. No one in the USSR is allowed to make a claim to be in a true communion with Lenin's spirit but the established ideologists. Unfortunately, these bureaucrats are unable to discern between Lenin's original writing and some quotations by him taken from the book by Otto Bauer, an Austrian socialist and his opponent, whose statements crept into the Central Committee's "Theses" on Lenin's anniversary.[4]

Lenin's Word

There can hardly be a more striking proof of the inference that true Leninism is dead in the Soviet Union, and that Lenin really meant what he wrote in 1922:

"I am afraid, I have committed a great offense against the workers of Russia because I have not interfered with sufficient energy and sharpness in the notorious question of 'autonomization,' which is, it seems, called the USSR."[5]

The slowly dying man attempted to salvage a part of his dream even though it was obvious to him that "the freedom to withdraw from the union, with which we justify ourselves, will prove to be nothing but a scrap of paper, incapable of defending the minorities of Russia from the incursions of the... Great Russian, the chauvinist, in substance a rascal and a tyrant, such as the typical Russian bureaucrat is."[6]

REFERENCE NOTES

[1]V. I. Lenin, "On the National Pride of the Great Russians," *Collected Works* (4th ed.; Moscow: 1964), XXI, 102-106.

[2]V. I. Lenin, "On the Question of Nationalities or 'Autonomization'," *Collected Works* (4th ed.: 1968), XXXVI, 605-611. This article, part of so-called "Lenin's Testament," was published for the first time in the Soviet Union in the Party organ *Kommunist,* No. 9 (1956).

[3]See article No. 24 in this collection.

[4]Reference is made to Otto Bauer, *Die Nationalitätenfrage und die Sozialdemokratie* (Wien: Verlag der Wiener, 1907), in which a proposal to solve the national question in the Austro-Hungarian Empire was developed.

[5]See note 2 above.

[6]*Ibid.*

16

THE JEWISH FACT IN RUSSIA

To open a new book on a Jewish question in Eastern Europe often amounts to opening an old wound; it does not tell you much new about the patient and it leaves you with an apprehension: where does this all lead us anyway?

The Jews in Soviet Russia Since 1917 is a different book. Basically historical in its intent, this collection of fifteen essays somehow helps to cure ignorance and heal anguish. That is why, contrary to what Professor L. Shapiro hints in his excellent introduction to it, the reader is left with a comforting impression about the immediate future of the Jews in the USSR. They are going to survive.

Even a cursory perusal of the book convinces you that the Jewish fact in the Soviet Union still exists and the "silent Jews" there are less silent than ever. During the last 50 years, Soviet spokesmen denied this stubbornly and vehemently at times. Maurice Friedberg quotes one such conversation from a Soviet novel which, however, reflects the political reality of the 1930s. A visiting foreign journalist, one Mr. Berman, asked a Soviet official about the Jewish problem in the USSR. "It does not exist!" — was the answer.

"But surely there are Jews in Russia?" he asked warily. — "Yes,

Reprinted with permission from *The Montreal Star,* July 18, 1970. A commentary on the book by Lionel Kochan (ed.), *The Jews in Soviet Russia Since 1917* (New York: Oxford University Press, 1970). 357 pp.

there are," the official replied. — "Then you have a Jewish problem" — "No, there are Jews, but no Jewish problem."

The same studied approach is being applied by Soviet authorities today. And together with other "unproblems". . .it is now tackled only by "underground" Soviet literature. Indeed, the painful dilemma of the Soviet Jew constitutes one of the central themes of that body of Soviet literature that has recently come to public attention in Russia and in the West.

The authors of the collection, under the general editorship of Dr. Lionel Kochan, Professor of Jewish history at the University of Warwick, set out to probe the depth and the forms of the problem. On the whole, they have succeeded in their efforts. The book is the first balanced study of the subject.

To give an inkling of the topics discussed, Professor Etinger introduces the reader into the human condition of Russian Jewry on the eve of the revolution. The demographic and occupational structure of the Jews in the USSR is analyzed by Professor Nove and Dr. Newth. The tragicomic drama of the Soviet attempt at localizing the "non-existing" Jewish problem by establishing a Jewish autonomous territory on the left bank of the Amur River (north of Manchuria) is unravelled by C. Abramsky. For those interested in the legal position of the Jews within the Soviet ideological and constitutional structures, there are two essays — one on Soviet theory and the other on practical application of the theory. Three essays deal with various aspects of Jewish literary achievements in three languages used by their writers — Russian, Yiddish and Hebrew.

Although differing in quality, most of the essays are well written by knowledgeable authors in the given field, and a sincere attempt has been made to see the other side of the coin in almost every subject discussed. The palm of achievement goes, however, to Joshua Rothenberg — for his essay on Jewish religion in the USSR and to Reuben Ainsztein — for his very informative essay on "Soviet Jewry in the Second World War." Even a well-read observer in Soviet subjects will share in the surprise of T. F. Fyvel who admitted in the *New Statesman:* "I had not known that in the Second World War there were over 50 Soviet Jewish generals."

But above all the reader will have become aware of the existence in the Soviet Union of a deep-rooted Jewish problem, the complexity and the intensity of which frustrated Soviet leaders from Lenin to Brezhnev. "In the 1950s," — writes Professor Rothenberg — they "concluded that the disintegration of Jewish identity in the Soviet Union had progressed to such a degree that with a suitable policy and a little effort the highly objectionable 'Jewish separateness,' both in the religious and national sense, would completely disappear."

This sentence contains the crux of the matter. Any "little effort" on the part of Soviet administration to solve the Jewish "unproblem" affects all Soviet Jews no matter how assimilated they may be, because the Jewish minority in the USSR constitutes both a nationality and a religious entity. The inability of the Soviet-Russian bureaucrats to see the fact and to adapt their policies to it led them to ever harsher administrative measures against their Jewish citizens who are being accused, as in the old days, of serving foreign interests.

An article on "Anti-Semitism in Soviet Russia" and another on the Soviet Jewish situation, "After the Six-Day War," represent an attempt of the editor to bring the volume up to date. But what is badly missing, in my opinion, is an essay on different roots of anti-Semitism in the areas of Jewish settlement and on the gradually changing social climate in that respect there. Since, until the Second World War the Jews lived mostly on the territory of Belorussia, Ukraine and Lithuania (under czarism, Russia proper was forbidden territory for the Jews), the problem begs for a scholarly probe.

It would show that one of the main causes of anti-Semitism among the non-Russians had been the tendency among the Jews to identify themselves with the dominant nationality, that is the Russians. As Professor S. Goldelman of Jerusalem put it, the Jews in 1917-19 would see their security only in the preservation of a unified Russian empire which would guarantee law and order for its citizens. Consequently, they would spurn all national aspirations of the minorities in Russia.[1]

In the Soviet Union the Jews have been again trying hard to live within the limits of the official ideology and hoping for the implementation of a system of law and order. But certain expanded opportunities for them in different fields of the new society had been counterbalanced by anti-Jewish administrative measures and by the glowing embers of anti-Semitism among

Soviet citizens, artificially fed by Soviet Russian bureaucracy.

Fortunately, the enlightened society of the non-Russian peoples is slowly getting wiser in this respect. One of the Ukrainian dissenters, S. Karavansky of Odessa (now serving a 25-year term in Mordovia) raised a mighty call for a redress of the injustices perpetrated by the regime on the minorities. Of the Jews he wrote in 1967: "Where are the Jewish theatres now, the newspapers and publishing houses, the schools?..." (The Jewish Theatre in Moscow was closed in 1949).[2]

And Ivan Dzyuba, a Marxist Ukrainian critic, made a public plea for Jewish-Ukrainian cooperation in the face of the policy of discrimination and Russification. At the Babi Yar anniversary on September 29, 1966, he declared:

> Our common past consists not only of blind enmity and bitter misunderstandings, although there was much of this.... The Jews have a right to be Jews and the Ukrainians have a right to be Ukrainians in the full and profound, not only in the formal, meaning of the word. Let the Jews know Jewish history, Jewish culture and language, and be proud of them. Let the Ukrainians know Ukrainian history, Ukrainian culture and language, and be proud of them. Let them also know each other's history and culture and the history and culture of other nationalities, and let them know how to value themselves and others as their brothers.

Dzyuba's speech was never reported in the Soviet press but it has reached the public with the help of private transcripts. In English, it was published for the first time in Canada, by *Commentator* (Toronto) in February 1968.

It would have been worthwhile including in this collection an essay on that recent development in the relations between the Jews and the second largest nationality in the USSR as the Soviet leaders continue the traditional policy of preventing any publicity of the ills afflicting the Russian empire. Such publicity is "the doctor" Russia needs badly, wrote one of Alexander Herzen's friends about 100 years ago.

By presenting the Jewish problem in the Soviet Union in a balanced scholarly symposium, Professor L. Kochan and the Institute of Jewish Affairs in London have done a service both to their own people and to the nationalities of the USSR, whose plight is being suppressed as an "unproblem" as well. Indeed, it is a service to the Russians themselves, as millions of them are among those who suffer because of the lack of the rule of law in their own police state.

REFERENCE NOTES

[1]For an analysis of the condition in which the Jewish minority found itself in the midst of the Russian Revolution and civil war and the attempt of the newly founded Ukrainian National Republic to provide a solution by way of a Jewish national autonomy within the Ukrainian state, see Solomon I. Goldelman, *Jewish National Autonomy, 1917-1920,* (Chicago: Ukrainian Research and Information Institute, 1968), 131 pp.

[2]S. Y. Karavansky, "To the Council of Nationalities of the USSR," *The New Leader,* LI, No. 2 (January 15, 1968), 12. Karavansky (b. 1920), a Ukrainian writer and journalist, was first arrested and sentenced to 25 years of hard labor in 1944. After serving 16 years, he was released in 1960 under a general amnesty. In 1965, in spite of the fact that the 25-year sentence was abolished in the Soviet Union by that time, Karavansky was re-incarcerated without trial to serve out the balance of his 25-year term for protesting Russification policy in the Ukraine.

17

EIGHT NATIONS DIE

The saying that the poor beetle a man treads upon feels a pang as great as when a giant dies, has acquired a new significance in this work by British poet and writer, Robert Conquest. His study of the tragic fate of eight nationalities within the Soviet Union, deported from their lands by the Politburo, presents the reader both with a lucid account of their historical tribulations and with an insight into the mechanics of the much-disputed Soviet "nationality" policy.

Concerned were Chechens, Ingushi, Karachai, Balkars, Kalmyks, Meskhetians, Crimean Tartars and the Volga Germans. The latter had been deported in 1941, the others in 1943–44.

Much has been written about the alleged disloyalty of these nationalities in the Second World War. But, as Khrushchev officially admitted at the Party Congress in 1956, this sweeping charge was mistaken.

Stalin blamed whole nations for the deeds of the few. He even planned to resettle the Ukrainians but they were too numerous to be deported in secret.

The small ones took the rap.

True enough, they were not physically liquidated as were the millions of victims in the Nazi gas chambers. But they sustained

Reprinted with permission from *The Montreal Star,* January 23, 1971. A commentary on the book by Robert Conquest, *The Nation Killers* (Toronto: Macmillan of Canada, 1970), 222 pp.

heavy casualties. Over half a million — mostly children and the aged — died while being deported to distant territories of the USSR: about one-third of the whole total of 1,600,000 persons affected.

Robert Conquest presents a true historical perspective of their experiences seen against the background of the Soviet theory on treatment of minorities in a communist federal state. All his statements are supported by documentary evidence, mostly Soviet.

The picture that emerges is gloomy: hypocrisy pervades all the declarations and comments by Soviet spokesmen on the subject.

If one is tempted to assert that the Kremlin only pursues the policies of czarist Russia in an endeavor finally to stabilize Russia's boundary somewhere in the Caucasus, then one should remember the following difference between the two regimes.

The czarist regime had spared the life of "its most intransigent opponent when he was finally captured." And it allowed publication of Tolstoy's objective account of the Caucasian hero, Iman Shamil; other Russian sources of the time (1850-60) also "give Shamil at least a certain admiration, however reluctant."

But under the Soviets, "facts of considerable importance can simply never be published anywhere if official policy so decides." The case of the 200,000 Meskhetians remained unknown in the West until 1969. The deportation of the Kalmyks involved an entire republic (about 140,000 people) but no public statement was ever made about it. As history in the USSR is continuously being rewritten, there is little chance for a casual Western observer to fathom the tragedy of the Soviet minorities. Especially today, when only big numbers seem to count and monstrous carnages alone deem deserving of public note.

Robert Conquest is inclined to place the responsibility for the killing of whole nations on the system itself: ". . . while Khrushchev condemned the policy pursued by Stalin in the matter, even he nowhere condemned in any way the structure of Soviet rule which made such a decision possible."

Here the author echoes General Petro Grigorenko's[1] sentiments, who warned the Crimean Tartars two years ago: "What was done to your nation was not done by Stalin alone. And his accomplices are not only alive but holding responsible offices."

Against this pessimistic assessment, however, there is some hope.

That in the Soviet Union itself such courageous people as Grigorenko, Karavansky, Iakir[2] and Kosterin[3] have raised their voices in defence of the persecuted minorities holds some promise.

Robert Conquest tries to put it into an all-European context this way:

> Where there is oppression ordered from outside and carried out largely by foreigners, the inevitable resistance will take national form — even though the original oppressive measures have no specific national character. This proposition, which has been largely forgotten by the Soviet leaders, seems to be the key to the enormous strength of national feeling in the Soviet bloc. The cases of Hungary and Czechoslovakia were particularly striking demonstrations of the theme.

He adds ". . . the Ukrainians now demanding their own rights have also expressed solidarity with the Crimeans — even though it is to the Ukraine that the Crimeans have lost their land. It is similarly striking that while Ukrainian nationalism had long a reputation of being anti-Semitic as well as anti-Russian, its latest manifestations strongly emphasize solidarity with the Jewish population which the Ukrainians rightly see as also suffering from various oppressive acts."

It seems that the beetles themselves, instead of being engrossed solely in their own miseries, have begun to show some comprehension of the sufferings endured by others under the giant's foot.

But do we?

REFERENCE NOTES

[1]P. G. Grigorenko (b. 1906), a retired Soviet Army major general, active in various protest movements of the 1960s, especially on behalf of the Crimean Tartars. In 1964, he was confined to a mental asylum for 14 months; released, he was arrested again for

dissident activities in 1969; was tried and recommitted to an asylum the following year where he was kept until his release in 1977. He now lives in the United States where he continues to work on behalf of the Soviet dissident movement.

[2]P.I. Iakir (b. 1923), an historian, son of well-known Soviet Army Major General I. E. Iakir who was executed in 1937; the same year, he was sentenced to 17 years in a hard labor camp; rehabilitated in 1956 together with his father, young Iakir became active in various protest movements of the 'sixties and 'seventies, and a member of the Initiative Group for the Defense of Human Rights in the USSR. Arrested in June 1972, P. I. Iakir was, together with another fellow dissident Viktor Krasin, an engineer, tried in a "show trial" during which both publicly "confessed" and recanted reportedly as a result of torture. Given mild sentences, they were paroled shortly thereafter.

[3]A. I. Kosterin (1896-1968), writer, former editorialist for *Trud, Gudok,* and *Izvestia.* Spent 17 years in Stalin's concentration camps; released and became active in the protest movements of the 1960s, especially in support of the reform movement in Czechoslovakia in 1968.

18

MAGADAN AND THE RISING
NEW HUMANISM

You wouldn't recognize him even if you bumped into him while boarding a bus or passing him on a downtown street. He looks just like any other Canadian who enjoys the many good things we have and who mildly grumbles about the weather or the spiralling prices and taxes.

I wouldn't be able to point him out to you either because I never met him. But I seem to know him very well, indeed — from his book.

Into the pathway of my thoughts he has stepped right from the pages of the memoirs entitled simply *Magadan* (Montreal: Chateau Books, 1971) — the man who made an involuntary journey straight down to the bottom of a human-made hell. And he came back, apparently with an undiminished zest for life; the sufferings that broke or bent many much stronger men have not impaired his human purposefulness either.

A naturalized Canadian, Michael Solomon was arrested by Romania's communist security police in February 1948 only to be handed over to their Soviet Russian overlords 10 months later. The latter were eager to get him into their claws because they believed him to be an "expert on Palestine" and a British spy at that.

Reprinted with permission from *The Windsor Star*, March 8, 1972.

The Romanian security men were not loath to making a few roubles and getting additional stripes for their "alertness" by selling to their protectors a co-citizen of Jewish origin, for some time a resident of Palestine under British rule.

When he landed, finally, in the abode of Soviet counter-intelligence at Constanta, Mr. Solomon was astounded to hear: "Don't be afraid. You are among the Jews."

Indeed he was. Facing him were: a colonel of counter-intelligence; a military prosecutor; a major; a lieutenant; and a translator — all with Jewish names and all speaking Yiddish to boot.

The translator, Sasha Roth, turned to these Soviet officers and, with studied indignation, pointed to Solomon's blackened hands — due to the much too tight handcuffs — and at his blood-covered face: "Look, what the Romanian bandits have done to this poor Jew."

Michael Solomon tried in vain to explain that it was the Russian guards that had mistreated him while transporting him from a Romanian prison. But his captors, being Soviet communist Jews were much too eager to impress upon their own superiors their ability for extracting secrets of state importance from the prisoner of their kind.

Later on, General Smirnov of the Soviet State Security arrived on the scene to try his hand in breaking the stubborn "British spy" whose only crime consisted of writing some good articles in Bucharest newspapers during the brief reign of King Michael after the Second World War.

Beria's Hell-gate

Since Mr. Solomon would admit only to knowing the English language and some British journalists — but no state secrets concerning a never-planned British aggression against the Soviet Union — onward he goes: to Far Eastern Siberia for 25 years. Magadan is the name of his final destination, a veritable hell-gate in Stalin-Beria's empire.

Many a country have I seen with plenty of human misery displayed before my eyes; and a great deal of misery fell to my lot as the due share of any man's destiny. But Michael Solomon's story of experiences on his road to Magadan shook me up, indeed.

For one, on the pages of his book I have met again some of my friends with whom I parted many years ago in the Ukraine.

Take Rev. Onufrii Ivaniuk. He was very close to the Metropolitan Andrii Sheptytsky who saved a group of Jews by giving them a shelter in the St. Iuri Cathedral buildings in Lviv, and on his country estate as well.

And why shouldn't I be moved by Mr. Solomon's description of the strike and resistance organized at Norilsk concentration camps by former Ukrainian insurgents (UPA)?

They fought against Himmler's SS troops during the wartime in the woods and mountains of West Ukraine; then they put up stiff resistance to Beria's NKVD troops. The remnants of the insurgents found themselves inmates of Norilsk and other Arctic construction sites, nowadays visited and praised by some innocent Canadians.

Those of the insurgents who survived the massacres arranged on orders from Comrade R. Rudenko, the prosecutor-general of the Soviet Union in 1953, were shipped to Magadan; and Mr. Solomon vividly describes the scene of their arrival there.

He frankly admits to not having shared in the "delusion" of the Ukrainian prisoners for the idea of a sovereign non-communist Ukraine. But who would in his circumstances, at the time when mighty Soviet armies had reached the heart of Europe, triumphed in the Far East, and when many Ukrainians served the Kremlin mob as servilely as did the Jewish communists who had mishandled him?

Yet, Mr. Solomon tries to be as objective as possible for a man who had never before lived in the Soviet Union and was bound to be puzzled by the complexity of internal cross-currents there. Therefore, one should not pay too much attention to some factual errors in his narrative. These can be weeded out in the next edition.

What should be commented upon here, however, is the painful aspect of Ukrainian-Jewish relations. I think, eventually there must be a more rational explanation of the anti-Jewish bias among Ukrainians, anti-communists and communists alike, rather than repeating the cliches about the traditional Slavic anti-Semitism for its own sake.

Without being aware of it, Michael Solomon helps the reader grasp that complex problem by not sparing even some from among his own ethnic group. Time and again he shows, by registering specific cases, that along with the good natured Soviet Jews there existed in the Soviet Union also another strain — the communist Jews of Russian hue. By their unswerving support for the cruel Soviet regime they alienated masses of Soviet Ukrainians (as well as Russians) from the Jews in general.

No Motherland

And the Ukrainians outside the Soviet Union would acquire a similarly wrong idea that all Soviet Jews were helping the Kremlin rulers in their effort at the Russification of Ukrainians and a total destruction of the Ukrainian nation — either by mass arrests and summary executions or by an artificial famine which, in 1933, caused about six million deaths in the Soviet Ukraine.

What these and other Ukrainians did not realize (but what clearly transpires from Mr. Solomon's narrative) was that there has been growing since the formation of the Soviet Union in 1922 a class of uprooted men; and these deracinees have been in power ever since.

They have no motherland of any kind; they don't care for any ethnic origin; they adorn themselves communists, but Marxism and Leninism are strange doctrines to them as well. They recognize only one creed and that is their own "power unlimited."

By sticking together and supporting one another in their various capacities — be it as party men or state bureaucrats — they form a mighty pyramid of Soviet power; politburo is its tip and its base consists of policemen and concentration camp supervisors. Under the weight of this pyramid, all the nationalities, with the Russians included, are staggering as no other part of mankind ever has.

From time to time, the pyramid needs some propping up against the ever opening cracks. Then a scapegoat must be found, and the Jews are nowadays as good for that as they were in czarist times when the old-order pyramid was also in dire need of diverting the people's attention from the pressing problems of the day. Ukrainians are usually played as a scapegoat for punishing so-called saboteurs and conspirators against the unity of the empire.

Against this background, it is encouraging to note that during the first post-Stalin decade the new generation of Ukrainians began turning toward humanization of relations among the nationalities of the USSR. For one, Ivan Dzyuba — a Soviet Ukrainian writer and critic who was arrested in January (1972) in Kiev along with 18 other Ukrainian progressive intellectuals — called upon the Ukrainians and Jews to find a common ground for the defense of their distinct cultural identities.

Speaking at the Jewish commemoration ceremony held at the Babi Yar site in September 1966, Dzyuba said:[1]

> Our common past consists not only of blind enmity and bitter misunderstandings, although there was much of this. Our past shows also examples of courageous solidarity and cooperation in the fight for common ideals of freedom and justice, for a better fate for all nations. We, the present generation, should continue this tradition and not the tradition of distrust and reserve....

Then he came out strongly for human rights of the Jews in the Ukraine as well as in the Soviet Union as a whole:

> The Jews have a right to be Jews and the Ukrainians have the right to be Ukrainians in the full and profound, not only formal, meaning of the word.... Let them know each other's history and culture and the history and culture of other nations; and let them know how to appreciate themselves and others as their brothers.

Any thoughtful reader, albeit superficially familiar with the changing complexion of the Soviet Union's multinational society, will discover similar grains of a growing mutual understanding among the oppressed nationalities even in the concentration camps, upon reading such memoirs as that by Michael Solomon.

A Sigh of Relief

His testimony is invaluable as another proof that the Soviet pyramid oppresses all the nationalities alike; that without these hard labor camps the pyramid of the deracinees in power would crumble; and that the suffering they cause only hastens the growth of a new humanism—of a faith that would replace both the established religious hypocrisies and the established Soviet communism. On closing Michael Solomon's book, *Magadan,* a sigh of relief escapes the reader's lips: "Thank you, God, for having spared me an involuntary journey to Siberia. And blessed be Thy name for the few survivors you have brought back from the road to Magadan. By their testimony, they give us all a rare chance to become and to act like true human beings: to know one another better and to cooperate more eagerly for the sake of those who are less fortunate than ourselves, be they Jews, Ukrainians, Lithuanians, Georgians or Russians."

REFERENCE NOTES

[1]For a full text of I. Dzyuba's address at Babi Yar, see "Ivan Dzyuba on Jewish and Ukrainian Destiny," *Commentator* (Toronto), XII, No. 2 (February, 1968), 12–15.

PART IV

UKRAINIAN NATIONALISM: FIFTY YEARS
AFTER THE OCTOBER REVOLUTION

EDITOR'S NOTE

Ukrainian nationalism is still alive. Fifty years of Bolshevism, using every weapon in its armory have failed to kill it.

The Ukrainian cause is not a terminal case.

19

UKRAINE: THE SPECTER
OF NATIONALISM

From its inception, the Soviet Union has been haunted by the specter of nationalism. Now, on the eve of the 50th anniversary of the October Revolution, the regime is still worried about the same, old, partly real, partly imaginary enemy. Official speakers still call on good Soviet citizens to be watchful and resist "recurrent bourgeois nationalism." Indeed, the nationality question in the Soviet Union, allegedly solved "once and for all on the basis of Lenin's policy" (Khrushchev, 1956), remains the greatest single obstacle to the creation of a "uniform community...advancing toward one goal, communism."

Today, nationalism manifests itself in the main in the resistance of the non-Russian groups to the swamping of their languages and cultures by the Russian. In some of the small but resilient federal republics, in Latvia, Armenia or Turkmenistan, for instance, such resistance has been remarkably effective. Even though Moscow has established a system of bilingual schooling with Russian as the first language, and *Pravda* and *Izvestia* have from time to time hailed the scheme as a huge success, the Russian language still is not much used. In Latvia, for instance, one-third of the school children now attend the bilingual

Reprinted with permission from *Commentator* (Toronto) X, No. 11 (November, 1966), 13-15, where it appeared under the title: "Ukrainian Nationalism Fifty Years After the Soviet Revolution."

schools. Yet a Ukrainian traveller, who was there as recently as last spring, noted with some awe that in Riga everybody spoke Latvian. Similarly, only Lithuanian was spoken in Vilnius.

This is not so in Kiev, capital of the Ukraine. People who speak Ukrainian in their homes prefer to use Russian in the streets in order not to arouse "the older brother," as the Russian authorities are called. Ukrainian caution in this regard undoubtedly stems from their long experience with purges of nationalists, some of which were also directed against the Politburo and members of the Ukrainian Communist Party. What is permissible in Russia, Latvia or Georgia could be a capital crime in the Ukraine.

A new generation of Ukrainians, however, free of the inhibiting experience of the purges, is coming to the fore in every field. The clandestine writers of Russia have defended the rights of the individual against collectivist dictatorship; Ukrainian clandestine literature nearly always refers to national freedom and dignity as well as to the rights of the individual.

The best known of the Ukrainian underground writers is Vasyl Symonenko (he died in 1963 at the age of 29).[1] He lashed out at the "hypocrites... who are trying to turn Marxism into a religion and a procrustean bed for science, art and love.... No single teaching can monopolize the intellectual life of Man." In his poems he denounced the Stalinist system that robbed the people of their dignity and reduced the peasants to becoming petty thieves of their own grain — the system that put unlimited power into the hands of little men.

In one of his poems he insisted on the right of Ukrainians "to converse with their Mother-Ukraine" without any interference from either Russia or the United States. Once at a public reading of his poems, he was asked what kind of independence he envisaged for the Ukraine. He replied, "I know only one Ukraine." Among friends he expounded the idea of a neutral Ukraine, and a specifically Ukrainian road to socialism.

Symonenko's poems and his diary were published posthumously in 1965.[2] At the time, a professor of Kiev University, Ivan Svitlychny, and a Kiev critic, Ivan Dzyuba, were accused of having helped to smuggle the anti-Soviet material abroad. Symonenko's mother was induced to declare in *Radianska Ukraina* that her son had been a faithful communist and had never intended to publish the poems or the ill-conceived diary. His friends, she said, were responsible for the mishap. These accusations coincided with the preparation of the Siniavsky-Daniel trial. Because the fate of the two Ukrainian critics received world-wide publicity, they have since been released.

Their detention, in any case, must also have had a good deal to do with their own non-conformist writing, some of it published in Ukrainian magazines in Warsaw and in Presov, Czechoslovakia. In fact, they never confessed to having any part in the Symonenko case.

The arrest of Svitlychny and Dzyuba climaxed a two-year-tug-of-war between the authorities and the youth of the Ukraine.[3] The year before, a fire had destroyed the library of the Academy of Sciences in Kiev and with it about 600,000 titles of Ukrainiana. It was said in Kiev that the fire department arrived mysteriously late and without the necessary equipment. An employee of the library was charged with arson. A protest pamphlet that circulated in the Ukraine claimed that the trial, conducted in secrecy without press coverage, was a farce.[4] Pohruzhalsky, the accused, was reported to have been indignant at the charges brought against him; after all, he said, many Ukrainian books had been systematically destroyed before and no one had been tried for it. A copy of the pamphlet eventually landed in the office of UNESCO director René Maheu.

Soon after, there was the Shevchenko incident. Each year a singing crowd gathers at the Taras Shevchenko monument in Kiev on May 22, to commemorate the transfer, in 1861, of the hero-poet's remains from Russia to the mound on the bank of the Dnieper. The czarist regime of those days had forbidden any manifestations of Ukrainian feelings. Now when Shevchenko monuments adorn Kiev and Moscow (and Winnipeg and Washington), it is once more "an offense to the great Russian people" to sing songs at his monument. A score of students went to jail for not heeding the ban. In the wake of the disturbances in Kiev and Lviv there followed more arrests, mostly among students and intellectuals. *Pravda* took note of this and charged that historians and party leaders in Lviv were responsible for the renascence of nationalism among Ukrainian youth.

Although the arrests had been made in secrecy so as not to awaken the curiosity of the foreign press, a large crowd gathered on the day when the group of prisoners was transferred by train from the Lviv prison to a camp in the interior of the Soviet Union. The prisoners were showered with flowers. Militia-men dispersed the crowd with fire-hoses which, on this occasion, were there on time and ready to operate.

Ukrainians have suffered too much from war and purges to engage much in the kind of daydreaming about revolution in which the *emigres* indulge. But events show that the nationality question has not been solved in the Soviet Union, not even to the degree that it has been in Tito's Yugoslavia. The people of all the republics quietly and stubbornly resist the Party's attempts at Russification disguised as promotion of "internationalism and Leninist friendship of people." In fact, the policy breeds more nationalism than it cures. There is one difference, though: The new nationalism seems to be free of the old violence-breeding fanaticism; in a way, it is political. A young Soviet Ukrainian explained it thus: "We grew up in the Soviet system and we have learned from Marxism about the common interests of working people. From our experience under the Nazi occupation we have learned to combat every kind of fascism. Under Stalin and his like we have learned to recognize the meaning of Lenin's warning to the Party about Great-Russian chauvinism...we want to be the equals of 'older brother' in the Union, and masters in our own republic. We have nothing to lose in this confrontation but our bondage; and we can regain our dignity as individuals and as a nation, exactly in the Leninist meaning...."

REFERENCE NOTES

[1]See note 5 to article No. 12 in this collection.

[2]*Ibid.*

[3]See note 6 to article No. 12 in this collection.

[4]For a complete text of the protest pamphlet, see *Suchasnist* (Munich), V, No. 2 (February 1965), 78–84. For an English text, see article "There'll Always be a Shevchenko," *Atlas* (January 1966), pp. 36–38.

20

UKRAINIAN NATIONALISM FIFTY YEARS AFTER THE BOLSHEVIK REVOLUTION

Fifty years ago this month, two strikingly different political entities rose from the ruins of the Czarist Empire. The forces of social change in Russia led to the establishment of a totalitarian Bolshevik state on November 7, 1917; social revolution in the Ukraine, with strong nationalist undertones, resulted in the proclamation, on November 20 of that same year, of the Ukrainian National Republic modelled on the British and Swiss democracies.

A conflict between these new structures was inevitable. Lenin recognized the Ukrainian Republic on December 17, 1917, but almost in the same breath he ordered the Red Guards to attack it from without and within. By then a general disillusionment with Russia had set in among the Ukrainians. Mykhailo Hrushevsky, the Ukraine's first President, explained their dilemma: "We had sincerely believed that in a new Russia the Ukrainian people would find the requisite conditions for its manifold development. Now we have become convinced that our ways differ from those of Russia, whether reactionary or revolutionary...the Ukraine has always stood in her history, culturally and poli-

---

Reprinted with permission from *Commentator* (Toronto), XI, No. 11 (November, 1967), 13-16.

tically, nearer to Western Europe. . . . If we wish to liberate our-selves from foreign violence, we must conform to the civilized West. . . ."

The West of the time had, however, little understanding of the aspirations of the non-Russian nationalities and attempted to support the idea of a united non-communist Russia. The ill-advised interventions of the Allies, like the earlier meddling of Germany, helped only the Bolsheviks, who suddenly appeared as the defenders of the people's "revolutionary gains." Thus the cause of the non-Russian peoples was lost.

The lesson of the almost three-year-long war between Russia and the Ukraine was not lost on Lenin. Recognizing the strength of nationalism, he agreed to the formation of the Soviet Ukrain-ian Republic, associated with Russia but having the right of secession. The same system was used with respect to Belorussia and the Trans-Caucasian Federation.

The formation of the essentially centralist Soviet Union, in 1922, deprived the Ukraine of her attributes of sovereignty won in 1919: the rights of amending her own constitution, deter-mining her frontiers, conducting foreign relations, organizing her armed forces, regulating her finances, and passing new legis-lation. With the ascendancy of Stalin, the centralist noose tightened even more. In 1937, the Kiev government comprised only six unimportant commissariats; its chief function was to rubber-stamp the decrees of Moscow and administer them. The Ukrainian Constitution reflected these basic changes in the Soviet Union; the confederation became in effect a monolithic Russian super-state.

By 1934, the central Politburo had restored as official doctrine the old nationalist concept of a single Russian people with a common history. The October Revolution was declared to be a Russian phenomenon with national purposes. Any manifestation of patriotism by non-Russians was branded as "bourgeois na-tionalism" and a crime against socialism. History was rewritten to show that the annexations of borderlands by czarist Russia merely represented progressive steps in the development of these countries and of Russia as a whole. Thus the 1654 Pereiaslav agreement between the Ukraine and Muscovy was interpreted as a voluntary and permanent union of the two peoples.

Moreover, Russian newspapers and schools were rapidly being

established in the Ukraine. Teachers, writers and artists were to glorify not only the communist system but also the traditional heroes of Russia. Dictionaries were rewritten to draw the Ukrainian language closer to the Russian. Those unwilling to submit were eliminated. In 1934 alone, 79 Ukrainian scholars and writers were shot and many others sent to concentration camps in Asia. The Great Purge of 1937 obliterated "an entire generation of political leaders, economic experts and cultural workers," says a historian of the period. The wholesale destruction of the Ukrainian peasantry had already been accomplished, in 1933, when over five million died in the famine resulting from the forced collectivization of farms.

Admittedly, the Ukraine's early communist leaders did make some effort to stem the centralist tide. Mykola Skrypnyk,[1] for instance, was an Old Bolshevik but he insisted on the "Ukrainization" of both the party apparatus and the administration in the republic; the Ukrainian language was to be the first official language. But in the early 1930's the Ukrainian Central Committee lost out in a struggle with Moscow against the harsh economic plans. Some of the Committee members thereupon committed suicide, others were deported or shot. Until 1953 no Ukrainian was allowed to occupy the post of First Secretary of the party in Kiev. According to Djilas, Yugoslav communist leaders took warning from this demise of the Ukrainian party officials; during their conflict with the Kremlin, in 1946, they refused to go to Moscow for fear they, too, would not come back alive.

In 1941, when the Germans invaded the Soviet Union's border territories, there were mass surrenders by units of the Red Army, Russian as well as non-Russian. But the Germans themselves were responsible for the turning of the tide. The atrocities they committed in the occupied countries impelled the people to fight for their survival on the Soviet side. The Ukrainians fought valiantly. Their achievements at the front, the existence of Ukrainian nationalist guerrillas (UPA), and the increasing restlessness in the Ukraine compelled Stalin to make some concessions. In 1944, the Soviet Constitution was amended to restore to the Ukraine and other republics the right to form their own departments of defense and foreign affairs. But only the Ukraine and Belorussia were sponsored by the Soviets as founding members of the United Nations. However, neither of the two republics has been recognized by any foreign nation, nor does Moscow encourage the idea. There have been feelers from the British and Sudanese governments which were silently rebuffed in the Kremlin. A feeble attempt by the Premier of the Ukraine, Volodymyr Shcherbytsky, to deal directly with foreign diplomats stationed in Moscow, led to his dismissal in 1963. Though he is now again at the helm in Kiev, he failed to obtain Moscow's permission for the Ukraine's participation in Expo 67 as a separate exhibitor. Such participation would have entailed a state visit to Canada by the Ukraine's representative and Moscow could not tolerate that. Recently, Alexei Kosygin declared that "no country in the world could claim to have solved the nationality problem as successfully as the Soviet Union. . . . No nationality in our country is discriminated against." The continuing evidence of underground ferment in the Ukraine makes nonsense of this boast.

True, the policy of Russification and economic integration is eroding the Ukraine's national identity, but there is still strong resistance to this process. That it exists, was recently revealed by a writer in the Russian-language paper *Pravda Ukrainy:* "We still meet people who consciously or sub-consciously stress national differences and individuality, thus hampering the progressive processes of drawing together nations and cultures." Behind these lines lies a story of continuing national consciousness among the non-Russians in spite of all "unifying" measures. In 1966, some 30 Ukrainian intellectuals and students were arrested and deported to Russia.[2] Earlier, a group of Ukrainian jurists had met the same fate for having prepared a brief calling for the practical implementation of the Ukraine's paper constitutional rights. There exists in the Ukraine a large clandestine literature similar to that in Russia.[3] Hand-produced articles, plays, poems, and stories circulate constantly, which cannot pass the censors of the state publishing organizations. Some of this material has reached the West and appeared in print; more is in process of being printed. The authorities clamp down with arrests and trials, but the young writers show a stubborn integrity.

Last May, there was a sit-in protest at the Taras Shevchenko burial mound on the Dnieper, and an even larger demonstration in Kiev. Students, who composed the majority of the demonstrators, raised demands that sound somewhat strange coming from citizens of a country where, supposedly, "the nationality problem has been solved." They wrote: "We demand the introduction of the Ukrainian language in all schools in the Ukraine, from kindergarten to university, as well as in all public institutions, from local town halls to ministerial offices." They also demanded minority rights for the seven million Ukrainians in the Russian Federation, deprived of their own language schools and newspapers while the Russians in the Ukraine enjoy all the privileges of a dominant race.

The older people, with long memories of purges and harsh suppressive measures, shake their heads in apprehension when young people state these problems so openly. But a member of *Komsomol* (the Communist youth organization) explains: "Why should we be afraid? To demand one's own rights is not a crime. And we are demanding only what is ours according to the promises made to our fathers and grandfathers in 1917. Why should we go on being cautious? There is a limit to cautiousness and after 50 years in the shadows the Ukrainians have reached that limit. . . ."

Are the leaders of the Soviet Union aware of the dangers inherent in the policies of rigid Russification and economic centralization advocated by the Russia diehards in the party? A year ago, *Pravda* warned that "total disregard for national characteristics could bring in its wake a dangerous outburst of the old nationalistic spirit." The fact is that this nationalistic spirit is still very much alive in every Soviet republic, despite the passing of 50 years since the Bolshevik Revolution.

REFERENCE NOTES

[1]M. O. Skrypnyk (1872–1933), Soviet Ukrainian party and government functionary; an associate of Lenin; identified with the so-called "Ukrainization period" in the Ukraine in the 'twenties and regarded as a leading Ukrainian national communist. Disillusioned, he committed suicide as the first phase of the Stalinist purges was getting under way.

[2]See Chapter V in this collection.

[3]See article No. 24 in this collection.

PART V

INTELLECTUAL DISSENT IN
THE UKRAINE

EDITOR'S NOTE

A new movement appeared in the Soviet Union. Call it, if you like, "intellectual dissent." It can be found among the Russian intelligentsia; it has had manifestations also in non-Russian republics, like the Ukraine.

The main vehicle of communication is samizdat (in Russian) or samvydav (in Ukrainian); meaning literally, self-published literature.

Examples are, the Russian-language "Chronicle of Current Events" and the Ukrainian-language "The Ukrainian Herald." In the Ukraine (and in other non-Russian republics), dissent has had a particular dimension: the defense of national rights, culture, and heritage in the face of Russification. The regime's response to this movement has taken the form of a variety of punitive measures. Some of Roman Rakhmanny's writings on the subject, by unusual paradox, exist in the Ukraine possessing a self-published literature of her own.

21

"EXCHANGE ALONG THE
50TH PARALLEL"

Of my nearly 500 commentaries published here in the last ten years, perhaps one-tenth reached the Ukrainian readers in the Soviet Union, Poland, Czechoslovakia, Romania, and Yugoslavia. Along with other "imported" writings, such as General D. Eisenhower's speech at the unveiling of the Taras Shevchenko monument in Washington and Pope John's encyclical, the articles were multiplied and circulated in typed and longhand transcripts by friends, among friends and for friends.

Mykhailo S. Masiutko, a teacher from the Crimea, was one of those accused of typing and distributing the "bourgeois nationalist literature from abroad." He argued both at the trial and in his letter to the attorney-general in Kiev that these essays were not anti-Soviet in content. "On the contrary, Rakhmanny in his article argues for strengthening and enlarging the powers of the present Soviet government in Ukraine," wrote Masiutko.[1] His co-defendant, Opanas I. Zalyvakha, an artist with a Siberian background, quotes from the same article a line saying that "we want to see the Ukrainian people masters in their own home and not just existing as an ethnographic non-entity. . . ."[2]

The article in question was prompted by a polemical message of Iryna Vilde, a Soviet Ukrainian novelist, who urged the

Reprinted with permission from *The Gazette* (Montreal), February 16, 1968.

133

Ukrainian Canadians in 1964, to face the truth and recognize
the "flourishing Soviet Ukraine." I countered it by comparing
the real autonomy of Canada's provinces with the paper sovereignty of the Ukraine in the Soviet Union, where (to quote
Lenin) "only the Great Russians were privileged to form a sovereign state." Since 1914, when Lenin argued thus against Rosa
Luxemburg, the situation has not changed, I charged in my
"Open Letter to Iryna Vilde."[3]

The article found the mark not because it showed something
new to the post-Stalin generation of Ukrainians, but because it
happened to coincide with their own observations. They had
seen and deplored the Russification of the Ukraine, Belorussia,
Latvia, Lithuania and other Union Republics; they objected, in
their essays, to the witch-hunting against "bourgeois nationalists." "There are no bourgeois Ukrainians, no bourgeois Jews,
no capitalist Tartars, no German landowners in the USSR.
There are only workers," wrote Svyatoslav Y. Karavansky, a poet
from Odessa.

Karavansky addressed a Petition to W. Gomulka, First Secretary of the Polish Communist Party, and asked him to use his
own influence to call an "international conference of the Communist parties of the world" in order to "define the principles of
Marxist-Leninist nationality policy." The conference should
"condemn   anti-Semitism,   Ukrainophobia,   discrimination
against nationalities" which are apparently practised by "various
Communist parties."

(The Polish Consul in Kiev accepted the petition; the Consul
of Czechoslovakia refused to forward a similar "appeal" addressed to the then President, A. Novotny.)[4]

For all his efforts to improve communist practices, Karavansky
received a term of 8 years and 7 months in a concentration
camp. About three months ago he was joined there by V.
Chornovil, sentenced for three years, because he wrote the
Ukrainian version of *Profiles in Courage* — 20 biographical
sketches of the dissenters.[5]

All these men and women, born and brought up under the
Soviet system, have been particularly wary of the recurrent Stalinism in the Soviet Union. About seven million Ukrainians in
the Russian Federation are still deprived of the language schools.
"The privileged position of the Russian language in Ukraine

breeds chauvinistic elements," declared Mykhailo M. Horyn, a psychologist, who was sentenced to 6 years of hard labor.

Yet the defendants' stand, both during their trial and in the concentration camps, points explicitly to the essential change in the mood and the structure of the Soviet "society of societies." The new generation in all the republics believes in freedom of speech, freedom to criticize and freedom to travel, write, and paint according to one's own desires.

The fact that they have accepted favorably the views of some non-communist writers from abroad, and have themselves succeeded in sending out to the West their highly humanistic messages, is in itself a victory.

The exchange of ideas along the fiftieth parallel running between Canada and the Ukraine is convincing enough.

REFERENCE NOTES

[1]Vyacheslav Chornovil (comp.), *The Chornovil Papers* (New York: McGraw-Hill, 1968), p. 144. See also, *Ukrains'ka inteligentsiia pid sudom KGB* (Ukrainian Intellectuals Tried by the KGB), (Munich: Suchasnist, 1970), pp. 90, 93-94, and 102.

[2]Chornovil, *op. cit.*, p. 128.

[3]For a text of the open letter, see *Suchasnist* (Munich), IV, No. 11 (November 1964), 122-27.

[4]Chornovil, *op. cit.*, p. 180-86.

[5]See article No. 22 in this collection.

22

THE CHORNOVIL PAPERS AND
INTELLECTUAL LIBERTY

The Chornovil Papers[1] is a compilation of documents dealing with the suppression of intellectual ferment in the Ukraine from 1965-67. Close to fifty Ukrainian writers, teachers, scientists and other members of the Soviet intelligentsia landed in the concentration camps of Russia in the winter of 1965-66, at the same time that two Russian writers, A. Siniavsky and Iu. Daniel, were on trial for their works published abroad. The trial of the Ukrainian intellectuals was never officially acknowledged.

Vyacheslav Chornovil, a 30-year-old reporter for Ukrainian radio-TV, was assigned to cover the secret trials at Lviv and Kiev, and in one case even to testify against a colleague on trial. He refused to take part in the "illegal proceedings" and was himself suspected and arrested. When released, he would not keep quiet about what he saw in the secret police offices, in the courtrooms and in the streets of Ukrainian cities.

In his Petition addressed to Petro Shelest, First Secretary of the Ukraine's Communist Party, and in his sketches of "Twenty Criminals," Chornovil raised some probing questions about Soviet society and the Stalinist policy of intimidation of Ukrainians, carried out under the cover of silence in both the press and radio-TV services.

Reprinted with permission from *The Gazette* (Montreal), July 27, 1968.

"When I began writing these notes," Chornovil says, "I had just one purpose in mind: to warn against the repetition (under different labels) of the terror of the 1930s." For all efforts to improve the so-called Leninist justice in the Ukraine, Chornovil got three years of imprisonment, later commuted to 18 months. Presently he is being held in Vynnytsia not far from Lviv where the Russians proposed recently to hold a two-party meeting with the leaders of Czechoslovakia about the "dangers of liberalization" which, allegedly has spread to Ukraine.[2]

But in the meantime Chornovil's friends, who had copies of his "notes," have managed to send them abroad to Poland, Czechoslovakia, Yugoslavia, Romania, and Hungary, to acquaint all their comrades with the recurrence of Stalinism in the Ukraine. Two or three copies reached North America, appeared in excerpts in various papers, and have finally been published in book form.

This book shows again that it is not enough to be a "good communist" but one has to be a loyal Russian as well. "For five years I studied faithfully Marxist-Leninist philosophy—just recently I passed my Master's exam in that philosophy. Then, all of a sudden and quite by accident I lay my hands on a Ukrainian book published abroad and I am accused of being a bourgeois nationalist... or I listen to a speech by the Pope on the radio and I become a Jesuit... or I read a leaflet from Peking and I become a follower of Mao Tse-tung...." Chornovil wrote the above about himself and other Ukrainian intellectuals accused, among others, of transcribing and circulating one of my articles.

The readers of that article and its author alike held the view that Ukraine, being a developed country with vast resources and technical knowhow, could be an independent country. If Belgium "enjoys independence: why does not the Soviet Ukraine," Mykhailo Ozerny, a teacher argued before his class, and for his views he was sentenced to six years of hard labor, although the Soviet Constitution guarantees the right of secession to the Ukraine and other Soviet non-Russian republics.

There were many other gross transgressions of the Soviet law by the present rulers of the Soviet Union. A reader will find it a fascinating experience to follow Chornovil's reasoning based on the law, the constitution, and Lenin, and aimed at the defense not only of Ukrainians, but of all the non-Russians discriminated against: Lithuanians, Estonians, Latvians, Jews, Tartars, Moldavians and the Volga Germans.

Among various statements in defense of the freedom of peoples and of individuals, the most striking ones are those by S. S. Karavansky and I. Dzyuba. The former indicts the Russian government for their suppression of peoples, and the latter calls for cooperation between Ukrainians and Jews on the basis of their mutual interest and similar sufferings.

The book is in want of an editorial hand, to make the reading more understandable to a person not familiar with the events. Professor Frederick C. Barghoorn of Yale University does not help much in this respect with his over-cautious introductory article. The whole issue is presented much more clearly and concisely by Z. Brzezinski of Columbia University. "Fifty per cent of the Soviet people is non-Russian. Among these, the Ukrainians are the most numerous and potentially the most powerful. It is not inconceivable that in the next several decades the nationality problem will become politically more important in the Soviet Union than the racial issue has become in the United States," says Professor Brzezinski.

In addition to being a moving human document, *The Chornovil Papers* focusses attention on this important political issue: intellectual ferment is a sure sign of the maturing of the non-Russian nationalities, some of them asking for greater autonomy within the Soviet Union and some eying their own road to self-government.

REFERENCE NOTES

[1]Vyacheslav Chornovil (Comp.), *The Chornovil Papers* (New York: McGraw-Hill, 1968). 246 pp.

[2]V. Chornovil was released from imprisonment on February 3, 1969, after serving 18 months of his three-year sentence. He was not allowed to work professionally as a journalist or literary critic, and had to earn his livelihood as a railroad worker. In January 1972, he was arrested again on charges of continued dissident activities and sentenced in February 1973 to 7 years of severe regime labor camp and 5 years of exile.

23

UKRAINIAN WRITER DZYUBA
CRITICIZES RUSSIFICATION

Another book written by an Ukrainian writer, Ivan Dzyuba, has been recently smuggled out of the Soviet Union and put into the hands of Western readers in an English translation.[1] Ivan Dzyuba's study implies that the more Russia changes the more it remains the same, at least, in its relations with its non-Russian territories.

Lenin tried hard to change this relationship and promised along with a just society for the working classes, self-determination for the oppressed non-Russians. But on his death-bed, in December 1922, he had to admit his failure on both counts. The ageless Russian bureaucracy, sprinkled only by a few internationalists of his kind, took control over the peasants and workers while the chauvinists in the party reverted to the familiar method of forced assimilation of the non-Russians. In his last three letters to the Central Committee, Lenin warned against the mistake of following these diehards whom he had dubbed scornfully "Russian *derzhimordy*" or big bullies. Soon after, however, Stalin was building up his personal power using these very elements in the party and state administration.

Now, 45 years since Lenin's warning, this 37-year-old Ukrain-

Reprinted with permission from *The Gazette* (Montreal), October 4, 1968.

ian writer charges that the present-day Soviet leaders are continuing the anti-Leninist policy of Russification of the Ukraine.
The arrests carried out in various Ukrainian cities in the fall of
1965 prompted him to voice his own warning. The victims then
were young Ukrainian intellectuals who expressed their dissatisfaction with the colonial-like status of their republic. Dzyuba, in
an extremely well documented essay, defends their right to "feel
anxiety about the fate of Ukrainian culture and the Ukrainian
nation," threatened by annihilation as much as all the other, and
much smaller, non-Russian nationalities of the USSR.

"The idea of assimilation of nations, the idea of a future na-
tionless society is not an idea of Scientific Communism, but of
that kind which Marx and Engels called 'barrack communism,'"
writes Dzyuba to the Soviet leaders, one of whom Petro Shelest[2]
of Kiev, has made a reputation for himself as a "hawk" of the
Politburo during the recent Czechoslovak crisis.

In the spirit of that reactionary tradition, Soviet leaders have
been busy promoting a process of Russification which is marked
by its own "special mechanics," says Dzyuba. First of all, there is
what he calls "the language blockage." Commercial relations in
all republics are conducted mostly in Russian. The party, Communist Youth League, trade unions, factories, business and
educational institutions "prefer" Russian to any other language.
The Soviet Army remains the most powerful instrument of the
process, as its language of instruction and command is Russian only, and its military traditions and aims are those of
Russia.

The so-called Soviet-Ukrainian schools "do nothing to instill a
sense of national dignity and feeling. . . . They do not even assure for the pupils a minimal knowledge of Ukrainian history
and culture."

But even these inadequate schools are few. In 1958, relates
Dzyuba, "even in the capital of Ukraine, Kiev, there were only
22,000 pupils in Ukrainian (secondary) schools but 61,000 in
Russian schools." In such large cities as Kharkiv, Odessa or
Donetsk, secondary Ukrainian schools are rather an exception,
says Dzyuba, himself a native of the industrial region of Donbas.

At the same time, economic over-centralization works against
the development of the Ukraine as a distinctive nation. "In our
country detailed economic statistics are for some reason kept

behind a triple lock and key. . . . Till 1958, the Ukrainian Soviet Republic did not compute its national income or national product."

Although Russians, and their Ukrainian collaborators in official positions, do their utmost to convince the Ukrainian public that their country gained from "the union with Russia," the Ukrainians appear to be more and more aware of their colonial status within the Soviet Union and since the ferment among the intellectuals more and more people are questioning the policy of "merging of nationalities."

Ivan Dzyuba, a sincere believer in Marxist-Leninist principles, has a warning for all those who have been trying to improve on Stalin. "He destroyed several million Ukrainians but did not destroy the nation. And no one ever will. You cannot go against history. . . . You cannot play at communism: you either have to put it into practice or betray it in the name of the one and indivisible barracks."

REFERENCE NOTES

[1]Ivan Dzyuba, *Internationalism or Russification?* (London: Weidenfeld-Nicholson, 1968), 240 pp. Also, 2nd rev. ed., 1971.

[2]Petro Iu. Shelest, First Secretary of the Communist Party of Ukraine (1957-72); member of the CC CPSU (1961-73) and of its Presidium, later renamed Politburo (1964-73). In May 1973, demoted and removed from his posts in the Politburo, CC CPSU and Soviet Government after being accused of being "soft on Ukrainian nationalism." See also article No. 27 in this collection.

24

CLANDESTINE SOVIET PAPER TELLS ALL

A promise of dignity and human rights for everyone, in a future just society under the flag of communism, was what made the Internationale a truly inspired anthem of the under-privileged population of Russia half a century ago—then in the throes of revolution. The song made the people aware, more than anything else, of their own self-sufficiency by proclaiming to all and sundry that their salvation was to be achieved, not through God, the czar or a hero, but through their own efforts alone.

Today, some 50-odd years later and with communist order well-entrenched in eight other countries of the world, the people of the Soviet Union are still pursuing the same elusive objective. And they are doing this literally (to borrow the phrase from the Internationale) "with their own hands."

To inform one another, and perhaps world opinion as well, about their grievances and the shortcomings of the Soviet system in the field of human rights, a group of public-minded citizens of the USSR is publishing a typed newsletter, *Samizdat* Chronicle, and circulating it clandestinely from hand to hand.

Samizdat means literally "self-publishing," and its impli-cations are obvious. The state, controlled by the Communist Party, owns all the means of publishing—from newsprint to the

Reprinted with permission from *The Ottawa Journal,* September 19, 1969.

distribution of printed items. Not a word can appear in print without being passed through the sieve of censorship. Thus, the only way to express oneself freely or to inform the public about some events, in the country or abroad, is to put out your own pamphlet or a newsletter.

Limited Means

To a prospective self-publisher there are very limited technical means available. The simplest to operate are typewriters and mimeographs, but even these are not easy to obtain. No wonder then, that Ukrainian dissenters had to turn to the pre-Gutenberg practice of copying their uncensored writings in longhand. For this effort, some of them were sentenced at a secret trial at Lviv, 1966, to up to seven years of hard labor.

Samizdat Chronicle differs from other self-publishing enterprises in that it is a newsletter of 15 to 20 pages, typed on regular size paper. The issues published during 1968 bear the heading: "The Year of Human Rights in the Soviet Union — A Chronicle of Current Events." Under the heading, there is a quotation from the Universal Declaration of Human Rights, Article 19: "Everyone has the right to freedom of opinion and expression; this right includes freedom to hold opinions without interference and to seek, receive and impart information and ideas through any media and regardless of frontiers."

The invisible editors of the Chronicle appear encouraged by the response of their readers to this effect. "After the publication of five issues," they wrote in the December, 1968, issue, "it is now possible to have at least a general idea of the manner in which human rights are suppressed in the USSR. This being so, not a single member of the Movement (for Human Rights) can regard the Year of Human Rights as over. The over-all objective — democratization — and partial task, fulfilled by the Chronicle — information — remain unchanged. Therefore, the Chronicle shall continue to appear in 1969."

Keeps Going

And they were true to their word. The Chronicle has kept on this year, with a slightly adjusted letterhead: "The Year of Human Rights in the Soviet Union Continues." But the same quote from the Declaration of Human Rights proclaims the right of every man to possess his own views and to express them either in private or in public, by any means and anywhere.

The language of the publication is Russian, in this case a *lingua franca* for readers of various nationalities both within and without the USSR. As to contents, the Chronicle is packed with reports on Soviet violations of human rights, regardless of the victims' nationality, race or belief.

Czechoslovakia's occupation by the armed forces of the Soviet Union and its allies occupied a central spot in the Chronicle's reporting last year. This year, the plight of the Crimean Tartars and thwarted Ukrainian aspirations, both cultural and political, are much in the limelight. Brief sketches of more prominent defenders of human rights in the USSR are presented along with information on suppressed publications. The April 1968 issue contained a brief review of other *samizdats* and their contents: discussion of arrests, protests, and social, literary and religious questions.

The editors of the Chronicle are extremely well informed about happenings in distant centers and regions of the USSR, including the concentration camps of Mordovia, and prisons in Russia and the Ukraine. They give a special report on Ukrainian and Russian prisoners' tribulations—ranging from stricter incarceration, through transfers to other camps and prisons, to (rarely) their release after sentences have been served.

Religious Persecution

There are also news items dealing with the renewed persecution of Baptists and Catholics in the Ukraine. "In January this year, the acting head of the clandestine Ukrainian Catholic Church, Bishop Velychkovsky, 70, was arrested."[1] This followed arrests of lower clergy and believers in the Western Ukraine.

A striking violation of human rights is presented by the administrative measures directed against those who had ventured to express in public (orally or in print) nonconformist opinions on current Soviet affairs or literary questions. Among those expelled from the Party or *Komsomol,* or fired from their jobs, for these transgressions, are journalists, teachers, artists, writers, engineers, scholars, factory workers and students.

The editors of the Chronicle, without displaying any emotions, record also the tragic self-immolations by those Soviet citizens who could not bear the pressures of the totalitarian system any more. Thus, in April this year, a student in Riga, Ilia Rens, set himself on fire while displaying under this city's Statue of Liberty a placard with the inscription: "Freedom for Czecho-slovakia!" His self-immolation has been preceded by a similar protest in the Ukraine: Vasyl Makukha, a teacher and father of two children, committed suicide by fire in a Kiev square last December, shouting "Freedom for the Ukraine."

Despite its contents and the irregular manner of its publication and distribution, the editors do not regard the Chronicle as illegal. They see only its "working conditions being limited by the peculiar concept of legality and freedom of information formulated in the years past by certain Soviet organs." Only for this reason, say the editors, are they unable to print their address like any other journal in the Soviet Union.

Chain of Contacts

But readers interested in making their Soviet society better informed, about events both in their own country and abroad, "should deliver to the Chronicle any pertinent information available to them." This can be done with the help of the very person "who has supplied you with a copy of the Chronicle; the same person will forward your report to his own contact. . . ." But there is a warning, too: "Do not try to follow up the whole chain of contacts by yourself because you may be suspected of being a police informer."

Thus, apparently, a chain reaction of thinking freedom-loving persons is being promoted from the murky depths of the totalitarian society. These public-spirited citizens, by acting as readers and correspondents at the same time, are trying hard to become better informed themselves and to share their knowledge with fellow citizens, concerning the state of human rights under the red banner.

By their unpretentious reporting and devotion to the truth, the editors of the Chronicle have succeeded in imbuing their readers with a feeling of optimism, in spite of all the shocking details about the seemingly invincible power of the regime. The reader is becoming aware of the multitude of honest people like himself, who are displaying such courage and human dignity that even an all-powerful Soviet state machine has not been able to intimidate them.

Opinion Growing

The significance of *Samizdat* Chronicle is unequivocal: within the realm of the Kremlin, public opinion is growing steadily and it is already challenging the community of totaly enslaved minds.

The situation is not unlike the one that had developed in Russia under Czar Alexander II, slightly over 100 years ago. One of the best minds among the dissenters of that period (the 1860s), Nikolai Serno-Solovevich, described the mood of society then in the following words, very applicable to the Soviet Union today:

> The present government awakened society with its partial reform measures, but did not give it an opportunity to express itself. But the need for expression is as important for society as chatter is for a child; therefore, society could not do anything else but to express its opinion, without waiting for permission to do so.

And this is why the march for human rights in the Soviet Union goes on.

REFERENCE NOTES

[1]Bishop Vasyl Velychkovsky of Lutsk (Ukraine), secretly ordained in 1963; twice imprisoned by the Soviet authorities (1945–1955 and 1969–1972); released from the USSR in 1972; died in Winnipeg, Canada in 1973.

25

WIVES OF SOVIET DISSIDENTS
LEAD A DIFFICULT LIFE

Of all the underprivileged women in the world, the wives of
Soviet dissenters merit the most commiseration, for their lot is
tragic.

They live in an industrially developed country and, theoreti-
cally, have all the guarantees of equal rights with other citizens.
However, the wives of Soviet dissenters feel compelled to fight for
the liberation of their husbands who are imprisoned in various
camps in the Soviet Union.

Their devotion is not even appreciated in their own country
and remains almost unknown beyond its borders. But that their
husbands deserve such an effort, most have no doubt. The dissenters are the men who not only believe in the principle of
human rights but also have dared to challenge the authorities in
the Soviet Union.

Thus, in the last eight years or so, such names as Daniel and
Siniavsky, Solzhenitsyn and General Grigorenko, Moroz[1] and
Karavansky became familiar to many a Canadian. But very few
if any know the names of the women who stood by them in their
most difficult moments when each wrestled in his mind with the
human dilemma: to speak or not to speak against injustice. Or
when the KGB men knock at a dissenter's door in the small hours

Reprinted with permission from *Winnipeg Free Press,* October 11, 1971.

147

of the night. Or when, months later on, in the courtroom where the government would hold a public trial to which even the defendant's wife may not be admitted.

But these women — wives, as well as mothers and sisters — chose to stand by their men when they have been sent away to prison for three to 15 years of imprisonment and hard labor, often supplemented by additional years of banishment from their region.

To stand by an arrested or sentenced man in the Soviet Union means literal hell for a woman. One becomes an undesirable social element in the eyes of the party. No publicity is involved. The woman soon must vacate the job she held before her husband's trial; a loss of living quarters is not rare. Children are discriminated against in school or at work. Existence on the brink of starvation is the only future for the dissenter's family. Relatives and friends remain to the dissenter's wife the sole hope for survival.

And yet, the wives of Soviet dissenters — be they Russian, Latvian, Ukrainian, Estonian, Jewish, Lithuanian or Tartar — find the necessary strength of spirit to defy their fate. They simply won't abandon their men.

Court appeals are sought. Petitions composed with the help of friends are sent to the attorney-general, to the republican legislatures and, eventually, to the Supreme Soviet of the USSR.

If this fails (as usually expected) appeals to prominent men of letters, to state-recognized artists and influential party members are directed. The rightful case of the imprisoned man is expertly laid bare. The argument usually rests on constitutional rights, the criminal code and the principles of the Universal Declaration of Human Rights which was endorsed by the Soviet Union in 1948.

Typed and hand-written copies of all these memoranda, appeals, petitions and protests — circulated from hand to hand — bring a moral pressure on the authorities. Soon, appeals addressed to the United Nations and "open letters" to humanitarian or professional organizations abroad appear both clandestinely in the Soviet Union and in some newspapers of the West. For idealism and faith in "international justice," these documents have no equal.

Through each document a fleeting image of a dissenter's wife seems to emerge, worn out with the struggle but still undaunted, as, for instance, Zinaida Grigorenko. After her repeated appeals to the authorities to release her 64 year-old husband kept in the mental hospital at Cherniakhovsk (formerly the East Prussian town of Insterburg), she addressed her plea to the world's psychiatrists:

> Who will stop this gradual murder? Evidently, in our country there is no such (legal) body. That is why I am appealing to you and pass on the request that my husband conveyed to me at my last meeting with him: 'Demand the repudiation of the false medical diagnosis on me, demand my immediate release.'

So did Giuzel, wife of historian Andrei Amalrik who was sentenced last November to three years in a hard labor camp.[2] She wrote to the Supreme Soviet: "I know my husband's strength of mind. Neither accusations nor conviction will break him mentally. But I also know that his health is poor and I fear for his life."

Soon, however, she had to turn to public opinion abroad: "All those who cherish the right of man to express views freely and to live in dignity, I am calling to help me."

The wives of Ukrainian dissenters have been even less fortunate. Their lot is reflected in the words of Raisa Moroz wife of the Ukrainian historian whose name came to haunt even some Canadian politicians on Parliament Hill in Ottawa. In her appeal to the Soviet Ukraine's boss, Petro Shelest, she wrote in October 1970:

> For four years I and my little son had been waiting for my husband, and the boy's father, to return from the imprisonment which had been inflicted upon him — as many people say — for more than dubious reasons. Now again, we are facing long years of separation. . . . Is it really necessary for the construction of the most just and humane society in the world?

Similar irony underlies the dignified and factual appeals by Nina, wife of Svyatoslav Karavansky: there was actually no case against this poet and translator who had already spent 15 years in Stalinist prisons. His "crime" was that he raised, in writing, the issue of discrimination against minorities in the USSR — the Jews, the Baltic nationalities, the Tartars, the Volga Germans — as a concomitant of the Russification being imposed on the larger nationalities, the Ukrainians and Belorussians, by the Kremlin.

And one is awed by the audacity of M. Ozerny's wife, a doctor herself and mother of two little boys. Already restricted in practicing her profession, because of her husband's arrest, she found it very hard to survive. She did not lose either her courage or dignity when she witnessed the court proceedings against her husband. After many months as a prisoner, he broke down and, in his concluding plea, asked tearfully for leniency. Mrs. Ozerny called out to her husband across the courtroom: "Mykhaile, don't cry!"

(High school teacher M. Ozerny got six years in a hard labor camp for discussing a hypothetical question in his history class: "If such a small country as Belgium is a sovereign nation, why is it that the Ukraine — a country comparable to France — is not?...")

Mrs. Ozerny's behavior recalls to our memory those women in the Soviet Union who are also in prison.

Daria Husiak[3] and Halyna Didyk[4] have been already 21 years in Soviet prisons for having dared to attend to the wounds of the Ukrainian resistance fighters. Kateryna Zaryts'ka-Soroka,[5] another movement supporter, has been 24 years in the "tombs of stone," to use S. Karavansky's description of Soviet prisons. They were joined there by hundreds of younger Ukrainian women who recently chose to stand up for human rights of Ukrainians.

There are thousands of men in the Soviet Union whose defense of human rights, for man and nation, is in itself a victory of the human spirit over the Soviet system. One must not forget that along with them, often standing by their men, there have been women — wives, mothers, and sisters — whose unpublicized self-sacrifice has made their men's feat possible.

REFERENCE NOTES

[1]See article No. 26 in this collection.

[2]Andrei Amalrik, author of the book *Will the Soviet Union Survive Until 1984?* (New York: Harper and Row, 1970), 94 pp. Amalrik was released and allowed to emigrate; he now lives in the West.

[3]Daria Husiak, a member of the Ukrainian resistance movement, condemned to death in 1950, later commuted to 25 years of imprisonment; released in 1975 at the expiration of her term.

[4]Halyna Didyk, condemned to death in 1950 for her role in organizing Red Cross units for the Ukrainian Insurgent Army (UPA), commuted to 25 years of imprisonment; released in 1971 as a second class invalid after having served 20 years of her term.

[5]Kateryna Zaryts'ka-Soroka, helped organize Red Cross units for the UPA; in 1947 was sentenced to death, later commuted to 25 years of imprisonment; released in 1972 after having served her full term. Her husband, Mykhailo Soroka, died as a political prisoner in a Soviet labor camp in 1971. See article No. 29 in this collection.

26

MOROZ ROCKS THE EMPIRE

OF SOVIET COGS

No other Soviet dissenter has ever spurred on so many young Canadians to appreciative re-thinking of their own democracy or to acting on his behalf as did Valentyn Moroz.[1]

The 35-year-old history teacher, now behind the bars of the prison in Vladimir (one of the toughest in Russia), never set his eyes on Canada's capital.

Yet, his name has been cropping up in news reports from Parliament Hill; it rings in every city the Soviet premier visits during his Canadian tour, and it must have been mentioned more than once in the conversations Mr. Trudeau and Premier Kosygin had on the two touchiest issues — the demanded migration rights for the Soviet Jews and the release of Ukrainian intellectuals from Russia's prisons.

(The assurance that the latter issue would be raised during the Ottawa summit was given by Mr. Trudeau to a group of Ukrainian-Canadian students who had been on a four-day hunger strike just before the Prime Minister was to address the Congress of Ukrainian-Canadians in Winnipeg, October 9, 1971).

Recently, one of Moroz's essays — "A Report From the Beria Reserve" — has been published in Israel by a group of immigrants from the USSR.

Reprinted with permission from *The Windsor Star*, October 21, 1971.

But a year ago nothing seemed to suggest his tremendous impact on so many young minds in so many different countries. Until then, he had been somewhat overshadowed by the dissenters whose works appeared abroad: by Vyacheslav Chornovil whose uncensored report on the secret trials at Lviv of 1966 — *The Chornovil Papers* — was published in Toronto; and by Ivan Dzyuba whose study *Internationalism or Russification* was published in Britain.

Born in 1936, Moroz was fortunate to survive the Second World War and the hunger and terror years in the post-war Ukraine. He was teaching history in the College of Education at Ivano-Frankivsk, Ukraine, and preparing his doctoral thesis when the KGB arrested him on the trumped up charge of "spreading anti-Soviet ideas" in 1965.

For four years he toiled in a forced labor camp of Mordovia where many Ukrainian, Jewish, Lithuanian and other "thinking people" — including such Russians as A. Siniavsky — have been compelled to slave.

But these years were not entirely wasted for Moroz, a Soviet-educated man who was also able to think for himself.

There and then, he enriched his understanding of the government system he calls "the empire of cogs." The experience resulted in "Report From the Beria Reserve," one of the most soul-rendering essays to come out from under the pen of a Soviet dissenter.[2]

"Stalin did not believe in cybernetics. But he has greatly contributed to this branch of science; he invented the programmed man. Stalin is the inventor of the human cog," wrote Moroz.

In a satirical manner, he explained how that came about.

"Once, the separation of the individual from the mass of matter signalled the beginning of life itself, the birth of the organic world. Presently, however, a reverse process began: the blending of the individual into the greyish mass — a return into solid non-organic and non-individual existence. Society has been overpowered by the inertia of facelessness. It is a crime to have a personality of one's own."

That is why Moroz and other imprisoned dissenters had been repeatedly asked by their interrogators to explain what seemed a puzzle to them: "Who do you think you are to yearn to become an individual in this society?"

Cogs Hypocritical

As intended, this essay, written in the nooks and crannies of a slave labor camp, reached the ruling circles in Kiev and was also brought to the attention of all the members of the rubber-stamp Supreme Soviet of the Ukrainian SSR.

Soon after, typed and written copies of the document began circulating all over the republic. Even more timid from among the older generation would nod in agreement while reading a line like this one:

> The ageless question—'Whither should I proceed?'—has been transmuted for the cogs (in the USSR) into a formula that requires no mental effort: 'Wherever they deign to order me.'

A writer himself, Moroz lashed the hypocrisy of the established Soviet writers, Russian and Ukrainian alike.

"The cog writes angry poems about the ashes of Buchenwald. . . . But the ashes of the victims burnt in the Siberian tundra do not affect the cog at all."

Neither do such programmed men notice another incongruity of their wretched existence, wrote he with scorn:

> All of us condemn the Nazi crimes perpetrated on the Jews but, at the same time, we all stroll coolly on the sidewalks paved with the tombstones which had been torn out of the Jewish cemeteries in quite a few of our towns. . . . Lecturers and postgraduate students had been walking over these flattened tombstones. . . . If by now some of them have obtained their Ph.D. degrees, then maybe even full professors are strutting over the names of the dead.

Moroz (whose name in English means "frost") has no pity, especially for the self-adjustable cog, the ideal Soviet creature who has no thoughts, no convictions or desires of its own:

"An obedient drove of cogs may be named a parliament or a scholarly association, and none of them would ever cause any problems or surprises. A cog that was appointed a professor or academician, will never say anything new. If he happens to astound someone, he will change his views with a lightning speed—within a day. A group of the cogs appointed to the International Red Cross will count calories in the diet of some African tribes but won't ever mention the starving people in their own country." In different Soviet Republics, that is.

Some of the former inmates of Soviet concentration camps are, perhaps, the most miserable of all the programmed men in the USSR, observes much saddened Moroz: "When a cog is released from prison, he immediately will write that he never spent any time there; he is apt even to call as liars those who had demanded his release."

But Moroz himself would never follow that well-trodden path of a regular Soviet cog.

After his release, in the fall of 1969, he kept expressing in public his strong beliefs in the dignity of men and their right to have their own personalities. Many regular cogs witnessed a senseless destruction of Ukraine's historic sites and cultural monuments by the officials who hate anything individual—be it an artifact, a person or a nationality. But it took a thinking man, Valentyn Moroz, to register a public protest against the barbarity.

In his essay "Chronicles of Resistance in the Ukraine" he noted that there was more involved in the people's defense of their customs and folklore than it appeared.[3] The people opposed the official attempts at creating a pseudo-universal society which Moroz described thus:

> America represents a deculturation process of all the ethnic elements that get into that melting pot. The Soviet Union, while entirely differing from the USA in other respects, has this one thing in common. . . . If you want to prove that you are 'a progressive,' you must disown your ancestry and quickly become 'a universal person' which in practice means a Russian.

In his last essay, "Amidst the Snows," written in February 1970, Moroz argued for the need to stand up and be counted whenever human and constitutional rights are threatened in one's country.[4]

As soon as the essay reached different regions of the Ukraine,

in uncensored copies, the KGB brought the author to the bar
and put him behind the bars of a prison. Sentence: nine years
plus five years of banishment from the Ukraine.

The second sentencing of Valentyn Moroz—on Nov. 17,
1970—shook the conscience of thousands of young people in the
USSR and all over the world.

The sentence (one of the harshest of this kind in the post-
Stalin Soviet Union) was pronounced by a court that had failed
to produce a single witness for the prosecution.

Chornovil, Dzyuba and a senior writer, Borys Antonenko-
Davydovych, had been forced to appear at the trial as material
witnesses. All three refused to testify against Moroz because the
trial was a closed one and thus, in their opinion, illegal in terms
of both the Soviet Union's and the Soviet Ukraine's laws.

Wife Dismissed

"In Stalin's time, I myself had been convicted twice in the
same manner and by a closed court like this one; once I was even
sentenced to death. I won't have any part in inflicting the same
injustice upon Moroz," declared Antonenko-Davydovych, an undaunted veteran of Soviet prisons.

Moroz's defense attorney, E. M. Kogan, who defended A.
Siniavsky in 1966, has proven that his client's activities had been
entirely within the Soviet law.

Moroz's wife, Raisa, stressed the same point in her appeal to
Petro Shelest, the Communist boss of the Ukraine and the man
who had bullied the Czechoslovak leaders at the fateful meeting
at Cierna on the Tisa in 1968. She wrote with a subtle irony:

> For four years I with my little son had been waiting for
> my husband, and the boy's father, to return home from the
> imprisonment which was inflicted upon him—as many
> people say—for more than dubious reasons. Now again, we
> are facing long years of separation.... Is this really neces-
> sary for the construction of the most just and humane so-
> ciety in the world?

For all her efforts, Mrs. Moroz was dismissed from her

teaching job by the time her husband had been transferred to the prison at Vladimir this past January.

As it is, many a Canadian may wonder about the high stakes of free thinking in the Soviet Union.

Others may ask: What significance does such resistance have if even people in the civilized world often are not aware of the dissident's feat?

But it is a fact that the young dissenters like Moroz have definitely shattered the weirdest of the Soviet myths: that there ever existed a homo Sovieticus, a truly Soviet man.

In spite of all the endeavors by the Kremlin rulers for more than 50 years—and at a shocking cost in human lives—the Ukrainians, the Jews, the Lithuanians and even Russians themselves (as witnessed by A. Solzhenitsyn) are successfully resisting the attempts at remodelling them into the programmed cogs in human forms.

Or, as Valentyn Moroz put it: "In the last decade, for the first time and to the great surprise of the KGB, public opinion has arisen."

Herein lies the significance of Moroz's self-sacrifice: the huge empire of cogs is rocking because this human cog would not keep silent.

REFERENCE NOTES

[1]Valentyn Ia. Moroz (b. 1936), Ukrainian historian, arrested in 1965 at the age of 29 for protesting Russification of the Ukraine, sentenced to five years in a severe-regime labor camp. Released in 1969, he was arrested again in 1970 for his criticism of the Soviet nationality policy in the Ukraine; he was sentenced to 14 years — six years imprisonment, three years severe-regime labor camp, and five years in Siberian exile. Reported near death in 1974 as a result of a 20-week hunger strike to protest prison conditions, which led Andrei Sakharov, Soviet dissident physicist to appeal on his behalf to Soviet President Brezhnev and President Carter. Moroz became a leading figure in the Ukrainian dissident movement and a symbol of the Ukrainian national liberation movement in the seventies. He was released on April 27, 1979 together with four other Soviet dissidents in an

"exchange" for two convicted Soviet spies and now resides in the United States.

²For a complete text of the essay, see *Boomerang; the Works of Valentyn Moroz,* ed. by Ya. Bihun (Baltimore, Md.: Smoloskyp Pub., 1974), pp. 7-60.

³*Ibid.,* pp. 91-124.

⁴*Ibid.,* pp. 63-89.

27

STALINISM REAPPEARS IN
THE UKRAINE COLONY

The Windsor Star Editor's Note — *Since its formation 50 years ago this year, the Soviet Union, which consists of 15 constitutionally sovereign republics, has been plagued by an apparently insoluble problem: the aspirations of its various nationalities to become real masters in their own republics.*

Thus, the Kremlin rulers are facing today the same specter of nationalism Lenin and Stalin did in their days. But the issue has become even more complicated for them by recent demands of many Russians themselves for granting human rights to all the Soviet citizens.

The complexity of the dual problem — nationalism and human rights — is reflected best in the events that recently took place in the Ukraine and which are analysed in the following article.

Petro Shelest,[1] the little emperor of the Soviet Ukraine, may not be aware of it, but he is naked. Not that he ever was disrobed by some ethnic Canadian with a personal or ideological grudge against representatives of the new Soviet class.

Isolated as he is from the West, Shelest must know Canada to be a nice country to live in but too hazardous for him to enter-

---

Reprinted with permission from *The Windsor Star,* February 12, 1972.

159

tain any thought of visiting it. For here dwell far too many Ukrainian-Canadians who are keenly aware of the injustices perpetrated on their kith and kin in the Ukraine.

By now, however, even those in the two countries sprawled along the 50th parallel, who had cherished some elusive hopes for a more humane treatment of the Ukrainians under the post-Stalin regime, have been brutally awakened by recent arrests in Kiev and Lviv.

Nineteen young intellectuals in these two main cities of the Ukraine were put behind bars in January and many more have been subjected to house searches and interrogations by the KGB, the Soviet internal security police.

The action came in the wake of Shelest's public call to party workers for ideological vigilance against those who allegedly are bent on undermining Soviet rule in the Ukraine, the second largest Soviet republic with a population of 47 million.

Shelest, First Secretary of the Communist Party of the Ukraine, is known as one of the more ruthless Soviet leaders. He became notorious in the West after the historic meetings between the Soviet Politburo and Czechoslovak leaders at Cierna on the Tisa and Moscow, in 1968. There, he furiously attacked Dr. F. Kriegel—the only Jew on the Dubcek Presidium—for his pro-Western liberal ideas.

Zest on Hatchet Job

Of course, Shelest acted on the orders of Brezhnev who chose for the occasion the role of a benevolent supremo who leaves a hatchet job to his underlings, as Stalin used to leave his to Kaganovich and Molotov.

But Shelest did his job with gusto and some inner conviction because he was seriously worried about any untoward influence of a 140,000-strong Ukrainian minority in Czechoslovakia on his own 40 million Ukrainian subjects.

The latter had been jealously eyeing the freedoms of thought and action just acquired by their brethren in Czechoslovakia. To stem the ferment from eroding the foundations of his not so little empire, Shelest eagerly cast his vote in the Politburo for sealing off Czechoslovakia — that historic gateway from West to East Europe — by an intervention of the Soviet Army.

And in order to placate about 800,000 students in the Soviet Ukraine, Shelest's establishment allowed them to prepare and hold a mass rally of their representatives in Kiev for the purpose of discussing youth issues of the decade.

Being the first (and last) discussion rally of Soviet students ever held in any Soviet republic, the Kiev three-day meeting in February 1969 was primarily designed to prevent the more dissatisfied among the less timid younger generation from swelling the ranks of active Ukrainian dissidents.

The ruse apparently failed as did the administrative measures introduced with the same objective in mind: the tightening of control on passenger traffic between Czechoslovakia and the Ukraine; the intimidation of Ukrainian visitors from countries in which a Ukrainian minority enjoys a dignified status (Canada, U.S., Yugoslavia and even Poland); official pressure on Russia's university graduates to settle in the Ukraine while Ukrainian graduates could find employment mostly outside their own republic — in the Asian parts of the USSR.

But all that only tended to underscore the subservience of the Kiev establishment to the Kremlin centralists at a time when Soviet youth had already lost its faith in both communist dogma and the Soviet kind of federalism.

Consequently, numerous uncensored pamphlets, appeals, political and literary essays circulated hand to hand with a growing persistence.

A bulletin, *Ukrains'kyi Visnyk* (The Ukrainian Herald) began to appear, bringing uncensored news about the officially unpublicized events in the Ukraine.[2]

This phenomenon closely resembled the one in the Russian Federation or those in the Baltic countries, with the former being more known and appreciated in the West.

And like his Russian or Baltic counterparts, a Soviet Ukrainian youth of today is loathe to look into the *Izvestia* of Moscow (The News) for hard news items or to search for some truth in the *Pravda Ukrainy* (The Truth of Ukraine).

He prefers finding his own sources of information, unpolluted by official interpretation; and he likes confronting his own views with the opinions held by unofficial persons.

In this manner, a semblance of independent public opinion has crystallized there in spite of the oppressive censorship.

To what degree, however, has this movement of minds in the Soviet Ukraine been influenced by the Ukrainians residing abroad?

The existence of well-organized Ukrainian communities in North America, Britain, Australia, France and Latin American countries has been a positive challenge to the independent-minded Soviet Ukrainians rather than a directive factor. As it is, an essential gap exists between the views held by Soviet Ukrainian patriots and those of the Ukrainian emigres with their descendants included.

Sincerity Brought Wrath

The emigres, almost without exception, oppose the idea that a viable sovereign Ukraine could be reconstituted on the Marxist-Leninist formula which is expounded and defended by all the spokesmen of Soviet Ukrainian dissent.

It is one of the major ironies of Soviet existence that it was Ivan Dzyuba, one of these recently arrested by the KGB dissenters, who had presented the definitive concept of that Leninist formula.

In his scholarly study *Internationalism or Russification?* that appeared in print only outside the USSR (in Ukrainian and English editions), Dzyuba contrasted the current Soviet practices in the Ukraine with the Marxist-Leninist theory of equality of nationalities in a communist system.

The practice has been roughly the same as under the Russian czars: to Russify all the nationalities of the Soviet Union.

Dzyuba made an ardent appeal to the Kiev leadership to return to the true Marxist-Leninist concept of internationalism as the only means of providing for the Ukrainian people equal status with the Soviet Russians, and of eliminating the entrenched chauvinism in the inter-ethnic relations there.

The sincere effort of Dzyuba brought only the establishment's wrath upon his head. But what particularly strikes an observer of the Ukrainian dissent movement is the self-confidence of its spokesmen. They seem to practise love of truth without fear.

Vyacheslav Chornovil, who was instructed by the state TV

network to prepare an official version of the secret trial of a group of dissidents at Lviv in 1966, produced from his notes a striking document for the public — 20 portraits of courage: the cases of the accused Ukrainian dissenters. (His book appeared in English translation in Toronto, 1968.) For this he served a two-year prison term.

Dissenters Jailed

Undaunted, Chornovil recently protested against willful destruction of the Ukrainian soldiers' cemeteries and war memorials by the Soviet administration at Lviv. In January, he was promptly re-arrested.

Another dissenter Anton Koval of Chernihiv, appealed to the Ukrainian Supreme Soviet in Kiev to restore the armed forces to Soviet Ukraine because, according to the constitution, the republic is supposed to have its own department of defense and should be represented at the Warsaw Pact councils.

Svyatoslav Karavansky of Odessa, now serving a 25-year prison term, was the first man in the Soviet Union to raise the case of small nationalities — the Jews, the Tartars, the Baltic peoples, the Moldavians, the Volga Germans, etc.

He appealed to the Communist parties of the world to formulate a charter of human rights for these peoples, along with the Ukrainians and Belorussians as a guarantee against the Russian preponderance. His wife Nina refused to abandon him to his own fate and continued appealing for a review of his case. For this she was arrested in the January round-up of Ukrainian dissenters.

Valentyn Moroz, a historian who became a subject of controversy even on Parliament Hill in Ottawa last Spring, is now serving his 14-year term in Russia. In his last address to his judges he wrote:

> If by putting me behind the bars you hope to create a vacuum in the Ukrainian resurgence, then you are mistaken. You must comprehend one thing: there won't be any vacuum there. The intensity of the Ukraine's spiritual potential is already sufficient to fill out any vacuum and to

produce new civic leaders for taking over the tasks of the imprisoned and of those who had left the public arena.[3]

Volodyslav Nedobora[4] of Kharkiv has availed himself of a
statement by a 19th century Russian dissenter Chaadaev when he
was faced with a similar set of official demands for blind
obedience to the rulers: "I have not learned to love my fatherland with closed eyes, bowed head and closed mouth. I believe
that a person can only be helpful to his country when he sees
clearly. I believe that the era of blind compliance with the laws is
now past."

Youth Dropouts

What is more, all the dissenters have protested against the traditional practice of punishing Ukrainian citizens by sending
them to prisons and concentration camps or compulsory settlement in Russia, as such a practice was another proof of the
Ukraine being a colony.

It is evident then that all these Soviet Ukrainians felt no great
need for any inspiration from abroad to grow up into as complete human beings as was possible under these conditions.

The realization of this fact must have come as a shock to
Shelest and his like: the Soviet system, renowned for its ability of
indoctrinating young minds, is beset by the problem of "drop-
outs" from the system.

But being a true Soviet bureaucrat, he would explain this
inherent malady of the Kremlin system solely by external
reasons.

In his harangue to the ideological activists in Kiev last November, Shelest blamed foreign radio broadcasts and other media
for the split of personality in the Soviet Ukrainian society.

These mass media have been partially successful, he said,
because they addressed their subversive idea to Soviet youth who
"have not gone through the school of class struggle and have not
acquired sufficient ideological training at work and at school."[5]

Moreover, a recent alliance between the Zionists and the
Ukrainian bourgeois nationalists is another factor in the process,
he said.

The Rattle of Chains

But Shelest's accusation was not the first one of the kind levelled at the Ukrainians who—like Karavansky, Dzyuba or Moroz—dared to stand up for the persecuted Jews and for understanding of their mutual tribulations in the Soviet cauldron of nationalities.

As early as August 1970, V. Bolshakov devoted his two-part article in the Moscow *Komsomolskaia Pravda*[6] to the charge that various Western sovietologists—such as Professor Labedz of London, Professor Brzezinski of Columbia University, and this writer—were busy spreading the Zionist philosophy of cosmopolitism and ideological nihilism.

Even though this kind of writing was not on the level, it still represented a debate in the struggle for the minds of Soviet youths who had been searching for new ideas and some more humane practices of self-government.

But after November 1971 Shelest's speech and the subsequent harsh sentencing of Russian dissenter V. Bukovsky,[7] even these words have been drowned in the rattle of prison chains.

So gone are the days when Comrade Shelest would strike a pose of an enlightened bureaucrat who deemed it necessary to admonish publicly even the Soviet Ukrainian Writers' Union. He said it was the members' sacred duty to develop the Ukrainian culture and preserve the Ukrainian language in the republic.

Gone are the days when his propaganda men would project him as an efficient administrator of the huge republic in which Ukrainians are living without ever dreaming of a breakaway from their "older brother"—the Russian people.

Ukraine Like a Colony

In those years, 1967–1971, communist followers in such countries as Canada would take heart from Shelest's "soft approach" to the thorny Ukrainian problem in the USSR.

In the imagination of Ukrainian-Canadian communists, few as they are today, the Soviet Ukraine seemed to be shaping itself into a sovereign state whose representatives at the United Nations appeared to feel more and more at home.

And the leadership of Canada's Communist Party breathed somewhat easier after its previous embarrassment over the reported neo-Stalinist practices in the Ukraine.[8]

It was to counter those reports which kept seeping through to the party's membership of Slavic extraction that a special fact-finding mission headed by Tim Buck, was sent in March 1967 to Kiev.

The delegation was reassured by Shelest and lieutenants that all shortcomings, if any, in the republic's life would be remedied.

But the cheering words could not prevent the Canadian observers from noticing what M. Djilas saw during his first visit to Kiev soon after the Second World War: the Ukraine was getting more and more to look like a colony ruled by decree from Moscow rather than by decisions made in Kiev on the basis of the needs of the Ukrainian population.[9]

Today, after the January arrests there, the old specter of Stalinism has re-appeared. Communists and anti-communists alike have come to realize the shocking fact: Petro Shelest is naked like the proverbial Chinese emperor.

But, at least, the naked truth is less confusing than any all-dressed lie. It has been known for some time that Shelest is eyeing a top position in the Kremlin as once did his former chief in the Ukraine, and now president of the USSR, Nikolai Podgorny.

Thus, the present tough line against dissent in the Ukraine only illustrates the unchanging human condition of the Soviet classocrats.

One can hope to reach the main center of decisions there only by divesting oneself of any humanity and by leaving behind all the sentiments one ever had for one's own people.

Once the people have been exploited as a collective stepping stone on the way up the Soviet bureaucratic pyramid, all that is needed is to wrap oneself up in the nakedness of sheer power.

From then on, the faceless KGB dummies remain the only companions of the classocrat until the sudden end of his career or his life. Whichever comes first.

Indeed, there has hardly ever been a greater chasm separating the rulers and the ruled than there is now in the Soviet Union as a whole and in each component republic. The Ukraine is only one of the most striking cases.

REFERENCE NOTES

[1]See note 2 to article No. 23 in this collection.

[2]*Ukrains'kyi visnyk* (Ukrainian Herald), a Ukrainian-language clandestine journal, began publishing in early 1970 to provide a vehicle for news about the national democratic movement in the Ukraine and a forum for Ukrainian dissidents. It is the Ukrainian equivalent of the Russian-language *Chronicle of Current Events* (see article No. 24 in this collection). Unlike the latter, however, *Ukrains'kyi visnyk* stresses questions of Ukrainian national rights.

[3]For a complete text of Moroz's last address at his trial, see *Boomerang: The Works of Valentyn Moroz* (Baltimore: Smoloskyp, 1974), pp. 1–6.

[4]Volodyslav Nedobora, an engineer; member of the so-called "Kharkov Group" of Soviet Ukrainian dissidents; wrote a letter to the United Nations in defense of the Crimean Tartars (1969); arrested and sentenced to three years of hard labor in 1970.

[5]*Radians'ka Ukraina* (Kiev), November 11, 1971.

[6]V. Bolshakov, "Sketches of an Ideological Front: A Pandora Box," *Komsomolskaia Pravda,* August 25 and 26, 1970.

[7]Vladimir Bukovsky (b. 1942), A Soviet Russian writer; committed to a psychiatric prison in 1965 for organizing a demonstration against the arrests of Siniavsky and Daniel (see note 3 to article No. 13); sentenced in 1967 to three years in a labor camp for organizing a similar demonstration against the arrests of Galanskov and Ginsburg; released in 1967, he documented the abuse of psychiatric treatment of political dissidents, as a result of which he was arrested again in 1971 and sentenced to seven years in prison and five in exile. In 1977, Bukovsky was released and allowed to emigrate in an "exchange" for the Chilean communist leader Luis Corvalán.

[8]See article No. 34 in this collection.

[9]Milovan Djilas, *Conversations with Stalin* (New York: Harcourt, Brace & World, 1962), pp. 119–20.

28

SUPPRESSION IN THE UKRAINE

Of the several hundred Ukrainians of every walk of life imprisoned in the Soviet Union during the first three months of this year, for alleged anti-Soviet propaganda, two may be of special interest to *Gazette* readers. Vyacheslav Chornovil, a Ukrainian TV correspondent, and Ivan Dzyuba, critic and author, were sentenced to twelve and five years imprisonment respectively[1]

Their cases make it clear that the Brezhnev-Kosygin regime intends to silence a whole generation of Ukrainian sovereignists before the decade of their quiet revolution ends in 1975.

It was in the spring of 1965 that Chornovil took notes at a trial of twenty Ukrainian intellectuals at Lviv district court. Soon after, he made these notes available to Ukrainian readers by means of the "samvydaw" (uncensored self-publishing).

In English, his report of the trial appeared in 1968. *The Gazette* was one of the first Canadian newspapers to comment both on the trial and Chornovil's book.

Recognition

Ivan Dzyuba gained world-wide recognition for his scholarly essay "Internationalism or Russification?" It appeared in print only outside the Soviet Union.

Reprinted with permission from *The Gazette* (Montreal), May 3, 1973.

Analyzing the situation in the Ukraine from a Marxist-Leninist point of view, Dzyuba found it wanting in more than one respect. With the help of some irrefutable evidence, he had proven that an outright Russification policy was being applied in every sphere of the Ukraine's life.

That policy, contrary to all that had been said and written by Marx, Engels, and Lenin, threatened the second largest nationality of the Soviet Union with cultural obliteration, Dzyuba wrote.

Meanwhile, "The Chornovil Papers" had laid open the inside machinery of the Soviet judicial system, in which a group of young Ukrainian intellectuals could be arbitrarily arrested and secretly tried for no other reason than deploring the gross acts of the Russification. For their strictly constitutional defense of the right of the Ukrainians to manage their own cultural affairs, these young men and women were sent to prisons and hard-labor camps for up to seven years.

Inadvertently, I became involved in their case because one of my articles, written in Montreal, was used as "evidence" against at least two defendants at the Lviv trial. As witnessed by Chornovil and other sources (both official and unofficial), the prosecution charged that the defendants had acquired, kept, copied, and presumably circulated that article, along with other "foreign anti-Soviet material," among the citizens of the Ukraine.[2]

Quebec's position of real sovereignty in certain matters was contrasted in the article with the bleak reality in the allegedly sovereign republic of the Ukraine. Although a founding member of the United Nations, the Soviet Ukrainian Republic is ruled by decree from the Kremlin, even in menial matters.

Since that ignominious trial, which was supposed to be secret but became known world-wide and debated by anti-communists and communists alike, the events in the Ukraine have only confirmed the findings of Chornovil and Dzyuba. In spite of their numerical strength as compared with other non-Russian nationalities, the Ukrainian people (over forty million in the Soviet Union) are under twofold pressure, from the centralist Kremlin administration and from the nine-million strong Russian minority that rules the Ukraine in the manner the colons once did in Algeria.

But Chornovil and Dzyuba were not the only ones to see the situation in its true colors. Their publicized stand was but an expression of the resurgent Ukrainian post-Stalin generation that got rid of the paralyzing fear of the "older Russian brother."

Two Trends

How to deal with these dissenters was an issue over which the once powerful Politburo member and Secretary-General of the Ukraine's Communist Party, Petro Shelest, stumbled and fell from power in April 1972.[3]

His tough treatment of the dissenters, whom he regarded as only the tip of a Ukrainian patriotic iceberg under the murky waters of the Soviet reality, made him extremely unpopular both in the Ukraine and abroad. But having done away with Shelest (partly to please President Nixon, who was about to visit Moscow and Kiev), the Kremlin establishment has retained his policy of unlawful suppression of the young people who were acting within their country's law.

Thus nowadays, the federal KGB resident in Kiev, with a special hotline to the Kremlin, supervises every sector of the Ukraine's life as if it were a region of Russia and not a constituent republic of the Soviet Union.

REFERENCE NOTES

[1]At the time of publication of this article, there were various reports circulating in the Soviet Union and abroad concerning Dzyuba's fate. After his arrest and detention, Dzyuba was released in 1973 upon publishing a "recantation." See note 6 to article No. 12 in this collection.

[2]See article No. 21 in this collection.

[3]See note 2 to article No. 23 in this collection.

29

SPIRIT UNDER OPPRESSION

I remember him clearly. He was five when the Nazis were ravaging the Ukraine.

Oblivious of danger, barefoot, carefree, Ihor Kalynets would chase the frisky, impudent hares through the golden-tinged fields under a genial blue sky. Or, making himself useful (as he thought), he threw pebbles like marbles at the crows which from the treetops were keeping an optimistic look-out for small stray fowl.

Now Ihor is 34, a poet, and in a Soviet jail.

Those Europeans who formed (under the patronage of the Nobel prize laureate René Cassin, in June 1971) an international committee for the defense of human rights in the USSR, claim that the Soviet "hard-labor camps" alone hold over one million men and women.

In his paper presented to the plenary session held in Brussels last February, Professor Peter Reddaway, of the London School of Economics, also pointed out that very large numbers of prisoners are being kept in jails, psychiatric wards, and areas of compulsory settlement. These, both in European and Asiatic Russia, are not accounted for.

In that nightmarish phantom category are Ihor and his wife Iryna.

Tried secretly and separately under the cover-all charge of being a party to "anti-Soviet propaganda," they were sentenced

Reprinted with permission from *The Montreal Star*, November 3, 1973.

to six and nine years' imprisonment respectively plus three years in exile each.

Their infant daughter is being taken care of by relatives whose fate is as uncertain as that of any Soviet citizen linked in any way to a person under the "temporary care of the police authorities."

What "crime" have the Kalynets committed?

Could it have been Ihor's boyish chase of a nationalized hare in one of the Ukraine's kolkhozes?

Was it the throwing of pebbles at state-owned crows?

The poet's "crime" was compounded by his love for the Ukraine and his openly expressed desire to promote a three-dimensional concept of Ukrainian identity in a society where everybody is obliged, at least to pretend, to be one-dimensional . . . a non-entity.

Ihor, one of the more talented Ukrainian poets, is read both in the Ukraine and in the Ukrainian diaspora.

Tradition meshes in his verses with the contemporary aspirations of Ukraine's youth: Their longing for uncensored self-expression in art and everyday life . . . their claim for human rights both on behalf of the inhabitants of the Ukraine without discrimination, and for authentic self-government.

These are all legitimate aspirations and pursuits even in the USSR — at least on paper.

Kalynets' poems, however, reached their readers through longhand, private transcripts in the pre-Gutenberg tradition rather than through the official printing presses.

His two collections of poetry, "stalled" or rejected by Soviet censors, have been published abroad. They are available in North America.[1]

The earlier collection of poems, entitled *The Opening of a Christmas Theater,* is enhanced by woodcuts — the work of a young artist born in prison, Bohdan Soroka, who somehow developed his talent in concentration camps.

His father, the architect Mykhailo Soroka, died before completing his 25-year term, in the hard-labor camp of Dubrovlag, Russia, last year.

Some recent immigrants to Israel from the Soviet Union (Avraam Shifrin, for example), remember Soroka as a man of integrity and a defender of prisoners' rights in Vorkuta and other places of detention.[2]

Kateryna Soroka (Mykhailo's wife and Bohdan's mother) was recently released from the same hard-labor camp after her own 25-year term.

Although she was kept in a camp close to the plot in which her husband Mykhailo has been buried, she was not informed of his death.

Only a number — not a name — marks his grave. Months later, prisoners brought the wife the news from another camp, says the Russian-language *Khronika*.

Thus, the arrest and the nine-year term of compound imprisonment of Ihor Kalynets' wife is no exception in the country which officially, every March, celebrates Women's Day.

But what puzzles an observer of the Soviet scene is the lack of justification for her sentence.

Iryna Kalynets' "crime" consisted of her giving moral support to her husband's ideas about the preservation of the identity of the Soviet Ukrainian, a citizen of the empire of the one-dimensional.

She had compassion for the Ukrainian patriots (intellectuals, workers, and kolkhoz peasants) imprisoned by "authority." She also dared express her indignation in such cases as that of historian Valentyn Moroz.

Moroz's name is known to many Canadians. It was brought to the attention of Canada's parliamentarians and its government in 1971, in connection with two diplomatic visits — Prime Minister Trudeau's to the Soviet Union and Premier Kosygin's to Canada.

A strong humanist, Valentyn Moroz was imprisoned for the second time in the autumn of 1970. The term: 14 years' imprisonment and banishment from the Ukraine.

According to recent reports, some unidentified common criminals allegedly with the connivance of the authorities of the Vladimir prison in Russia, set upon him with knives.

As to the esteem in which this defender of human rights is held by the young Ukrainians, witness the lines dedicated to Moroz by Ihor Kalynets in his more recent collection of poems. They read:

> *I wish this book*
> *were to you, for an instant at*
> *least,*
> *Veronica's cloth on the road*
> *to Calvary.*
>
> *I wish this book*
> *like Veronica's cloth, reminded*
> *us*
> *of the grace*
> *of your face.*

Taking the key from Ihor Kalynets' verse, I too wish I could reach readers with the following words:

Ihor Kalynets does not remember me. I never saw his wife. I did not meet Bohdan Soroka. He was born and grew up in captivity. I knew, however, his mother when she was a student and already a Ukrainian patriot.

But writing about them today in Canada, I perhaps immodestly wish this article were like St. Veronica's cloth to my fellow North Americans, reminding them of those striving to retain their spirit under oppression.

REFERENCE NOTES

[1]See, Ihor Kalynets, *Poezii z Ukrainy* (Poems from Ukraine), (Bruxelles: 1970); and *Pidsumovuiuchy movchannia* (Reassessing Silence), (Munich: 1971).

[2]Avraam Shifrin, *Chetvertyi vymir* (The Fourth Dimension), (Munich: Suchasnist, 1973), pp. 307–309. Shifrin, sentenced to 25 years by Soviet authorities as an "Israeli-American spy"; spent 10 years in Soviet concentration camps and 3 years in enforced exile; released in 1966, and in 1970 emigrated to Israel.

30

UKRAINIANS VIEW CANADA AS
THE LAST HAVEN

What with inflation, taxes and strikes which make many
Canadians somewhat uneasy in their own country, Canada still
remains about the only haven of good hope for quite a few
people in Eastern Europe.

Recently, at least two Ukrainian prisoners of conscience in
Russia's hard labor camps and prisons have renounced their
Soviet citizenship and asked the Supreme Soviet of the USSR to
permit them to emigrate to Canada.

Vyacheslav Chornovil, 38-year-old radio and TV journalist,
tried twice and sentenced to two separate prison terms on the
convenient charge of "waging anti-Soviet propaganda," is known
to quite a few Canadians. His book containing collected letters,
petitions and protests of 20 Ukrainian intellectuals, appeared in
English seven years ago nowhere else but in Toronto.[1]

The book revealed to Canadian readers that there existed
a spiritual link between the Soviet Ukrainians and Ukrainian-Canadians in their mutual desire to preserve both Ukrainian culture and identity. Canada, with its fair treatment of
the French fact, appeared to the Ukrainian freethinkers
a convincing example of a practical solution to any confron-

Reprinted with permission from *The Winnipeg Tribune*, January 17, 1976.

175

tation of different ethno-cultural entities within a larger structure.

Even for these modest thoughts the young freethinkers were arrested, tried, and sentenced to harsh terms of imprisonment and banishment from the Ukraine. Vyacheslav Chornovil was tried later on for having refused to testify falsely against some of the accused.

Re-arrested

After having spent three years in a prison, Chornovil was released. But, in January, 1972, he was re-arrested together with several hundred other Ukrainian intellectuals, students and workers who opposed the Kremlin policy of a Soviet melting cauldron.

The extent of these arrests and the severity of sentences prompted some observers to charge that the KGB (Soviet secret police) was intent on making a "cultural desert in the Ukraine" from which every year thousands of professional people are being sent out to remote regions of Russia anyway.

In his letter to the Supreme Soviet, Chornovil charged that he was "physically tortured" by the secret police. "Ill, weakened by my hunger strike, I was shackled and then kept outside in the frost, naked, for over three hours."

This has not deterred him from informing the Supreme Soviet of his intention to emigrate: "I have already appealed to the Canadian Government to grant me Canadian citizenship and to take steps towards my release and my departure from the USSR. But I have no doubts that the (prison) authorities have not had it forwarded."

Chornovil did not renounce his spiritual Ukrainian citizenship.

"I will, in the event of a change of my citizenship, continue to consider myself a citizen of the Ukraine, to which I shall return as soon as Ukrainian patriotism is no longer considered a crime there and is removed from under the 'supervision' of the KGB."

The case of another prisoner, Danylo L. Shumuk, is more complicated, although he has some relatives in Canada. Shumuk, a former member of the Komsomol (Soviet youth organization), went over to the Ukrainian nationalist insurgents during the Second World War and upon its conclusion was arrested by the Soviet police.

He served about 10 years for that "interlude" in his life, was amnestied and then arrested again for writing his "memoirs." Since January 1972, he has been in a prison camp.

Danylo Shumuk has also asked the Supreme Soviet to relieve him of Soviet citizenship and let him emigrate to Canada. In the meantime, his relatives in Canada have brought his case to the attention of the Canadian Government.

"Having been deprived of my freedom and my Motherland (Ukraine), I have no need for the citizenship, because without freedom and a homeland that citizenship is superfluous for me," explained Shumuk in his letter a few months ago.

Others Join In

Copies of these letters written by the two prisoners have been delivered from hand to hand in the Ukraine for some time, and recently they have reached the people in this country as well. But Chornovil and Shumuk are not the only ones who have expressed, in writing, their confidence in Canada.

In addition to a number of Ukrainian prisoners, some prominent Russians did the same. Alexander Solzhenitsyn visited Canada a few months ago to look for a suitable place to settle. Reportedly, he liked what he saw here.

"Last Refuge"

And former Stalin prize winner Viktor Nekrasov, while on a Canadian tour last April, told me: "Canada seems to be the last refuge for the freedom-thirsty people of Eastern Europe."

All these statements are echoing an observation made by a prominent Soviet chemist, Mykhailo Klochko, back in 1961, during an International Congress of Chemists in Montreal. He said: "I think, I would forego even the United States for Canada if and when I had a choice."

Two days later, in Ottawa, he asked for asylum in this country and was granted it.

Freedom to travel or settle in the land of your liking, is now as important as freedom of speech and belief to many of these people.

It is on the minds of millions standing on the shores of expectations in the countries of their unwanted, compulsory citizenship. But what made Canada loom large and, perhaps, even "sublime" in their thoughts, was twofold.

The freedom of choice this country has been offering to all its citizens in every walk of life and regardless of cultural background; and the persistent campaign waged by Canada's representatives at various international forums, including the Helsinki Conference for a speedy application of the principle of free movement of people, ideas, and information across all national borders.

By an unexplained human osmosis, the news about Canada and her stand on human rights has penetrated deep into the closed Soviet society and evoked an unexpected response even among prisoners.[2]

REFERENCE NOTES

[1]See article No. 22 in this collection.

[2]Soviet reaction to this article, though belated, appeared in a paper published in Donbas, the industrial region of the Soviet Ukraine. See Ie. Korchagin, "A Haven for War Criminals," *Vechernyi Donetsk,* August 17, 1978.

31

THE TALE OF TWO ARCHIPELAGOS

Two distinct archipelagos of human misery and compassion coexist along the fiftieth parallel that spans Canada and the Soviet Union.

Thousands of people living freely on their ethno-cultural islands across Canada are tied together by invisible threads to their kin on the "islands" of the Soviet penal system now known as GULAG.[1]

Only rarely a voiceless letter "from beyond" manages to reach the inhabitants on this side of the invisible divide. But every time it does, it shakes their lives like a private earthquake.

You may not be aware of it, but a close neighbor of yours may be one of those "Fridays" from whom some "Robinson" on a Soviet penal island is expecting a letter, in vain.

Like Evhen Pryshliak who has relatives both in Montreal and Toronto.

Now 62 and an inmate in a forced labor camp of Perm, in the Urals, Pryshliak spent half of his lifetime in the prisons of powers which overrun the Ukraine, Poland, Germany, and Russia.

A strong believer in human rights and sovereignty for every nationality under the sun, Evhen Pryshliak opposed the Nazi

Written for and distributed by the Southam News Services, this article appeared in several newspapers across Canada. Here it is reprinted with permission of the Southam News Services and the *Edmonton Journal* (March 6, 1976).

Germans almost from the moment they entered the West Ukrainian city of Lviv, at the end of June 1941.

For this he was arrested and would have found death either there or in one of the concentration camps of Germany if the Ukrainian underground had not sprung him out of the Lviv prison.

I saw him fleetingly during that interlude of his free life when he was urging his nationalist colleagues to help liberate Jewish medics and mechanics from the ghettos in various Ukrainian towns. The newly formed armed detachments of Ukrainian insurgents felt a dearth of such personnel. And his advice was put into practice more than once, and with good results.

The re-occupation of the Ukraine by Stalin's armed forces in the summer of 1944 did not cool off Evhen Pryshliak's revolutionary ardor. He was one of those who managed to keep up the flame of the Ukrainian liberation movement well beyond Stalin's demise and into the period of his successor Nikita Khrushchev.

Reportedly, it was the notorious English journalist-turned-Kremlin-spy, Kim Philby, who contributed to the destruction of the underground network in the Carpathian mountains region, then under Pryshliak's supervision.

But the speculations aside, Evhen Pryshliak withstood all the pressures and temptations of the Kremlin security machine. Never would he become a "linear man" of the Soviet mold.

Former Soviet prisoners, such as Avraam Shifrin[2] of Israel or the Lithuanian seaman Simas Kudirka[3] who spent some time with Evhen Pryshliak in the system of GULAG archipelago, speak highly of his integrity.

"Evhen Pryshliak has remained a three-dimensional human being in spite of the harsh treatment allotted to him by his jailors," Simas Kudirka told me during his brief visit to Montreal a few months ago.

It is not easy to achieve such a dignified status among numerous prisoners and under the terrible conditions in the Soviet prisons and camps described by Alexander Solzhenitsyn.

When re-reading Evhen Pryshliak's letter to his Montreal relatives a few days ago, I hardly sensed a shade of self-pity in his words.

Perhaps you too have joined those who have decided not to write to me because this might jeopardize my legal release upon the completion of my term....

Of course, I realize that some of the letters addressed to me might have been seized by the administration (of the camp). But anyway, it is well-nigh impossible for a prisoner to further his own case because his life conditions are entirely independent of him....Moreover, one cannot simply cast off one's own half lifetime, to say the least....

Well put, indeed. Particularly by someone who, at 62, after three prison terms under three different foreign regimes has still preserved human dignity and faith in humanity.

Evhen Pryshliak's 25-year term is due to run out, legally speaking, in 1977. His relatives in Canada, like the relatives of other Soviet political prisoners, have a tormented life. They are torn between a desire to do something on his behalf and their caution lest these attempts at intercession impair his chances for survival and possible legal release.

But the prisoners on the Soviet archipelago neither falter in their determination nor are they aware of such a dilemma. Thus recently about 80 of them went on hunger strike; and 25 Ukrainian dissenters imprisoned in forced labor camps of Russia officially renounced their Soviet citizenship. Two of them declared they want to emigrate to Canada.

And from those living on the "free archipelago" of Canada and elsewhere, they demand to raise their voices of protest against the mistreatment of political prisoners in the Soviet Union.

Together with the recently released mathematician Leonid Plyushch,[4] they seem to believe in Robert Burns' dictum that man's inhumanity to man ought to make countless mourn; and protest.

That is, on both archipelagos of human misery and compassion along the fiftieth parallel which spans the two countries divided by the Arctic Sea—Canada and Soviet Union.

So similar and so infinitely different.

REFERENCE NOTES

[1]GULAG — *Glavnoie upravleniie ispravitel'no-trudovykh lage-rei* (The Main Administration of Corrective Labor Camps), a Soviet government agency in charge of the penal system — the concentration camps, where both criminal and political prisoners are kept. This acronym was used by Aleksandr I. Solzhenitsyn, himself a former inmate of these camps, for his multi-volume world-famous work *The Gulag Archipelago* (New York: Harper & Row, 1973-76), 3 vols.

[2]See note 2 to article No. 29.

[3]Simas Kudirka, a Lithuanian seaman who jumped the Soviet fishing boat in Boston harbor and was handed back to the Soviets by the US Coast Guard. Tried for treason and sentenced to death, which was commuted to 10 years of imprisonment, Kudirka was released when it was established that he was a former US citizen. He now lives in the United States.

[4]Leonid Plyushch, a mathematician-cyberneticist and a Ukrainian dissident; for his active participation in the civil rights movement in the Ukraine and the USSR, was sentenced to an indefinite term in a special psychiatric hospital (a form of Soviet punishment for political dissidents); released after three years (1973-76), and allowed to emigrate; he now lives in Western Europe.

PART VI

INTERNATIONAL COMMUNISM AND UKRAINIAN NATIONALISM

EDITOR'S NOTE

The improbable happened. The once monolithic communist camp has splintered into separate nation-oriented and competing communist power centers.

National communism has become a reality in almost every communist ruled state as well as among non-ruling communist parties.

Two of these—the Soviet Union and China—have locked themselves in an ideological and political struggle. Political propaganda and polemic have become the main instrument of this internicine cold war.

Inevitably, the Ukrainian question became involved.

32

UKRAINIAN DISSENTERS BEING HEARD

Leaders of the 66 Communist parties who were trying in Budapest to strengthen communist unity in the world were not surprised when they received an appeal signed by a dozen Soviet citizens on behalf of the imprisoned Russian dissenters. What some Western observers had suspected for some time, these communist leaders had known all along — in even more detail. For the last seven years the Soviet leadership has been striving to stem the revisionist trend both in Russia and in the Ukraine, the largest republics in the Union.

Uncensored publications, petitions and protest letters, written by young Ukrainian Marxists — both imprisoned and those still at large — have been circulated all over the Soviet Union, and recently they have spilled over into the West.

Some party oficials of the communist countries actively helped the Russian and Ukrainian dissenters in bringing their messages to the attention of "the civilized world's opinion."

When Svyatoslav Karavansky, a Ukrainian poet-translator from Odessa, wrote a Petition[1] addressed to First Secretary Gomulka of the Polish Communist Party, asking him to arrange for an "international conference of the Communist parties of the world," Polish officials forwarded the petition to Warsaw. There, the Poles did not mind leaking its contents to the West. Karavansky proposed that Gomulka use his "prestige and influ-

---

Reprinted with permission from *The Montreal Star,* March 19, 1968.

185

ence" to call a conference which would ban, once and for all, "anti-Semitism, Ukrainophobia, and discrimination against minorities" practiced by various Communist parties in their lands.

Czech communist officials were not too eager to help, but they did diligently study the case of the non-Russian nationalities in the USSR. So did the Hungarians and Bulgarians; even the East Germans showed an appreciable interest in the problem. Romanians, though not too enthusiastic about Ukrainians (Bucharest still covets the Ukrainian province of Bukovyna, united with the Soviet Ukraine since 1940), thought it useful to transmit Karavansky's Petition and other uncensored information to the West as it raised the question of the Moldavians in the Soviet Union.

Chinese Voice

The Chinese leadership ventured even further. Having watched inscrutably the Soviet scene for a number of years, Peking decided to put a word in defense of Ukrainian and other non-Russian dissenters.[2]

Last November, when the Soviet Union celebrated the 50th anniversary of the Bolshevik Revolution, a Peking broadcast in Russian hurled accusations directed at the Moscow leadership: mass arrests had been conducted in the Ukraine and "many people are still kept in fascist-like concentration camps." The reference was to the camps of hard labor in the Mordovian Autonomous Soviet Socialist Republic (part of the Russian Federation) where Daniel and Siniavsky are kept, along with about 40 Ukrainian dissenters sent there between 1961 and 1966; last November Vyacheslav Chornovil joined the group for having exposed the secret trials of these Ukrainians in a pamphlet that has just reached the West.[3]

Thanks to these and other publications, all the communist countries became aware of the one, and perhaps the only, true Marxist axiom which states that no people oppressing other nationalities can be free. Moscow trials of Russian intellectuals demonstrated the truth of the statement once again as the Russians themselves were faced with the "peril caused by trampling on man in our country," to quote the appeal sent to the Budapest meeting in February.

But there are other nationalities suffering in the Soviet Union from recidivist Stalinism. Svyatoslav Karavansky, in his second Petition addressed to the Council of Nationalities of the USSR, lists some "pressing problems that should have been of primary concern" to the Council.[4]

He asks, "Where are the Jewish theaters now, the newspapers, the publishing houses, and schools?" And what about "Ukrainians and Moldavians being severely restricted in their right to a higher education...." In his opinion, the expulsion of 900,000 Tartars from the Crimea was an "act of open injustice that no argument can excuse." And he rejects the notion that "the Germans of the Volga region were responsible for the Hitler's crimes."

Baltic Injustice

Undeterred by the severe sentence of eight years and seven months of hard labor he received at a secret trial in 1966, Karavansky reminds the Council of the injustices committed on Baltic peoples. Estonians "were deported *en masse* to Siberia," and "even at this time, 25-year sentences were being served primarily by Ukrainians, Lithuanians, Latvians, Estonians, and Moldavians. Why is there no pardon for them?" charges Karavansky.

Another Ukrainian writer, Ivan Dzyuba, made an impassioned appeal to the Jews and Ukrainians, calling on them to cooperate because, living side by side, they have been faced with the same danger of cultural and physical obliteration. The address, given during the memorial service in the sinister Babi Yar on the outskirts of Kiev on September 29, 1966, was not published by the Soviet papers, but it is being read avidly in transcripts in the Ukraine, and recently it has reached the West.[5]

This is another hopeful aspect of the ferment within the communist camp and particularly in the Soviet Union. In spite of the fact that these young people grew up under a totalitarian regime, they have developed a deep human understanding of their neighbor's plight.

Thus, Ukrainian patriots of today are not possessed exclusively with the problems of their own people; they are able to pick up the cause of other nationalities as well and to raise the issue before their own authorities and the leaders of other communist countries. The latter showed enough wisdom not to suppress the truth.

Victory of Spirit

And this is the greatest victory of the human spirit over both fascism and Stalinism. It explains the mystery of the cracks in the walls which up to now have divided the communist countries from one another; that is why some vital information on what the Peking broadcast referred to as "police terror" over the non-Russian peoples in the USSR was able to reach the West more quickly.

But what about the nations of the West? In this respect they have fallen somewhat behind the communist countries. A few years ago a group of Ukrainians tried to pass on some information about "mass arrests in the Ukraine" to the embassy of a Western country in Moscow, for transmitting to the "civilized world's opinion."

After a brief exchange of words with the embassy staff the young men left and, in the street, they were immediately arrested right in sight of the embassy. No Western paper ever printed a word either about the incident or about the arrests going on at that time in the Ukraine. "The civilized world" has only recently become aware of the struggle raging on the barricade of human rights within the Soviet Union.

REFERENCE NOTES

[1]For a complete text of the *Petition,* see V. Chornovil (Comp.), *The Chornovil Papers* (New York: McGraw-Hill, 1968), pp. 180–86.

[2]See article No. 33 in this collection.

[3]Source cited in note 1 above; see also article No. 22 in this collection.

[4]For a complete text, see S. Y. Karavansky, "To the Council of

Nationalities of the USSR," *The New Leader,* LI, No. 2 (January 15, 1968), 12-15.

[5]For a complete text of I. Dzyuba's address at Babi Yar, see "Ivan Dzyuba on Jewish and Ukrainian Destiny," *Commentator* (Toronto), XII, No. 2 (February, 1968), 12-15.

33

PEKING'S INVOLVEMENT WITH

THE UKRAINE PROBLEM

Throughout its history, the Ukraine has been a bone of contention between her powerful neighbors more often than any other European country.

In the old days, the Mongolians, Hungarians, Poles, Turks and Muscovians had made their claims upon the Ukraine; in more recent time, Nazi Germany and Soviet Russia crossed swords over it.

Today, Red China seems to enter cagily into the fray by consistently raising the Ukrainian problem against Peking's enemies in the Kremlin.

At the very outset of economic and political differences between the two communist giants, Peking was reluctant to use the plight of the oppressed Ukrainians (or any other East European nationality) in the Soviet Union as its lever in the ever deteriorating relations with Moscow. The difficulties caused by Chinese occupation of Tibet had put Peking somewhat off balance in this respect. The year was 1959.

But the Chinese strategists could not have overlooked the Russian build-up along the Soviet-Chinese border and especially

---

Reprinted with permission from *The Montreal Star,* May 10, 1969, where it appeared under the title "Peking Raises Ukraine Problem in War with Moscow Enemies."

in the region facing the province of Sinkiang. Using the much-publicized Nikita Khrushchev's pet project of making "the virgin lands of Kazakhstan" a wheat producing land, the Russian strategists have transferred well nigh a million young Ukrainians, Lithuanians, Belorussians, Estonians and Latvians to the region. Promises of better wages, threats and harsh administrative measures helped to make the project a bureaucratic success.

Thus, two objectives were achieved. The unruly non-Russian republics were somewhat cowed by the removal of many potential rebels against Kremlin domination. At the same time, the Soviet Union's "soft underbelly" in Central Asia has been considerably hardened to balance the industrially more developed and militarily stronger Sinkiang with its nomads crossing the border to and fro.

When ideological issues had topped all the other Peking-Moscow controversies, the Red Chinese began adding to their verbal arsenal the accusations about Russia's non-Marxist nationality policy toward its minorities. The Ukrainian problem came up at an appropriate time. When the Soviet Union celebrated the 50th anniversary of the Bolshevik Revolution, Radio Peking informed its listeners in the USSR about the "fascist-like concentration camps" in the Russian Republic where many Ukrainians were still being kept.

After this and similar propaganda fencing failed to achieve much result, the two fell to actual armed conflict. The encounter on the Ussuri River this year was indeed a bloody one, even for such ideologically related countries. And both have been eager since to make the most of it in the propaganda department.

The Kremlin leaders tried to steal a march on the Chinese by placating the Ukraine's public opinion and arousing patriotic feelings in every section of the Soviet society. They have recently pardoned Vyacheslav Chornovil, after 18 months in prison, the Ukrainian journalist who defied, in 1967, Soviet authorities by reporting on secret trials of intellectuals in the Ukraine.

At the same time, *Literaturnaia Gazeta* of Moscow, in an unprecedented move, published (in its March 12, 1969 issue) a photo of a plaque erected at the graves of the fallen Soviet soldiers on the Ussuri River. Any reader can tell from the names on the slab that about half of the slain soldiers were Ukrainians.

Peking then came out with its own long-range charge. In a broadcast directed to the Soviet Union and later in a special article published by the *Peking Review* of April 4, 1969, the Chinese charged outright that the Kremlin leaders were continuing the chauvinist policies of the czars: "Fascist white terror reigns in Soviet society today," says the article entitled significantly "New Czars' Social-Fascist Tyranny."

Ukrainians have been known as tough soldiers and produced able military leaders. Such names as Marshal A. Grechko, Marshal K. Moskalenko, Marshal A. Ieremenko, the chief defender and liberator of Stalingrad, or the late Marshal R. Malynovsky who led the impressive campaign against the Japanese Kwantung Army in 1945, are familiar not only to the Europeans but to the Chinese as well. So are the Ukrainian partisans who have carved for themselves quite a niche in the history of insurgency by their exploits both against the Nazi Germans and the Soviet Russians during World War II and immediately after it.

It would be unwise to provoke the feelings of these warrior people and to mobilize them "on the wrong side of the front" in a Soviet-Chinese military conflict when and if it comes. This explains the double approach of the Kremlin strategists trying to please the Ukrainians with a carrot of liberalization and, at the same time, arousing their wrath against "the Chinese atrocities."

The Chinese may soon step up their campaign of words and point out that the present-day leaders of Moscow are trying to bleed the Ukrainians white by pushing them into the frontline against China, a more progressive and friendlier nation than Russia. And the Chinese strategists will perhaps think twice before arranging for an attack on a post manned by the non-Russians, so as not to force them against their own will into the arms of the Russian bear.

Ukrainian-Canadians have had conscientious objections against Canada's intention to establish diplomatic relations with Red China. Today, they may have second thoughts about the issue. Some, at least, see an advantage in bringing to another country's attention the true facts about the Ukraine. Ukrainians may yet find an unexpected ally in Communist China.

34

CANADIAN REDS HAVE HARDEST TIME
EXPLAINING POLICIES

Of all the Communist parties toeing the Moscow line today, the Communist Party of Canada has the hardest time explaining its course to the motley crowd of its multi-ethnic followers.

At the 20th convention of the CPC, held in Toronto last month, Secretary-General William Kashtan was pressed by various members to clear up the "striking contradictions between the party's stand on the nationality question and the harsh reality prevailing in the Soviet Union."

As usually happens, his woes were partly of his own making.

On the occasion of the 50th Anniversary of the Bolshevik Revolution, William Kashtan declared in Moscow's *Pravda* that "the very existence of the Soviet Union strengthens national and democratic forces in Canada that are fighting for the real independence and sovereignty of our country and its foreign policy...." Moreover, according to the Secretary-General of the feeblest of all the political parties in this country, French-Canadians have been "studying attentively solutions of the question of nationality in the Soviet Union."[1]

Reprinted with permission from *The Ottawa Journal,* June 7, 1969.

Youth Wondering

But it is exactly this realm in which Kremlin leaders have fared worst during the first half of a century of the Soviets in power. The Russo-Czechoslovak confrontation has only brought into the open the problem which is still puzzling young minds in the Soviet Union.

One of the Soviet Ukrainian intellectual dissenters whose voices have reached the West, Ivan Dzyuba, put it squarely before the tough Kiev leader, Petro Shelest: "Many people in the Ukraine, especially those of the younger generation, are wondering what is amiss with the nationality policy in the Soviet Union."[2]

Himself a sincere believer in Marxism-Leninism, this 37-year-old literary critic came out with a somewhat startling answer. Quoting extensively from the works by Marx, Engels, Lenin and even Stalin, Dzyuba — in his scholarly study *Internationalism or Russification?*[3] — has demonstrated that in fact there is no internationalism in the communist commonwealth of equal nations, called the Soviet Union; sheer forced Russification of the non-Russian peoples is applied there as systematically as it was ever done by czarist governments before the Revolution.

Linguicide is the order of the day. In addition to anti-Semitism, crass "Ukrainophobia" pervades the country of victorious socialism, says Dzyuba. A 6,000,000 Russian minority in the Ukraine has all the privileges of the dominant nationality which shows no consideration either for the Ukrainian language or culture.

Although millions of books and newspaper copies are imported into the Ukraine from Russia, that minority has its own newspapers and local supply of Russian books published at the cost of the Ukrainian republic. Russian language schools are created in the Ukraine as fast as it is possible to build them; Ukrainian schools are converted into bilingual ones.

The Russian minority succeeded even in preventing the teaching of science subjects in Ukraine's institutes and universities in Ukrainian; Russian is used in spite of protests by students, teachers and parents, expressed in individual and collective appeals to the Kiev and Moscow authorities.

No Ukrainian

At the same time, the Ukrainian minority in Russia (about 7,000,000 strong) has no Ukrainian classes in their local schools, no newspapers or books published in Ukrainian. For a Ukrainian in the Russian SFSR, it is even difficult to subscribe to a paper from the Ukraine.

A "special mechanics" of Russification tends to disperse Ukrainians all over the Soviet Union. The vacuum created thus in the Ukraine is immediately filled by Russian migrants or Russified minorities.

The Soviet Army still remains the most potent single Russifying factor in the USSR. Even the Russian Orthodox Church has a role to play in the "process of merging" various nationalities into a monolithic Russian super-state.

What Stalin admitted to have been unable to achieve by purges and mass resettlements, his successors are trying to attain by a system of inner economic pressures and cultural discrimination. No wonder then that, as Dzyuba shows it, since 1913 the number of Ukrainians has increased only by 3,000,000 — from 37 to 40 million, in 55 years.

Although hit the hardest, Ukrainians are not the only victims of the process of a forced assimilation glossed over by the cliches extolling the "brotherly union of peoples" under the Marxist-Leninist flag. From the works by other Ukrainian dissenters — like S. Karavansky, V. Chornovil, V. Moroz — the tragic fate of Soviet Jews, Latvians, Lithuanians, Estonians, Belorussians, Moldavians and Germans has also become known to the people beyond Soviet borders.

That is what has caused ferment among the communists both in the Satellite countries and in the West. Their leaders and intellectuals had acquainted themselves with appeals and protest essays written by Soviet Ukrainian dissenters and calling for "outlawing of any discrimination against minorities in all communist countries."

Thus, fear of the potential Russification of the whole communist bloc prompted Romania, Czechoslovakia and Poland to readjust their policies in this respect. But the Kremlin leaders acted under an even greater stress; they were afraid to lose their grip on all of the non-Russians in Eastern Europe, and therefore they decided on a military intervention in Czechoslovakia.

The Communist Party of Canada has been watching the events in Eastern Europe with great apprehension. Its ethnic membership has been pressing on the leadership to explain "What is wrong with the nationality question in the Soviet Union."

When their outcry about the ruthless suppression of Ukrainian intellectual dissenters between 1961-67 has become too loud to be silenced by disciplinary measures, the CPC sent a special fact-finding delegation to the Ukraine. Headed by Tim Buck, the delegation returned from its visits to Moscow and Kiev with more doubts than it had when leaving Canada.

It has seen Russification on the march everywhere, promoted by the ageless Russian bureaucracy Lenin had complained about more than once; it has learned that the Ukrainian communist dissenters had been dealt with more harshly than anybody else in the Soviet Union, and for a lesser offence: their sentences ranged from two to 15 years of hard labor, and at least one of them received a death sentence (later commuted to 15 years prison term).

No wonder then, that the Report of the delegation published last year in Canada, both in English and Ukrainian, could not stem the exodus of Ukrainian-Canadians from the party ranks.[4] Moreover, the whole Slavic wing of the CPC has been badly shattered since.

The confrontation between Czechoslovakia and Russia has put an even greater strain on the Communist Party of Canada, as events have decidedly proven that both in the Soviet Union and in the communist camp of the allegedly equal nations the internationalist god is as dead as his prophets, Marx and Lenin.

What is alive, however, is — according to Ivan Dzyuba — the spirit of the Old Russia, with its all national and international objectives. Canadian communists have hardly any reason to boast about the Soviet Union being a perfect example of a multi-national and multi-lingual nation. Russia still is, as Lenin used to say, "a prison of nations."

REFERENCE NOTES

[1]*Pravda,* November 7, 1967.

[2]I. Dzyuba, *Internationalism or Russification?* (London: Weidenfeld-Nicolson, 1968), p. 5.

[3]See article No. 23 in this collection.

[4]"Report of Delegation to Ukraine," (Central Committee Meeting, Communist Party of Canada, September 16, 17 and 18, 1967), *Viewpoint* (Toronto), V, No. 1 (January, 1968), 1-13.

35

KREMLIN STRATEGISTS WORRIED
ABOUT ETHNIC VARIETY

If the Soviet Union ever goes to war with China, the Russians will have to strike at the enemy with all their might just to survive the conflict. By now, the Kremlin leaders must be aware of their predicament: they cannot allow themselves the luxury of the mistakes Nazi Germany committed in her war against the Soviet Union, by hitting their enemy—as Dr. Goebbels ruefully put it—with their "left hand."

But even if they decide upon using nuclear weapons, it will remain doubtful whether the Kremlin would be able to master the needed "right-hand-blow" against China. With their own empire seething with discontent, there are reasons to believe (and the Chinese seem to know this) that Soviet Russia's "right-hand" would be then partially disabled by the problem that has been dogging Moscow leaders for over 50 years. It is the same, as yet unresolved, nationality problem which Lenin was frantically trying to solve in his dying day.

Out of necessity, a Soviet-Chinese war would be fought solely for Russian nationalist aims, with preservation of Russia's last territorial acquisitions in Asia being the foremost among them.

Reprinted with permission from *The London Free Press* (London, Ontario), January 30, 1971, where it appeared under the title "Non-Russian Soviets Perplex Kremlin Strategists."

Public opinion among the international Left, to say the least, would favor Peking rather than Moscow in such a conflict, because the Chinese appear to have preserved a closer affinity with "true Marxism-Leninism," especially when cast in the role of a victim of Russian aggression.

The Kremlin rulers would then be left with very little, if any, room for maneuvering. In spite of its self-assumed title of defender of the proletarian class, its proud army bears too deep an imprint of nationalist stigma. Under a new name and led by a new set of commanders, the Soviet Army still is the most conservative of all the Soviet state institutions, rivalled in its conservatism perhaps only by the established Russian Orthodox Church. Under the Soviets, the allegedly internationalist army has not shed a single feather from its inherited plumage of czarist military traditions.

Mindful of these traditions, the Kremlin leaders deprived the Soviet Ukraine of its own Red Units even before Stalin made himself an undisputed master in the USSR. The same thing happened to the Don and Kuban Cossacks, as well as to the Transcaucasian republics. Military traditions of no other nationality are recognized or permitted to take root within the union of allegedly sovereign socialist republics. Thus, in various positions both in the USSR and within the Warsaw Pact system, Ukrainian and Belorussian generals and marshals must represent the "single and indivisible Russian Army," without any hint at military contributions to defense by the Ukraine or Belorussia, the two republics most exposed to any attack from the west and south-west.

And it was the Soviet Army's objections that prevented the Soviet government from implementing its own constitutional amendments of 1944, which restored the Union Republics' right to establish their own defense departments. Even Belorussia and the Ukraine, the only two other Soviet founding members of the United Nations, were not allowed to make use of this constitutional prerogative.

The looming Russian-Chinese conflict prompted the party and military leaders to drop almost all internationalist pretenses. They are doing their utmost to instill strong Russian patriotic convictions into the minds of all Soviet citizens, old and young alike.

Since January 1968, when a revised Universal Military Service Law was put in force, military indoctrination of school children—between 14 and 16 years of age—has been intensified. The program of physical fitness in public schools includes instruction in hand grenades, fencing, judo and some forms of close combat. Special classes of "young guardists" are being formed in various schools and these are put under supervision of local military colleges.

(One such group at the 71st Kiev school is attached to the Suvorov Military Academy.)

Young student clubs, "Friends of the Soviet Army," maintain close relations between their schools and local military establishment. Excursion to military barracks are more and more superseding the once obligatory visiting of kolkhoz farms by school groups and their teachers. Councils for Military and Patriotic Education have been hastily organized in colleges and universities, with professors—veterans of the Second World War—and the senior students who have finished their regular military service as obligatory members.

In this military preparedness campaign for Soviet youth, the Chinese are projected as the most dangerous potential enemy of the Soviet Union's territorial integrity. It can hardly escape the attention of reflective people there that this potential external threat is being exploited by the Kremlin leaders in a similar manner, and for the same objective, as it was exploited by the czarist regime about 65 years ago, as a unifying factor for the Russian empire strained by social, economic and political dissent.

The potential Soviet-Chinese war conflict would be a "patriotic Russian war" and as such it is viewed by many non-Russians in the USSR with great misgivings.

"But what is in it for us?" asks a Soviet Ukrainian when asked about the possibility of such a shooting war. "Give me one reason why we should die for the Ussurian or Vladivostok region as our grandparents were compelled to die for Manchuria and Port Arthur in the war of 1904 or for the Dardanelles in the war of 1914-17?"

Indeed, there has been hardly any tangible progress in the relations between the dominant Russians and the other nationalities of the Soviet Union, that would justify a repetition of such a supreme effort by the latter. The traditional policy of Russi-fication of the old and newly acquired non-Russian territories make Soviet reality today essentially the same as it was in the pre-revolutionary times. In this respect Russia has not changed.

But what has changed, is the non-Russian nationalities them-selves. They still occupy areas of major economic and military importance and numerically they are much stronger than their "grandparents" were under the czars. Today, there are more non-Russians than Russians in the Soviet Union, no matter how doctored their census is. And the national self-awareness of Ukrainians, Belorussians, Georgians, Armenians and of various Asiatic peoples has a much wider popular basis than it had at the dawn of Soviet power. Their political aspirations have struck roots into each stratum of their advanced societies.

To be sure, they have ceased to be just amorphous masses of semiliterate peasants of 1917-21, that would fall prey to the dialectics of a more advanced urban proletariat of Russia. Today, the non-Russians possess a considerable technical know-how of their own, and their republics have highly developed in-dustries. Their experts — from agriculture through industry to chemical and space research — could not be easily replaced by Russians, if, for example, Ukrainians and Estonians decided on starting passive resistance or slackening the effort in a war (using Lenin's terminology) labelled an "anti-peoples war."

The manpower of the non-Russian nationalities is vital to the Kremlin in any confrontation with China.

Their potential military value to the Russian strategists could be calculated on the basis of the contribution made by the Ukrainians in the Second World War. Although no absolute figures were published on the subject, it is at least known that over 4,500,000 Ukrainians fought in the ranks of the Soviet Army, over 2,500,000 of them were decorated for bravery; and, of the latter, 2,300 received the order Hero of the Soviet Union, the highest Soviet military award.

It is significant, that these scanty data were made public by the present leaders of the Soviet Union right after they had re-moved Khrushchev from his power position, in October 1964.

There was, evidently, some concern in the Kremlin as to the attitude of at least one non-Russian nationality, if the new leaders felt the need for wooing the Ukrainians.

But could they be sure of a loyal response of the non-Russians in case of a Russian patriotic war against China?

What with their haunting memories of the destructive German *Drang nach Osten,* combined with an apparent unwillingness of the West to recognize their countries as distinctive nations, Ukrainians and Belorussians seem to be cast in the role of the most natural allies of the Russian people. But who wants to be taken for granted or treated as a subordinate nationality, insulted daily and deliberately Russified in the same confederation he is supposed to uphold and defend with his own blood?

Certainly, the younger generation of the non-Russians would not acquiesce in the status of second-class citizens as readily as their fathers (terrorized by the Stalin-Yezhov-Beria gangs) used to do for about three decades. On the contrary, the young people want the Soviet constitution to be amended so that it would be more representative of the changed role and mood of the non-Russian ethnic components of the Union.

Some of their speakers took recourse to Lenin's theoretical teaching and reminded the Kremlin leadership of the fact that Lenin never underestimated the danger of alienating the non-Russians by the chauvinist policies so much in use in the Old Russia. Unfortunately, says Ivan Dzyuba, a prominent Soviet Ukrainian dissenter-author, nothing has changed since the time when in the 1920s Lenin's comrade-at-arms, M. Skrypnyk, charged that the Russian Army under the Soviets still remained "an instrument for the Russification of the Ukrainian and the whole non-Russian populace."[1]

Recently, another Soviet Ukrainian dissenter, Anton Koval, addressed an appeal to the Supreme Soviet of the Ukrainian SSR in which he urged this legislative body to recover the Ukraine's right to possess its own armed forces within the framework of the Union army. The demand must have come as a shock to the meek members of this republican council used to acting only as a rubber stamp for the party leaders.[2]

But similar charges and demands to abandon the traditional policy of building a monolithic Russian empire out of a dozen distinct founding nations, have been ringing in the last few years through all the non-Russian republics. The critics of the Kremlin policies point out in particular Moscow's attempts at saturating the non-Russian regions with Russian immigrants while the local population is being enticed or forced to leave for Siberia, central and far eastern regions of Soviet Asia.

As a result of this compulsory migration, between 1945 and 1959, the number of Russians in Latvia rose from 10 percent of the total population to 26 percent; in Lithuania, from two percent to eight percent; in Estonia, from eight percent to 20 percent. In the Ukraine, the number of Russians increased by 300 percent as compared with the census of 1926. At the same time, Ukrainians are strongly represented in Kazakhstan and in the Amur-Ussuri region, opposite China.

The partial results of the 1970 Soviet census confirm the trend.[3]

But spreading of Russians all over the non-Russian republics creates social and political problems rooted in inter-ethnic and economic discrimination. Ukrainians, Moldavians, Belorussians and the Baltic nationalities complain that Russian immigrants tend to occupy all the more important administrative positions in their republics and grab all the lucrative economic possibilities for themselves. Bad blood thus produced will not contribute to the inner strength of the multinational empire facing a Chinese colossus of the same ideological hue.

This weakness of the Soviet Union is well known to the Chinese strategists and they are hitting at the giant's clay foot represented by the non-Russian element. Some time ago, the Peking *People's Daily* did not hesitate to revive Lenin's description of Russia as being "a prison of nations," and the Ukrainians are repeatedly mentioned in the Chinese polemics, as being oppressed by the "new czars." To counter the charge, a Soviet-operated Radio Peace and Progress had been trying to exploit the theme of the allegedly unjust treatment of the non-Chinese minorities by the Peking regime. The accusation concerns a sprinkling of Uighur and Turkic tribes in Singkiang and the Mongols of Inner Mongolia.

Peking, however, has a much tighter case for the non-Russian nationalities to put at the Kremlin door, and long before a shooting war would start the Russians could lose the war of words.

There is enough evidence for the charge that the Soviet federal system has been watered down to a meaningless constitutional formula on paper. And there is a wealth of documents written by Soviet dissidents who furnish proof that even the slightest indication of cultural or political aspirations on the part of the non-Russians is being treated by the Kremlin as treason against Russia.

To quote only two cases, a KGB interrogator (as reported in Dzyuba's essay *Internationalism or Russification?*) derided his Ukrainian victims in a Russian concentration camp: "Why, you seem much too anxious to become a Bulgaria of your own. . . ."[4] And Anatoly Marchenko, in his book *My Testimony*, tells of three Lithuanian students being tortured to death in the same concentration camp. The KGB officers kept yelling at them: "Come on, free Lithuania. Crawl on, you are about to get your independence."[5]

How long people can take it in peacetime is hard to tell. But in wartime these animosities may assume dangerous proportions. A situation may arise not unlike one forecast by Lenin for the enemies attacking his Soviet state. He said: "As soon as the international bourgeoisie raises its hand against us, its own working class will grab tightly the same hand and hold it."

Whenever the Soviet Union faces China as its ideologically related enemy, the Russian aggressive war effort may be stalled by the hand of the angry non-Russian peoples.

REFERENCE NOTES

[1] I. Dzyuba, *Internationalism or Russification?* (London: Weidenfeld-Nicolson, 1968), p. 136.

[2] Anton Koval, "Open Letter to the Deputies of the Soviets of the Ukrainian SSR," (April 1969), *Suchasnist* (Munich), IX, No. 10 (October, 1969), 99–103.

[3] Reference is made to the initial report on the Soviet census issued at the time this article was published. Subsequently, complete census report was published. See, *Itogi vsesoiuznoi perepisi naseleniia 1970 goda* (Results of the All-Union Population Census of 1970) (Moscow: 1972), Vol. I.

[4] Dzyuba, *op. cit.*, p. 211.

[5] A. Marchenko, *My Testimony* (New York: E. P. Dutton, 1969), 415 pp.

36

THE ESCALATORS OF MADNESS

Responding to a telephone call from the secretary-general of the World Congress of Free Ukrainians in Toronto, Russian academician Andrei Sakharov promised to take up the case of the imprisoned Ukrainian historian, Valentyn Moroz, along with other similar cases on the list of his Moscow Committee for Human Rights in the Soviet Union.

Professor Walter Tarnopolsky of the Toronto York University, has already collected an impressive list of prominent Canadian names under a petition on Moroz's behalf prepared by the Committee for Human Rights he is heading.

The expulsion of Nobel prize winning writer Alexander Solzhenitsyn from his homeland was but a surgical operation that resulted in chopping off only the tip of a large multinational body of a newly-formed public opinion in most of the 15 Soviet republics.

While Solzhenitsyn, for a change, was going up on an escalator to be spirited out of the Soviet Union, many Soviet citizens were riding the escalators which were bringing them down to prisons, asylums for the insane, hard labor camps, or the districts of "voluntary settlement" in remote regions of the Kremlin empire.

Reprinted with permission from *The Gazette* (Montreal), April 13, 1973, where it appeared under the title "While Diplomats Smile, Soviets Are Imprisoned in Stalinist Madness."

The Ukraine, the second largest and most developed among the Soviet Republics (with a population of 47 million on a territory comparable to that of France), once again appears to be the main supplier of the "human goods" for the escalators of totalitarian madness.

After the mass arrests of Ukrainian intellectuals last year, a selective system of imprisoning Ukrainian patriots has been applied since. That system is netting more and more men and women from both intellectual and peasant-worker strata of the society.

Both the United Nations Commission on Human Rights and Amnesty International have, independently, collected impressive records of the identified prisoners in the known post-Stalin places of detention.

Plight Neglected

But while the cause célèbre, that of Alexander Solzhenitsyn and of his two famous supporters, Andrei Sakharov and Roy Medvedev, is being given well-deserved publicity in the West, the plight of these lesser known freethinkers of various ethnic backgrounds is neglected.

Consider the case of Valentyn Moroz, a 37-year-old Ukrainian historian and essayist. He is being kept in the toughest Russian prison at Vladimir on the Kliazma River. His prison term of nine years has an additional rider: Five years of banishment from the Ukraine to an undetermined place, probably in the Arctic region of the Soviet Union.

The harsh punishment was meted out to Moroz, at his second secret trial, for his outspoken advocacy of the sovereignty of any individual, that is: The right to think, to speak, to do creative work and arrange personal affairs according to one's own national and cultural background.

Valentyn Moroz made some headlines in Canada three years ago.

Mass Demonstration

First, when Prime Minister Trudeau was caught on the horns of a dilemma — to raise Moroz's issue with the Kremlin authorities or not to raise it during his visit to Moscow and Kiev in the spring of 1971. Then, retreating before the unyielding Ukrainian-Canadian students in Winnipeg, Mr. Trudeau agreed to intercede in Moroz's behalf during his talks with Soviet Premier Kosygin visiting Canada later in 1971.

Recently, Ukrainian-Canadian students staged a new mass demonstration in front of the Soviet embassy in Ottawa, proving that their interest in the fate of that freethinker has not diminished.

(They were moved to confront once again the silent walls of the embassy by the reports received from former inmates of the prison at Vladimir in which Moroz is being kept prisoner.)

"Some of the criminals set upon Valentyn Moroz with their knives, apparently having been goaded by the prison authorities. . . . Raise your voice in defence of this great humanist," — urge recent Jewish emigres from the Soviet Union who, like Anatol Radygin,[1] have settled in Israel.[2]

Thus, Jewish escapees from the escalators of madness are in a way, repaying their moral debt to this Ukrainian intellectual who once rose to urge the Soviet regime to grant a more humane treatment to the Jews in the Ukraine. Moroz wrote in part: "All of us condemn the Nazi crimes perpetrated on the Jews, but, at the same time, we all nonchalantly stroll on the sidewalks paved with the tombstones which had been taken out of the Jewish cemeteries in quite a few of our towns."[3]

In a similar way Valentyn Moroz accused Soviet authorities of wilfully destroying Ukrainian landmarks, including the cemeteries of Ukrainian soldiers at the city of Lviv.

When members of the Komsomol (Soviet youth organization), on orders from "the center" (in Moscow), began confiscating and destroying even the traditional Ukrainian Easter eggs *(pysanky)* — in stores and on village bazaars, Moroz publicly denounced that barbaric attempt to obliterate the most essential symbol of Ukrainian culture, with its roots imbedded in the pre-Christian era.[4]

Preserve Identity

Not unlike Alexander Solzhenitsyn defending the very essence of Russian culture, Valentyn Moroz seems to epitomize by his protests the will of the Ukrainian people to preserve their own identity in spite of all the attempts of a foreign establishment at annealing the Ukrainians and other nationalities into an amorphous mass.

It is, then, to the credit of Canadian young people that they have been able to recognize the value in the heroic stand of the two intellectuals of two different nationalities.

Solzhenitsyn's case took a more favorable turn, as he is at least safe himself and his family has joined him in exile.

Meanwhile, Valentyn Moroz, like thousands of other free-thinkers within the Soviet Union (Ukrainians, Jews, Estonians, Georgians, Latvians, and many Russians as well) is facing the KGB inquisitors who are not satisfied with keeping him behind bars.

What they want from Moroz is a confession of his "guilt" and a written declaration of his repentance. These used to be conveniently extracted from most of the prisoners in the good old days of Stalin's rule.

Now, any Canadian who is sincerely yearning for a lasting peace and cooperation between the nations of the East and the West must keep in mind the harsh fact of hardly changing Soviet reality.

Diplomatic Game

While the diplomats exchange smiles and pieces of paper, many Soviet citizens are being brought into prison wards by the escalators of the same Stalinist madness.

To acquiesce in Solzhenitsyn's expulsion would mean to become an involuntary accomplice in the crime which was recently defined by that intrepid Russian lady writer, Lydia Chukovskaia. She called such silence, supporting the only important Soviet law — "the law of the preservation of muteness."

The least one may do is to ask oneself the question Professor James Eayrs of the University of Toronto put before his Canadian readers two years ago: "Khrushchev denounced the crimes of Stalin. Kosygin denounced Khrushchev's crimes. Who denounces the crimes of Kosygin?"

REFERENCE NOTES

[1]Anatol Radygin, Soviet captain of a fishing vessel and a poet; arrested and tried in 1962 for attempting to flee from the USSR, he spent ten years in Soviet prisons and labor camps; released and permitted to emigrate to Israel.

[2]This portion of the article was inadvertently omitted during printing in *The Gazette.*

[3]*Boomerang; the Works of Valentyn Moroz,* ed. by Ya. Bihun (Baltimore: Smoloskyp, 1974), p. 31.

[4]*Ibid.,* p. 118.

37

THE SECOND CIRCLE OF TERROR

This is one of the weirdest and, in Canada, least understood paradoxes of the grim Soviet reality: The heartier the handshakes Soviet diplomats exchange with their Western counterparts at various "peace and co-existence" conferences, the harder becomes the pressure of the Kremlin rulers on their own citizens. The more free-thinking people of that Union of the 15 allegedly sovereign republics are the first to bear the brunt of increased oppression.

Against such an unwanted result of the much praised but somewhat sterile detente a Soviet Russian writer, Vladimir Maksimov,[1] warned West Europeans just a few weeks ago.

In his "open letter" to Heinrich Boell, the West German Nobel prize laureate, Maksimov wrote that "only the Almighty knows what price are we going to pay" for the current rapprochement between West Germany and the Soviet Union.

Soon his uncensored opinion was strengthened by a more familiar and, perhaps, more authoritative voice from behind the *detente curtain.* The voice of the Soviet nuclear physicist Andrei Sakharov.

Almost at the same time, Piotr Iakir and Viktor Krasin, two Soviet Russian protesters better known in the West, were put on

---

Reprinted with permission from *The Gazette* (Montreal), September 5, 1973, where it appeared under the title "Soviet Intelligentsia in Peril."

trial in Moscow, after having been softened by the secret police sufficiently to plead "guilty to anti-Soviet agitation."[2]

In these circumstances, novelist Alexander Solzhenitsyn deemed it wise to tell two Western reporters that his life was in danger.

"If I am declared killed or suddenly mysteriously dead, the world could conclude I have been killed with the approval of the KGB or by it," declared the author of the novel *The First Circle*.

Thus, screened by diplomatic smiles and wrinkles from the public eye of the West, Soviet Russian dissent has entered its second circle.

Until recently, mostly the non-Russians had been on the receiving end of the poisoned fruit from the detente plant. Several hundred Ukrainians — most of them intellectuals, students, and journalists, as well as many Baltic nationals, were sent to jails and hard-labor camps after Prime Minister Trudeau and President Nixon made their separate visits to both Moscow and Ukraine's capital Kiev.

Now, the Russian free-thinkers begin to feel the backslaps of the official Soviet hand swinging towards "peaceful co-existence" with various countries of the West. Apparently, the Kremlin leaders have concluded that it was safe for them to strangle the dissent movement now without endangering their precious foreign trade deals, wheat and all.

Even so, one must realize the fact that the Kremlin onslaught is directed, as yet, against the upper planks of the barricade of freedom whose main body is still hidden under the official Soviet uniformity. A quick glance at the writings of such protesters as Anatoly Levitin (Krasnov),[3] Ivan Iakhimovich,[4] Vladimir Lukanin,[5] Vladimir Dremliuga,[6] or Natalia Gorbanevskaia[7] will prove even to a sceptic that dissent has a wide base in the Russian masses.

All these average Russians scaled their scaffolds voluntarily. They were not afraid to face long-term prison and hard labor sentences; some were sent into psychiatric police wards for "mentally deranged."

Vladimir Dremliuga, at his trial in Moscow, was speaking for all of them when he explained why he did demonstrate against the Soviet occupation of Czechoslovakia: "All my conscious life I have wanted to be a citizen — that is a person who proudly and calmly speaks his mind. For 10 minutes I was a citizen."

Regrettably, the voices of such idealists have been muffled in most mass media in the West, at least recently. Meanwhile, the continuous strangulation of the democratic segments in most Soviet republics is the grossest Soviet Watergate of the atomic age.

In practical terms, these voices of dissent prove that even in the Russian republic, which dominates the other fourteen republics, there are people who want to establish in their own country *the rule of law* as against the present rule of self-appointed persons.

These dissenters want a democratic system with human relations between the government and the governed. Moreover, as the clandestine "Program of the Democratic Movement of the USSR" informs its readers, they also demand that "all the peoples forcibly attached to the Russians (in the Union) be granted their basic and inalienable rights," including self-determination under the UN guarantees.[8]

Thus, the celebrated Lenin's axiom that "every nation consists of two nations—the oppressor and the oppressed," is applicable even to his own creation: the Soviet Union, allegedly a country of the victorious socialism. Because even in the Soviet Russian Republic—the mightiest component of the Union—there are today two Russias: a despotic Russia, that of the Communist Party establishment, and the rebellious Russia of the oppressed.

It is impossible to foretell the outcome of this confrontation within the Russian nation between the powerful Kremlin establishment and the budding Russian democracy.

But Iuri Galanskov, the Russian poet-dissenter who died last November in the hard-labor camp of Potma ("with the approval of the KGB or by it"), wrote the following sentence in his article, addressed to the Kremlin leaders:

"You may win this battle but you will lose war; war for democracy and Russia."

REFERENCE NOTES

[1]Vladimir Maksimov (b. 1932), Russian writer; emigrated from the Soviet Union in 1974; chief editor of *Kontinent*—a journal published in Russian, English, French and German by

former Soviet dissidents in exile (Solzhenitsyn, Siniavsky, Nekrasov, Galich, Brodsky, *et al.*).

[2]See note 2 to article No. 17 in this collection.

[3]See note 2 to article No. 13 in this collection.

[4]Ivan A. Iakhimovich (b. 1930), philologist; model collective farm chairman in Soviet Latvia; author of appeal to Suslov, which cost him his job; supported the Dubcek regime in Czechoslovakia (1968); arrested in 1969 and confined to a psychiatric hospital; released in 1971.

[5]Vladimir Lukanin (b. 1945?), arrested in 1969 for protesting Soviet occupation of Czechoslovakia (1968), committed to a psychiatric hospital.

[6]Vladimir Dremliuga (b. 1940), worker; arrested for protesting in Red Square Soviet occupation of Czechoslovakia; released and permitted to emigrate to the United States (1974).

[7]Natalia Gorbanevskaia, member of the Initiative Group for the Defense of Human Rights in the USSR; arrested in 1969 for protesting in Red Square Soviet occupation of Czechoslovakia and committed to a psychiatric hospital in 1970.

[8]The Program of the Democratic Movement of the Soviet Union (DMSU) was drawn up and issued in October 1969 by the members of DMSU — a union of political dissidents in Russia, Ukraine, and the Baltic States. The program, among others, proposes the reorganization of the USSR along democratic lines with the recognition of national rights of the non-Russian nations. In 1970, the group also published its *Tactical Principles* which called on its members to change from open to clandestine mode of operation.

PART VII
UKRAINIANS IN DIASPORA

EDITOR'S NOTE

A persecuted country, struggling for emancipation, needs a diaspora.

A diaspora, in search for identity and self-preservation in the midst of (often well-intended) assimilatory environment, needs a second home.

Why?

Because a diaspora and its relationship to a mother country underscores mutual responsibilities. They can share pride. They can divide sorrows.

Roman Rakhmanny expands the postulate, particularly in the North American context, stressing the importance of the umbilical cord.

38

THE SAGA OF THE
YOUNGEST BROTHER

Of all Ukrainian folk epics, called *dumy,* the Tale of the
Three Brothers' Escape from Azov presents perhaps the most tragic episode in the life of Cossack Ukraine.[1] Who in our
adolescence would not shed a tear while reading, perhaps in a
secluded nook, the poetic narrative unfolding before our eyes:

> *From the Town of Azov, from oppressive slavery*
> *Three brothers are fleeing;*
> *Two of them mounted, and the third on foot,*
> *As if he were a total stranger...*
> *Trying to keep pace with them,*
> *Leaving footprints of blood,*
> *He is shedding his tears,*
> *He is imploring his brothers with words:*
>
> *"My closest kin, my own brothers...*
> *Wait for me a little while.*
> *Take me along with you,*

This article was originally published in the Ukrainian-language journal, *Suchasnist*
(Munich), V, No. 10 (October 1965), 93-105. It was translated and made available
for public distribution by the Joint Publications Research Service, US Department of
Commerce, Report No.: JPRS 33, 292, December 13, 1965.

Toward Christian settlements,
Give me a short lift at least . . . .

Remember, reader, how shocked you were. How, in your young thoughts, you simply refused to believe it possible for any Ukrainian not to come to the succour of his younger brother in dire necessity. But the two did exactly that:

Because we neither would escape ourselves
Nor would we save thyself.

But now we have become men hardened by many of life's tribulations and we seem at least to have acquired some insight into certain things.

Life is much more complex than such direct feelings infusing our youthful day-dreams. A human may find himself in a marginal situation when, face-to-face with what he considers invincible powers, he feels entirely alone, forsaken by God and kin alike. Poets, novelists, playwrights as well as some perceptive film producers have tried often enough to fathom that human condition. If our own writers were endowed with a spark of creative ingenuity, they too would discover episodes in the lives of their Ukrainian compatriots worthy of the genius of a Sophocles or Shakespeare. As it is, however. . . .

Beyond Good and Evil

Here we are not merely concerned with the artistic aspects of this remarkable tale beautifully rendering a "marginal situation" in a strict philosophic sense. The tragic fate of the Youngest Brother, abandoned by his two older brothers on the desolate and arid frontier steppe of the Old Ukraine, is recalled here bearing as it does strikingly vivid resemblance to the present condition of a large segment of the Ukrainian people. On seeing a tragic occurrence one may often recall a certain book, read long ago, a mirror of the occurrence. For indeed, a well written story is but a slice of life itself — past or future.

The Tale of the Three Brothers' Escape foreshadowed, almost prophetically, the serious situation of the Ukrainians living beyond the borders of the Soviet Ukraine—in the Russian Soviet Republic, in the Polish, Romanian, and Czechoslovak People's Republics. How many Ukrainians are currently residing there? Who knows? There are no reliable official statistics. The governments of these republics do not appear anxious to provide such figures. Why? Because the fact of figures hampers their drive to assimilate the Ukrainian minority. Does the Soviet Ukrainian government in Kiev show greater interest in clarifying the problem? Some 40 years ago this issue was vigorously pressed both in Kiev and Moscow by Mykola Skrypnyk, the Old Bolshevik and member of the Soviet Ukrainian government. At the 12th Congress of the Russian Communist Party held in Moscow, June 1923, he inquired:[2]

> Why did seven million Ukrainians living within the borders of the Russian SFSR have no guaranteed human rights to safeguard and develop their own culture? Why, of some 500 Ukrainian-language schools recently opened there, over 300 had been already shut down while the secondary schools (of the *tekhnikum* type) with instruction in Ukrainian are subject to phasing out in the near future?

Skrypnyk quoted instances showing that regional leaders in the Russian SFSR had suppressed all manifestations of Ukrainian culture in those districts with a high proportion of Ukrainians. Thus, the provincial Communist Party Committee of the Voronezh *oblast* gave the following reply to the inquiry by the Central Committee of the Russian Communist Party: "To organize a Ukrainian section, even for the purpose of party agitation in the *oblast,* would be very inopportune."

The Kursk *oblast* Party Committee maintained "such an attempt was altogether redundant." But the Kuban *oblast* Party Committee, directing a province inhabited by 2,273,000 Ukrainians, "would not even bother to reply" to the inquiry of the Central Committee in Moscow.

> "On the whole, what kind of cultural services were provided for the Ukrainians living on the territory of the Russian SFSR by 1923?"—asked Mykola Skrypnyk. He offered the following facts: "In the last two years only two

single brochures in Ukrainian were published in the whole
of the Soviet Russian republic. One of these we received two
days ago. It contains resolutions of the First Congress of the
Soviets of the USSR. The other brochure is an anthology of
poetry. In my opinion, this is a far cry from what is needed
by these seven million Ukrainians."

Mykola Skrypnyk, speaking in Moscow, June 12, 1923, added
that Russification of Ukrainians in the Russian republic had
been conducted mostly by the Red Army.

As a result of the last mobilization about 60,000
Ukrainians residing in Russia proper joined the Red Army.
But what language is being used to instruct them? Are any
educational or cultural activities carried out in Ukrainian?
No, the Army remains the instrument for Russifying the
Ukrainians and other minorities. . . .

Four momentous tides of change swept across the Soviet Union
since Mykola Skrypnyk formulated these arguments for the
Kremlin leadership. The Stalin Constitution was proclaimed;
the Second World War was fought; and both the post-Stalin
thaw and the Khrushchev "liberalization" relevant to the
nationality question shook the confederation of Soviet republics.
But the situation of the Ukrainians in the Russian SFSR has not
improved; on the contrary, it deteriorated. On the territory of
what is allegedly the most progressive state in the world, built by
the "most humane Russian people," the Ukrainians do not have
a single Ukrainian-language school nor are they allowed to
organize Ukrainian-language classes in Russian schools. Deprived of their right to publish any Ukrainian newspapers, they
even dare not dream of opening a Ukrainian school of the
collegiate type.

The Russians in the Ukrainian Soviet Republic, however, are
provided with all types of Russian-language schools and with
every assistance for developing Russian culture; even a separate
association of Russian writers exists in the Ukraine. Thus, the
Ukrainians in Russia continue to suffocate under the traditional
czarist system of Russification.

"The Russians alone should not be blamed for the situation.

You mustn't forget the timidity of our Ukrainian people. Instead of defending their own rights, they prefer suffering humbly," — a visitor from the Ukraine told me.

That may be so, but their "timidity" is deeply rooted in the realization that there is no one to stand up for their rights. They are entirely on their own, deprived of the legal protection usually provided for a stranded minority by the government of their Old Country.

The government of the Soviet Ukraine in this respect shares part of the responsibility for the oppression suffered by the Ukrainians in Russia.

To a certain degree that guilt must be shared also by the cultural circles of the Ukrainian Soviet Republic, party members in particular, because implicitly, in their thinking, they have erased from the "census" well over seven million of their own people to the advantage of the Russians. Mykola Skrypnyk was a Bolshevik and a faithful party man himself but he never forgot he was a Ukrainian. He defended the interests of the Ukrainian people on every all-Union council and thereby at least attempted to act as a true Communist of Ukrainian nationality. The present day administration of the Ukrainian SSR, however, has failed to demonstrate even such tokens of good will. And the intellectual circles of the same republic have not dared to prompt these bureaucrats to take some practical steps to protect the Ukrainian minority in the Russian SFSR. Indeed, they have deliberately abandoned their compatriots (forced settlers, migrants, and deportees in the Russian SFSR) on that new "Black Trail"[3] which leads them into a modern mode of slavery — Russification.

In a similar situation, comparable to the moral existence outside the power of good and evil, live the Ukrainians of the Polish People's Republic. According to our own incomplete data more than 400,000 Ukrainians call themselves citizens of that country. They do not, however, possess equal rights because their cultural needs are both disregarded by the authorities and restricted by their fellow citizens. Only one periodical publication in Ukrainian appears in Poland: the weekly *Nashe Slovo* (Our Word) together with a monthly supplement *Nasha Kultura* (Our Culture). But many Ukrainians in Poland fear to subscribe to the journal because local authorities and fellow citizens would make

their life even more miserable for having openly declared themselves persons of Ukrainian culture.

Apart from few exceptions, teaching children the Ukrainian
language is not permitted, and no courses on Ukrainian civilization or linguistics are given by any institution of higher learning.
As of now, there are no textbooks of Ukrainian literature for university students, not even in Polish. Publications of this kind
have not yet been authorized by the responsible Polish department, and neither the government nor the intellectual leaders of
the Soviet Ukraine ever thought of filling the existing void.

Much is being said and written, both in Soviet Ukrainian
papers and radio programs produced for foreign consumption,
about ever growing cultural contacts between the Ukraine and
Poland. One would expect this, naturally, since the two
countries are close neighbors ruled by the same doctrine. Moreover, Warsaw and Cracow are so close to Kiev and Lviv that
there should have been many opportunities for impressing upon
the Polish leaders the need to consider the plight of the
Ukrainian minority. Alas, the lot of these Ukrainians is in many
respects no less somber than under the "reactionary" regime in
prewar Poland.

Against such a background the recorded experiences of the
Ukrainians in Poland reflect their grave sense of frustration as,
for instance, when you are told that in Warsaw you cannot obtain any Ukrainian newspapers from the Soviet Ukraine. Polish
distributors won't order these periodicals from Kiev themselves,
and Soviet Ukrainian book trade officials would not cater to "a
few Ukrainian readers in Poland." Ukrainian observers from
Poland also report that "there is an abundance of Russian-
language books and periodicals in different Warsaw bookstores."

No wonder that Polish citizens of Ukrainian origin are reluctant to ask for a regular supply of Ukrainian books and
periodicals in Poland. In practice, a bizarre process is noticeable: Soviet Ukrainians visiting Poland may acquire some specific Ukrainian publications from the Polish-Ukrainian book
funds.

Thus, the existence of the Ukrainian SSR as a Ukrainian communist state is of no assistance to the Ukrainian minority either
in Russia or in Poland. The Soviet Ukraine has failed to evolve
into a source of cultural energy that by its cultural values would

sustain all the Ukrainians scattered over the outlying districts of the Polish People's Republic.

The Older Brother's Guilt

They have been broken up and forcibly uprooted from their native soil and resettled on the Recovered Territories of Western Poland right after the Second World War — an accomplishment of the Bierut regime, with the connivance of the Soviet Ukrainian authorities in Kiev. For more than 600 years the Ukrainians of western Ukrainian borderlands — Pidliashshia, Kholm, Peremyshl, and Lemko regions — successfully resisted Polish ethnic pressure. After these six centuries of pressure and resistance, the Poles could boast of only a narrow strip of land, about 15 miles wide, they had conquered from the Ukrainian highlanders in the Carpathians, the Lemkos. Without over-whelming support of Stalin's Russia, and the timidity of the Kiev administrators, the Bierut regime would probably have not been able to suppress the valiant people either. As it was, however, following a three-year-long struggle, most Ukrainians from the mentioned borderlands were deported to former Eastern Prussia and to other previously German-held lands where they would be robbed of any chance to foster their own way of life, or even to preserve what is allowed constitutionally at least in the Soviet Union — ethnic culture according to the formula of "socialist in content and Ukrainian in form."

Some try to justify that inhuman form of oppression per-petrated against the Ukrainians within the Polish People's Republic by citing the activities of the Ukrainian Insurgent Army (UPA) on the territory between the Buh and Sian Rivers during 1946-1947.

No one denies that the insurgency may have irked both Warsaw and Moscow and, eventually, may have prodded them into taking a concerted action against the underground network there. But it is also true that foreign oppression in the first place not so much the sentiments of the local Ukrainian population in the contested regions spawned the elements of insurgency there. It was not UPA's activity in the years 1946-47 that resulted in the slicing off of these borderlands from the Ukraine. The Moscow

leaders handed over these lands to their Polish ally in 1943, at
the Teheran Conference, with President Roosevelt and Prime
Minister Churchill conniving in the deal. The Yalta agreement
(February 1945) ultimately sealed the fate of the frontier lands
without taking into consideration the Ukrainian population.
They had not been asked what citizenship—Ukrainian or
Polish—they would prefer. At the time of the two international
conferences, the UPA waged no "provocative" military action
west of the Buh and Sian Rivers. Thus, no valid reason existed
for uprooting the Ukrainian population of Pidliashshia, Kholm,
Peremyshl, and Lemko regions in 1947-48 and for settling them
by force over the northern and western parts of Poland without
any legal right to return to their native land.

One may ask why is it that even after the de-Stalinization of
1956 in the USSR the Kiev government did not try to have the
border between the Ukraine and Poland rectified? Was it not the
Soviet Ukraine's official writers who explained that this borderline was drawn by Stalin alone "without consulting anyone?"
Moreover, why have no diplomatic steps ever been taken to regain, for the deported Ukrainians, at least the right of an
unimpeded return to their native districts?

We are aware of the fact that the government in Kiev did not
take any part in determining this borderline, even indirectly,
either in 1943 or 1945. It was not consulted by the Kremlin
rulers. But neither did the Soviet Ukrainian leaders register their
objections to the new and more unfair "Curzon Line" devised by
Stalin and Molotov.[4] The Kiev leadership deliberately washed its
hands of any involvement in the problem of the Ukrainians in
Poland. But so it must be admitted did the Soviet Ukrainian
intellectuals who, in psychological terms, went even further than
that.

Even a superficial perusal of the maps and geography textbooks published for use in the Soviet Ukraine schools exposes the
fact of both Russification and Polonization of the names of
towns, cities, rivers, and lakes by Soviet Ukrainian authors.
(Often, owing to poor knowledge of Polish, even some genuine
Polish names are distorted, but *always* in a Russian manner.) For
example, one of the oldest cities of the Ukraine, Peremyshl, has
been rendered in Ukrainian transcription but pronounced
wrongly in Polish. The City of Kholm, founded by Ukrainian

King Danylo Halytsky in the 13th century, also bears the Polonized name *"Khelm"* in the Soviet Ukrainian geography textbooks. Similarly, the Sian River is registered on Soviet Ukrainian maps as *"San,"* a Polish rendering of the river's name.

Soviet Ukrainian intellectuals responsible for these mutations could have acted under duress or intimidation by the proverbial "Muscovite terror." A policy of Russification is currently applied in the Ukraine by the Soviet centralizers; but does there stand behind every Ukrainian intellectual, day and night, a Russian with a bayonet and orders to Russify Ukrainian place names? It is even more certain that Moscow does not direct the intellectuals to Polonize geographic names. Do Polish authorities influence the thinking of Soviet Ukrainian intellectuals in this respect? Before 1939, when Western Ukrainian scholars lived and worked within the Polish Republic, they were exposed to various kinds of official pressures. But even then it was possible to resist such pressure, provided the intellectual involved possessed a measure of personal and national dignity. To mention one such case: a Ukrainian geographer in inter-war Poland was deprived of his professorship at the University of Cracow for having worked on the publication of an atlas of the Ukraine. This was the reaction of Polish authorities to his refusal to Polonize Ukrainian place-names or to doctor statistical data dealing with the Ukrainian minority in Poland. The professor, however, would neither submit to the arbitrary demand nor would he bend under pressure.

Today in the sovereign Soviet Ukraine, Ukrainian geographers and teachers attempt to educate the new generation of Ukrainians that the lands just beyond the Buh and Sian Rivers "were always" originally Polish lands and so bear "native" Polish names. Those explaining this strange behaviour of Soviet Ukrainian intellectuals by their loyalty to the doctrine of the so-called "progressive merging of nationalities under communism" should be asked: If so, why then should every attempt at closing the gap between various nationalities be usually achieved at the expense of the Ukrainian people? And how is it, that it was always a Soviet Ukrainian intellectual who failed to protest (in a scholarly manner) against such unfair practices often offering a helpful hand in implementing that illegal policy so damaging to the interests of the Ukrainian nation? If one praises the "progressive" structure of the Polish People's Republic, should one not also raise some objections against the oppression of the Ukrainian minority?

It seems that such officials and scholars of the Soviet Ukraine act like the oldest brother did in the tale of three brothers escaping from the fortress of Azov. He explained his own practical reasoning to the younger one:

> *Our old folks, father and mother, will be gone some day*
> *And we'll divide their land and cattle into two parts;*
> *The third won't then complicate things for ourselves....*

But crafty fate often makes short shrift of such egoistic designs. No sooner had these words escaped from his lips than this happened:

> *It was not the cries of the black-winged ravens,*
> *But the yells of the Turkish Janissaries*
> *Charging from behind the mound.*
> *They shot and hacked the two brothers*
> *And took back with them their mounts and their spoils.*

For a parallel, one doesn't need to look far. Sly fortune took similar revenge on a similar "older brother" — literary critics, party and state officials in the Soviet Ukraine of the 1920s who ferociously attacked their sincere Ukrainian compatriots for alleged ideological mistakes.

Mykola Zerov, Mykola Khvylovy, Valerian Pidmohylny, Mykola Kulish, and many others were accused and condemned by those critics — in the newspapers and at public rallies — long before the Soviet Russian police began arresting the "deviationists."[5] But the triumph of the over-zealous brothers was shortlived. In the early 1930s, those same critics and officials were felled by the same power-axe.

Thus, the highly instructive aspect of the old Ukrainian *duma* should be kept in mind also by our contemporaries who occupy positions of authority in Kiev and other urban centers of the Ukraine. Today they tolerate the intolerable policy of assimilation of their brethren in the Russian SFSR (in Siberia, along the Amur River, in the Voronezh, Bilhorod, and Kuban regions) as well as in Poland and Romania. Tomorrow, they may have to acquiesce in the Russification of the entire Ukraine, with accompanying diminution of their own authority. As a Ukrainian saying has it, if a tree grows slanted then even goats can climb it. Already even Moldavia is able to Moldavanize its Ukrainian population. If the Ukrainians of Romania have for the present a breathing spell from authorities, it is only because the latter raised their claim to Bukovyna—the Ukrainian province of the pre-war Romanian kingdom. The Romanian authorities are trying to convince the Ukrainians of that region—now an integral part of the Soviet Ukraine—that life used to be "much sunnier" when they were citizens of Romania (that is until 1940).

The negligence of the Kiev authorities is best illustrated by the case of the Ukrainians in Czechoslovakia whose situation has recently ameliorated. These inhabitants of the Priashiv (Presov) province in Eastern Czechoslovakia have been granted relatively advantageous opportunities for ethnic-cultural self-expression. Books and periodicals are being published there in Ukrainian; Ukrainian-language schools have come into being; and recently they have obtained permission to broadcast in Ukrainian. The Ukrainians in Poland and other neighboring communist countries eagerly listen to these programs dealing with the life and activities of the Ukrainian minority in the Czechoslovak People's Republic. Even these modest opportunities loom large when compared with their own privations in that respect. Thus, only thanks to the passivity and incomprehensible indifference of the Kiev administrators has the Soviet Ukraine not evolved into a magnetic pole to which all Ukrainians in foreign lands would gravitate. By this failure, the Kiev regime undermined its own position within the system of the Soviet confederation as well.

What then should be done to assure some legal protection for the Ukrainian minorities in the communist countries? The first step would be to establish consular and, later on, ambassadorial representations of the Soviet Ukraine in these countries; diplomatic channels provide best lines of communications between two sovereign nations faced with such a sensitive problem. Even the least developed African nations are making use of that instrument in international relations. The Ukrainian SSR alone has failed to direct its own foreign relations, and its spokesmen continue to shy away from exercising the republic's constitutional rights. Recently, the Foreign Minister of the Soviet Ukraine, Luka Palamarchuk, made a feeble attempt to rationalize this failure by suggesting specific ideological considerations, asserting that the Ukraine has already attained the summit of its sovereignty and that it maintains its diplomatic relations through the intermediary channels of the all-Union department of foreign affairs. But what he would not mention was that the Supreme Soviet restored to the Ukrainian SSR, in 1944, its previous right to enter into diplomatic relations directly. For this purpose a ministry of foreign affairs had been formed in Kiev. Moreover, the same constitutional amendment (passed under the Stalin-Molotov rule) also provides for a separate Ukrainian department of national defense.

Since the "rule of Soviet law" has been reinstated in the Soviet Union, as Soviet spokesmen would have us believe, it is even stranger that the Soviet Ukrainian authorities have not availed themselves of this right. On the contrary, they seem deliberately to avoid asserting themselves. To placate their own citizens, a ridiculous substitute of the so-called "expanded relations with foreign nations" is being touted. What does it mean in practical terms? There are indeed in Kiev consulates of Poland and Czechoslovakia to protect the interests of their respective citizens. But it is less known in the Ukraine that the Soviet Ukrainian government does not have its own representatives accredited either to Warsaw or to Prague. The only semblance of foreign diplomatic relations is preserved by a special embassy of the Soviet Ukraine at the United Nations where the Ukraine's status is no match for that of Mongolia or the Congo. Incidentally, there also exists a Society for Maintaining Relations with the Ukrainians in Foreign Countries. Composed of intellectuals and party activists, it addresses its propaganda to the Ukrainians in *non*-communist countries.

The Supreme Soviet of the Ukrainian SSR, which should be the voice of the Ukrainian people, keeps docile silence in this matter. So do Soviet Ukrainian experts on international law or other intellectuals, whether of the old or younger generation. It is that slavelike silence that conceals the tragedy of more than seven million Ukrainians left to their own devices beyond the borders of the Ukraine, in other communist countries, abandoned without the benefit of any international legal safeguards and without that moral support usually expected from a Mother Country.

Or to return to our analogy: the oldest brother who possesses all the legal and material advantages has failed to become a substitute parent to the underprivileged youngest brother.

It would be difficult to find a parallel negligence anywhere in the world. But, then, it is not easy to find in other folklore literatures a tragic epic comparable to the Ukrainian Tale of the Three Brothers' Escape From Azov, reflecting classic simplicity and poetic style of the Bible. One is tempted to ponder: who knows, perhaps we — Ukrainians — do live in a world of our own, separated from the rest of mankind, beyond the limits of good and evil.

The Middle Brother's Guilt

But the Ukrainians living in the West are also responsible for the vicissitudes of the youngest brother. Like him, the Ukrainians of Canada, the United States, Australia, Britain, France, and Latin America are in no way dependent on the support of the "oldest brother" in their endeavors to preserve themselves as a cultural-ethnic entity. Up to now, they have been able to keep their own organizational structures, to stand up for their own rights, and even to contribute to the common weal of the Ukrainian nation. From the "oldest brother" — the Soviet Ukrainian who appears to be in the saddle because he possesses his own republic — they have received nothing but slanderous invectives, threats, and crafty obstacles devised by the Soviet Ukrainian republic.

Nevertheless, we are ready to admit that if the Soviet Ukrainians ever gained the status of a sovereign nation, then it would be much easier for the Ukrainians in the West to bring up their younger generation in the Ukrainian idiom and in accordance with Ukrainian cultural traditions. In educating the young nothing can replace the impact of Mother Country existing as a sovereign state. There is hardly a substitute for the natural influence of a specific spiritual nationality manifesting itself by its state and cultural institutions. The Ukrainian minority in any Western country would acquire much greater cohesiveness and specific characteristics if there existed a real power behind them — a sovereign Ukrainian nation as a fact and not a fog. In the absence of such moral support, the Ukrainian communities in the West are obliged to continue to rely only on their own resourcefulness.

Since the Ukrainian community in non-communist countries has been able to stand on its own feet (regardless of all the setbacks in the Ukraine), its responsibilities increase rather than decrease. Why? Because we have almost unlimited opportunities for developing Ukrainian culture in the countries of our settlement. We own numerous periodicals (in Ukrainian and other languages) not restricted by censorship. We have established scholarly societies and developed extensive economic and financial structures. We have produced a cadre of young intellectuals imbued with Ukrainian spiritual values and ideals. Having also secured for ourselves a high standard of living, virtually unknown to any previous generation, we are in a position to exert ourselves for benefit of our brethren in the communist countries.

The underprivileged condition of that "youngest brother" is commented upon from time to time in our Ukrainian papers published in Canada, the United States, Britain, Argentina, and Brazil — main emphasis usually on the persecution of the religiously minded Ukrainians in the communist countries. These news items and comments seem to ease the conscience of readers and editors alike, because they appear to be a proof of their participation in the all-Ukrainian effort of self-liberation. But the only real attempt at defending the human rights of their brethren has been made so far by the Ukrainian-Canadians who hail from the Lemko region of the Ukraine. They have for instance constituted a Society for the Defense of Lemkivshchyna. As for other regions detached from the Ukraine in the same manner — Kholm, Peremyshl, and Pidliashshia — these seem to have been forgotten even by their own emigres.

Who would raise the question of the Ukrainians in Romania and Russia? Granted, Professor Volodymyr Kubijowycz in his valuable demographic studies on the population of the Ukraine and other Soviet republics does not allow that problem to be completely forgotten. He reminds his countrymen all over the world that there are some Ukrainian communities also along the Amur and Ussuri rivers in the Far East. Naturally, scholarly works have much less impact on the general public than do the regular media of mass information.

Thus, whoever excites public criticism of the Kiev authorities for their neglect of the Ukrainians living outside the borders of their republic, must at the same time remind the organized Ukrainian communities in the non-communist countries that their own responsibility for these people is no smaller than that of the Soviet Ukraine's ruling circles.

We need to remind ourselves, at the same time, that far too much time and effort is being wasted on vague universal problems. Our "globalists" in the Ukrainian SSR are preoccupied with such problems as Cuba, Vietnam, or the Congo. On the other hand, the "globalists" among the Ukrainians in the West are anxious to share in attempts at "solving" the problems of China and Korea while some of them earnestly confess their anxiety about the future of the United States and the whole of mankind.

None of these misguided "idealists" on both sides of the curtain that divides the Ukrainian nationality into two opposing forces, seems to remember a very simple fact: that the United States, Vietnam, China, Cuba, and Korea became and still are sovereign nations without any help from Ukrainians. These nations need no such support to remain masters of their own affairs. While standing on guard against some "global windmills," we neglect the reality of urgent Ukrainian problems.

Much time and energy is consumed by our continuous search for an absolute Ukrainian unity. At present, a debate is going on about the need and the feasibility of forming a World Congress of Free Ukrainians.[6] There are those who sincerely believe that as soon as the Ukrainians in the West declare themselves obedient to a single leadership, all will be solved.

Purely formal or mechanical unity, without our united society ready to act as an organic unit on behalf of every Ukrainian individual or group in distress, would only furnish us with yet another empty framework for honorific posts to be occupied by different factional leaders. An ability to present a common front even without any specific world organization whenever there arises an all-national emergency is the only true manifestation of a mature society, even more so, of a nation.

The Ukrainians in the countries of the West have already

ceased to be a motley crowd of emigrants concerned about bread alone. Today they form, to a high degree, integral parts of society in the countries of their settlement. From this advantageous position we all can and should act as citizens of these free countries so as to alleviate the lot of our brethren under the communist regimes. It is of no use today to brandish old defeatist slogans about the "total destruction of the Ukraine" or, on the other hand, to boast that Ukraine's flag remains in our strong hands as unblemished as ever. Whoever continues to sing this emigre song instead of *doing* some constructive work resembles the middle brother from the Cossack *duma*.

Instead of helping his barefoot brother, he continued to ride on with the oldest brother and all he did was from time to time hack with his sabre some branches off the bushes along his trail. Once they reached the treeless steppe, he would tear a few strips out of the expensive colored cloth, booty from the Turkish town of Azov. In this way he hoped to mark the way to freedom for the unfortunate youngest brother:

> *So that he may find his way*
> *And, following our trail,*
> *He may yet reach the homeland*
> *Of his father and mother, and of his kin.*

Such a ragged and incidental assistance was of no avail. Upon seeing the strips of the familiar cloth, the youngest brother lost all hope for survival; he died of grief, because he had thought:

> *It is no accident*
> *That the cloth lies scattered along the trail.*
> *This is a sure sign*
> *That my brothers have been despatched from this world.*

An analogous conclusion may be drawn by our Ukrainian brethren in the communist countries, outside the Ukraine, if they perceive the empty stance of their two older brothers — truly "mounted horsemen" in every respect. For they have never received any assistance from the Soviet Ukraine.

From the Ukrainians in the West they are getting, now and then, only strips of propaganda cloth. Should not they infer from all this that the end is near — for their two brothers as well as for themselves?

The Ukrainians in the open societies of the West need to undertake a combined mass drive for the protection of their brothers separated from the Ukrainian nation. One is wary of memoranda submitted by dozens of isolated political groups. But a single appeal to the United Nations Commission on Human Rights signed by the Ukrainian Church hierarchy and leaders of all political and civic organizations may stir the public opinion of the world; the basic points of that appeal should be summarized and submitted to the governments of the countries with Ukrainian segments in their populations; all public, humanitarian, and cultural institutions should be acquainted with the content of these appeals.

The leading Ukrainian organizations in North America, the Ukrainian Canadian Committee in Canada, and the Ukrainian Congress Committee in the United States, could take particularly effective steps toward convincing their respective governments to lend a helpful hand in this matter.

Canada and the United States maintain diplomatic relations with the communist countries which comprise a Ukrainian minority. It might be possible through diplomatic channels to obtain from the government of Poland, Romania, the Russian SFSR, and Czechoslovakia permission for Ukrainians who would like to emigrate to North America. Every year Canada admits a number of immigrants. The required quota for 1965 has been set at 150,000 persons, according to the Minister of Immigration John Nicholson. Because of the improved economic conditions in Britain and Western Europe, it is not easy to find suitable immigrants there. Eastern Europe, however, is overpopulated and the Ukrainians there, for one, live under difficult conditions. They could be admitted to Canada where favorable conditions already exist for their integration with the Ukrainian-Canadians. Planned and reasonable communities in the countries of the West, may contribute substantially to easing the lot of our underprivileged brothers.

Joint efforts may create the preconditions needed for a possible resettlement of a large number of Ukrainians from Eastern Europe to North America. World opinion may then become aware of the "human condition" in which a section of our people has found itself through no fault of its own. This would provide for a strong pressure to be applied on the government of the Soviet Union as well as the governments of satellite countries which may also be induced to grant the Ukrainian minority within their borders a better chance to live as human beings.

At the same time, the Kiev government would find itself under normal pressure to recall its own duty to take care of the youngest brother in the hour of his dire need. The followers of the Soviet system both in Canada and the United States (the so-called Progressives but actually Communists of Ukrainian origin) will feel the pressure as well. They may find themselves obliged to demand from the Soviet authorities some assurance of a better deal for the Ukrainians in the Russian SFSR and other communist countries. If they do not raise such a demand, they would have to admit their own helplessness vis-a-vis Moscow and, thus, in the eyes of public opinion expose themselves for what they have been all the time, obedient servants of the Kremlin.

In a parallel action, moral pressure on Kiev could be exercised through visitors from Ukraine. Nowadays, at last, Ukrainians residing in different countries are able to meet one another without any rancor and in a friendly fashion exchange their traditional greetings "with bread and salt." It is also reassuring that they can sigh compassionately during public readings of Ukrainian poetry and at colorful folklore presentations. But these encounters must not result only in creating the unreal mood that prompts everybody to keep silent about the most painful Ukrainian problem out of fear that truth may hurt somebody's susceptibilities.

By all means, let's keep talking and by our incisive questions concerning the most essential Ukrainian problem, let's gently press the hearts of the visitors from Ukraine as we heartily press their hands upon greeting them. If they respond in a human Ukrainian voice to the youngest brother's plea, this shall be our proof that their heart is Ukrainian indeed, as we do remember how that brother was pleading with his more fortunate brothers in the steppe:

> *My dear, my own brothers,*
> *Beautiful like turtledoves.*
> *Stop for a while, let your horses graze,*

Wait for me a little while,
Take me with you
To Christian settlements,
Give me a lift, at least part of the way.

Now, our youngest brother is calling us. The plea concerns the urgency to safeguard human rights for Ukrainian minority in the Russian SFSR, Poland, Romania, and Czechoslovakia; the right to develop their own Ukrainian cultural values. Whoever among us fails to respond to that plea, by word or by deed, will be as responsible as the whole establishment of the Ukrainian SSR for the abandonment of his youngest brother on the arid, hungry, and lawless Black Trail of foreign oppression.

Readers will react differently to this essay clad in the poetic form of the Tale of the Three Brothers' Escape from Azov.

Those who smugly enjoy their prosperity in their adopted countries may sigh with an air of detachment: "Well, but what can we do? Any involvement in the issue would only put an unnecessary burden on ourselves without avail." Others will reply in a congenial manner: "Is it fair to criticize our compatriots in the Ukraine so severely?" On their part, they may retort by asking us why we had not stayed with them in the Ukraine to defend the human rights of the Ukrainian people right there?

Still other readers, confused by the trappings of their ideological beliefs, would hastily cover their ears so as not to hear the voice of their own brother from the Black Trail. For some of these the Chinese may seem to be the closer kin; and to many others the Soviet Russians may have appeared to be brothers in a more veritable way. To most of them, the solidarity of international left extremism may mean much more than the solidarity of the whole Ukrainian nation.

There will be those too who, having grown up in the shadow of the Anglo-Saxon traditions of cosmopolitanism and scepticism, would observe with a condescending smile: "We wonder whether it will ever be possible for a Ukrainian to write anything without the traditional Ukrainian emotionalism."

But fortunately, the general reader who prevails on both sides of the curtain of great silence will respond to the expressed thoughts here in the manner the youngest brother in the *duma* story did. Upon finding the strips of the rich-colored cloth he pressed them to his heart as a sincere gift from his brothers. Thus, these readers are going to embrace the thoughts by their souls and will join me in saying relevantly:

> Verily, without the searing feelings of responsibility for the chances of our youngest brother we shan't ever become a mature nation. So lead us, merciful God, unto the Ukrainian trail of dignity. Free us from foreign oppression — economic, cultural, and political. But above all, help us free ourselves from our own spiritual slavery. So that we may finally become Ukrainians not in name alone. Help us to feel and act as a single and closely-knit family of men and women eager to stand together in need. So that to each of us the name 'Ukrainian' radiates the warmth of dignified pride. So that at last we shall become as anybody else — a nation like any other nation in the world.

Indeed, unless we experience this keen emotion in our daily lives, we shall never escape from the realm of "beyond good and evil." Nay, we may turn into something like the three brothers eternally fleeing from the slavery of the Azov fortress.

REFERENCE NOTES

[1]*Duma* — Ukrainian folk ballad or epic tale, normally associated with the Cossack period (16th and 17th centuries), recounting Cossack heroic deeds in their struggle against the Tartars, Turks, Russians, and Poles, and lamenting the fate of Ukrainian frontier settlers falling victim of Tartar attacks and abduction into slavery. For a complete text of "The Tale of the Three Brothers' Escape From Azov," see Plisetsky (comp.), *Ukrains'ki dumy ta istorychni pisni* (Ukrainian Dumy and Historical Songs), (Kiev: 1944), pp. 54–62.

[2]*Dvenadtsatyi s'iezd Rossiiskoi Kommunisticheskoi Partii (bol'shevikov); Stenograficheskii otchot* (Twelfth Congress of the Russian Communist Party (Bolsheviks); Stenographic Notes), 17–25 April 1923 (Moscow: 1968), pp. 569–73.

[3]Allusion is made to the strategic highway, called "Chornyi

shliakh" (The Black Trail) which the Crimean Khanate Tartars used to conduct their raids deep into the heart of populated Ukraine and carry their booty and slaves back to the Crimea during the sixteenth and seventeenth centuries.

[4]Reference is made to the Curzon Line—an international boundary authored by Lord Curzon and adopted by the Supreme Allied Council in Paris (1919) as Polish frontier in the east, but rejected by Poland. The German-Soviet border (1939-1941)—the so-called Ribbentrop-Molotov Line—roughly followed the configuration of the Curzon Line as does also the present Polish-Soviet boundary agreed upon at the Yalta Conference (1945). Neither the original Curzon Line nor its later successors respected the ethnic delineations between the Polish and Ukrainian nations. In fact, large segments of the Ukrainian ethnic territory were incorporated into Poland. See: US Department of State, *Foreign Relations; The Paris Peace Conference, 1919,* (Washington, DC: USGPO, 1942), XIII, pp. 793-94; and *The Conferences on Malta and Yalta, 1945* (Washington, DC: USGPO, 1955), pp. 975-82.

[5]Reference is made to Soviet Ukrainian literati: Mykola Zerov, neo-classicist poet and literary critic, arrested in 1935, died in Siberia; Mykola Khvylovy, literary critic, committed suicide in 1933 in the face of persecution in the Ukraine; V. Pidmohyl'ny, writer, arrested in 1934, died in Siberia; Mykola Kulish, playwright, arrested in 1934, died in Siberia.

[6]World Congress of Free Ukrainians was, eventually, founded in 1967 by representatives of Ukrainian communities in various countries of the West. Its moral basis coincides with the ideal of Ukrainian spiritual unity as expressed in this essay.

39

THE PRAGUE GROUP OF UKRAINIAN NATIONALIST WRITERS AND THEIR IDEOLOGICAL ORIGINS

What Ukrainians need most is "to know Europe and to be known in Europe." This observation was made in 1873 by the editor of *La République française* in commenting on an article about Ukrainian literature.[1]

The truth of the observation never struck Ukrainians more clearly than immediately after their failure of 1917-21. The leading representatives of the Entente displayed such obviously meagre knowledge and understanding of Ukrainian aspirations that all Ukrainians could see plainly why their cause had received so little consideration, in spite of the proclaimed principle of self-determination. From that time on, Ukrainians were keenly conscious of their separation from the rest of Europe and their lack of contact with their neighbors.

The generalization quoted is probably as fallacious as any other, but the two aspects it suggests played a considerable role in shaping Ukrainian attitudes and literary trends. Some Eastern

Reprinted with permission from Miroslav Rechcigl, Jr. (ed.), *Czechoslovakia Past and Present, Vol 2: Essays on the Arts and Sciences* (The Hague: Mouton Publishers, 1968), pp. 1022-1031. This article was originally a paper presented at the Second Congress of the Czechoslovak Society of Arts and Sciences in America, Inc., at Columbia University, 11-13 September 1964.

Ukrainian writers urged their colleagues to orient themselves toward "the civilization of Newton, Goethe, Byron, Darwin and Marx" and, on that foundation, to build a truly Ukrainian concept of communist culture.[2] For Western Ukrainians, to be known in Europe, and to know Europe, was to become part of Europe, assimilating European technical and cultural achievements to further the aspirations toward national identity of a people who had for centuries belonged to Europe.[3]

The post-Versailles order offered Ukrainians few opportunities for significant contacts with Western Europe. Internal developments in the Soviet Union hardly favored any practical application of the idea of an independent "Ukrainian road to socialism," and even less, one based on European culture. The Ukrainians living in Poland, Romania, and Czechoslovakia were also compelled to struggle for their existence as a distinctive national and cultural group. Indeed, "the 1919 settlement roughly reversed the earlier (pre-war) positions, with the single exception that the Ukrainians remained the underdogs."[4]

Here was fertile soil for breeding resentment and revisionism. A Ukrainian nationalist literature, as much concerned with ideology as with art, developed in the early 1920's and reached its maturity in the late 1930's. One aspect of this development is of special interest today: the Prague center was the most productive and influential of the three emigre centers of Ukrainian nationalist literary production; the other two were in Lviv and Warsaw.

To a student of Czech-Ukrainian cultural relations, the statement should not be altogether surprising. Beginning with Havlíček-Borovský, Czech men of letters have sympathized with Ukrainian yearnings for Western Europe and a European cultural *risorgimento*. When the Ukrainian language was suppressed by the czarist regime, Taras Shevchenko's works were published in Prague in 1876. Ivan Franko's activity in Ukrainian-Czech relations found hearty support among Czech intellectuals,[5] and during the Ukrainian war of liberation, Czechoslovakia maintained a friendly neutrality toward the Ukrainian National Republic.

When the Ukrainian effort collapsed, thousands of Ukrainian refugees flocked to Czechoslovakia. Units of the Ukrainian national army, unwilling to surrender to either the Red Army or

the victorious Poles, retreated in military formation into Czechoslovakia. Some refugees came from Vienna; many drifted from
the Polish prisoner-of-war camps. Eventually, Prague, Mecca of
the Slavic emigres, absorbed most of them.

The Czech government treated emigres of various nationalities
generously and supported them financially. The economic
aspect of this aid has been discussed elsewhere.[6] Here, it suffices
to say that the Ukrainian emigres received their share of help
and tried to make the most of it. Soon there were more than
twenty Ukrainian professional, educational, and scholarly
institutions; among them were the well-known Ukrainian Free
University, the Ukrainian Economic Academy (at Poděbrady),
Drahomanov Teachers Institute, Artistic Studio Mako and the
Ukrainian Historical-Philological Association. Ukrainian emigre
scholars held two congresses in Prague (one in 1926, another in
1932) because there they were able to express their views freely
and without any interference from the government.[7] Although
Ukrainian enthusiasm for their national cause is proverbial,
without the financial assistance of the Czechoslovak government,
and without its support in their ventures, many of the Ukrainian
plans would not have been realized.

Most Ukrainian students had lost their best years during the
war and needed retraining in order to cope with modern society.
To take care of the influx of penniless Ukrainian students, the
Czecho-Ukrainian Committee was formed in 1921; Dr. Jaroslav
Bidlo was its chairman, and Dr. Jan Kapras (later minister of
education in the Prague government), its treasurer. The
Committee administered government assistance to Ukrainian
students, of whom there were 1,896 in March 1924, with 1,255 in
Prague alone. "The living conditions for Ukrainian students
were best in Czechoslovakia, where the cultural efforts of the
Ukrainian emigres had the most secure basis," says Symon
Narizhnyi, historian of Ukrainian emigration.[8] By 1931, over
1,660 Ukrainians in Czechoslovakia had received their diplomas
from Czech and Ukrainian institutions of higher learning, and
the graduates succeeded in integrating themselves in the life of
the Republic or that of the neighboring countries. Among them
were some of the writers whose ideological background and artistic efforts we are going to discuss. They had grown up in the free,
expansive atmosphere of Prague's academic life, circumscribed

only by the organizational and ideological limits set by the Ukrainians themselves.

Most of the students were members of the Ukrainian Academic Association, founded in 1919. Soon the Association initiated a central council of all Ukrainian student organizations in Europe (CESUS). Thus, Prague became the hotbed of Ukrainian nationalistic thought; there, plans were laid for the "opening of the window into Europe" and into the sources of Western European culture and socio-political thought.[9] In these efforts, such as they were, the Ukrainians were helped by Czech student organizations. Because of this help, Ukrainian student representatives were able to present their case to the International Students Confederation and to secure for their Association a seat in the assembly of the Confederation (1921). When, at the All-Slavic Student Congresses held in Prague (1922 and 1928), other Slavic delegations attempted to eliminate the Ukrainians by means of the nation-state principle, the Ukrainian representatives received support from the Czech student delegation.[10]

In 1923, the Ukrainian students in Czechoslovakia founded a monthly magazine, *Studentskyi vistnyk* (Student Herald), as a forum for the expression of their ideas. In addition to news and organization affairs, the contents included ideological, social, literary, and historical topics in the late 19th-century tradition of Eastern-European journalism. Its circulation was small, but it reached most of the emigre Ukrainian students in Europe.

Thus the student movement in Prague joined, and to some degree preceded, the nationalist student movement in Lviv. There, another group of Ukrainian nationalist writers began to form around the journal, *Literaturno-naukovyi vistnyk* (The Literary and Learned Herald). That venerable monthly was founded there in 1898 as a scientific and literary publication of the Shevchenko Scientific Society. Mykhailo Hrushevsky, Ivan Franko, and Volodymyr Hnatiuk had made it an outstanding magazine that attracted the best of Ukrainian writers and intellectuals at the beginning of the century. Its significance and influence in the development of Ukrainian literary and political thought was immense.

After the revolution of 1905, when control of the press was somewhat relaxed, publication of *LNV* moved to Kiev, but in 1914 it was suppressed, like all other Ukrainian publications in

Russia. In 1917, Hrushevsky resumed publication of *LNV,* but he was never able to rebuild its former influence and significance.[11]

In 1922, *LNV* was reestablished with financial help from a group of former officers of the Ukrainian National Army, and Dmytro Dontsov became its editor-in-chief. For the next decade, *LNV* became the forum of Ukrainian writers living and working outside the Soviet Union. These poets, novelists, historians, critics, and scientists represented all shades of literary and political views. Soon Dontsov's rightist views were challenged by three venerable Ukrainian democrats then living in Prague, the poet, O. Oles, the historian, Mykhailo Hrushevsky, and the publisher, M. Tyshchenko-Siry.[12] Eventually, Dontsov's views prevailed in *LNV,* and by 1933, he had gained complete control of the publication; it then appeared under the shortened title of *Vistnyk* (The Herald).

Dontsov's ideas were akin to, and partly borrowed from, the ultraconservative French writers, Maurice Barrès and Charles Maurras. Ukrainian liberalism he defined as an "atrophy of the instinct to dominate." He summoned the Ukraine's younger generation to a "reappraisal of values;" a complete break with the "effeminate ideas of the nineteenth century;" the acceptance of the concept that only "the stronger has the right to survive;" the primacy of will over reason. In 1924, he posed a dilemma to his readers: "Unless we cease to behave like a herd of cattle," he said—unless there emerged a group of people able to provide manly leadership—the Ukrainian masses would follow the communists, who seemed able to satisfy them in that respect.[13]

In the reappraisal, the most urgent task of the elite was to free themselves from the tenets of "foreign ideologies." The worst of these was the Tolstoyan philosophy of non-action, or the *sansara* of the Indian philosophers. It was necessary to revive and fortify the energy of the Ukrainian people, to make every Ukrainian conscious of his soil, his race, his traditions, and national group. "In our historic controversy with Muscovy," he said, "we do not combat any particular form of government or empire. What we face is the philosophical concept of the nation-as-conqueror, a messianic nation which, beneath the most diverse transfigurations, will always find expression for that concept."[14]

In the reappraisal of values, and in the regeneration of the

Ukrainian nation, literature should play the chief part. But as Dontsov saw it, Ukrainian literature was struggling through a crisis, its aesthetics crippled by a "worship of only one god, Beauty;" "the god of Energy" was neglected, heroic emotions were rejected, and the truly tragic was missing from Ukrainian art. The only salvation for the Ukrainian people and their literature was a return to the dynamic traditions of the 17th century and the Kievan Rus' period of Ukraine's history. He had no quarrel with the forms of Ukrainian art, but the content, he alleged, was poisoned by Russian and "Eastern" influences.

Now, these were clear-cut statements and slogans, even if they were biased; and they found a responsive audience, especially among the emigre students and all those young Ukrainians who resented the inability of the older liberal generation to reestablish the Ukrainian sovereign state, and who found consolation in the revisionist mood that had begun to creep over Europe. But in terms of literature and aesthetics, Dontsov would have been crying in the wilderness had not the young writers in Prague embraced his ideas as their own.

All that united the group of nationalist writers in Prague was the place where they lived and worked, and their sharing of the hazy *Weltanschauung* known as Ukrainian nationalism.[15] When, in the early 1920's, Dontsov was making his "revivalist" calls from Lviv, the writers of the group were still studying or just making their first steps toward Parnassus. Indeed, some passed away, leaving behind only fiery traces like falling meteors, mere promises of what they might have produced.

Among the latter were Maksym Hryva, Mykola Chyrskyi, and Iurii Darahan. Hryva, once a nationalist insurgent in the northern regions of Ukraine, left only a few poems in *Derzhavna natsiia,* published in Poděbrady. Chyrskyi wrote short dramatic works and poems. But of much greater talent was the other veteran of the Ukrainian national army, Darahan.[16] Like Hryva and Chyrskyi, he began writing poetry in a Polish prisoner-of-war camp; he might be regarded as the founder of the Prague group. His contribution was the poetic infatuation with the Kievan and Galician periods of Ukraine's history which, until then, had been seen from a strictly Populist point of view. Darahan was the first to extol the romanticism of princely statehood and the vitality of Rus-Ukraine. His only collection of poems, *Sahaidak* (The Quiver), appeared just before his untimely death in 1926.

Another "discoverer of our history," as Malaniuk called him, was Oleksa Stefanovych, whose poems show a strange eschatologic mood and little overt nationalism. Although he lived and worked in Prague, Stefanovych actually belongs to the Catholic group of Lviv. In Prague, there appeared two collections of work by this none-too-prolific, but original, writer: *Poezii* (Poems), in 1927, and *Stefanos,* in 1939.

Darahan and Stefanovych, in a way, influenced Oksana Laturynska, who revived the dim Lithuanian period in the history of Volhynia. She "reached accomplishments only attained by exceptional artists. The accomplishment is in her personal style. . . a severe sparsity of words, symbolism, and historicism," says Malaniuk.[17] Moreover, she successfully translated some poems by the Czech poet, Pavel Javor.

O. Olzhych was an archaeologist with a degree from Charles University, and associate editor of the nationalist monthly, *Proboiem,* published in the capital from 1933 till 1943, when it was suppressed by the Nazis. For his anti-Nazi activities, Olzhych was arrested by the Gestapo and tortured to death in the Sachsenhausen concentration camp, in July 1944. The second of his three collections of superb poems, *Vezhi* (Towers), was published in Prague.

Akin to Olzhych in her association with the nationalist group, but at the opposite extreme as an artist, stood Olena Teliha. She studied art in Prague and had begun to publish her poems in *LNV* by 1928. She was a faithful follower of Dontsov's ideas, and never tired of explaining the role of women in developing the new energetic Ukrainian. In 1942, she was arrested by the Gestapo in Kiev and summarily executed, along with other Ukrainian nationalists including her husband, and Ivan Irlavsky, a young Carpatho-Ukrainian whose poems, *Moia vesna* (My Spring), appeared in Prague in 1940. Teliha's ideological views and the aesthetics of her art were undoubtedly formed during her stay in Prague, that true forge of Ukrainian nationalism in the 1920s.

The greatest poet of the period, and "one of the finest craftsmen in the Ukrainian language" today,[18] Evhen Malaniuk, also passed through Czechoslovakia on his way up to the Ukrainian

Parnassus. While still studying for his degree in hydro-engineering at the Ukrainian Economic Academy in Poděbrady, he published his first collection of poems *Stylet i stylos* (Stiletto and Stylus) (1925). Malaniuk was responsible, more than anyone else, for the development in the Prague group of a highly cultured style. His influence was also felt in the Soviet Ukraine; indeed, he served as a spiritual bridge between the Kievan Neoclassicists and the new generation of Ukrainian writers abroad. He also tried his hand at translating the poems of Josef S. Machar[19] and *Písně otroka* by Svatopluk Čech; moreover, he seems to have developed close relations with both Machar and Karel Čapek. Even if his influence seemed to wane in the 1930s (with the rise of Iurii Lypa, O. Olzhych, and Leonid Mosendz), Malaniuk always commanded the respect of all Ukrainian nationalists.

Unlike Malaniuk, who settled eventually in Warsaw, Leonid Mosendz spend most of his writing life in Czechoslovakia. But, like Malaniuk, he obtained his degree (in chemistry) from the Poděbrady Academy and contributed poetry and prose to *Vistnyk* in Lviv. In his short stories, he convincingly depicted human beings in marginal situations—torn between heroism and the weakness of their human nature. During the war, he cooperated with the Ukrainian anti-Nazi and anti-Soviet underground. Mosendz's long novel on a biblical theme *Ostannii prorok* (The Last Prophet), shows the author's disillusionment with the nationalist extremism of the pre-war period.[20]

Ulas Samchuk, a Western Ukrainian who is now in Canada, lived in Czechoslovakia from 1929 to 1939 and studied at the Ukrainian Free University in Prague. Though he was published in *LNV*, he did not see eye-to-eye with Dontsov on many issues. The first part of his trilogy, *Volyn*, and the novel, *Maria*, have been translated into French. *Volyn*, which deals with the life of Ukrainian peasants under two foreign regimes, is the finest novel of the inter-war period and belongs among Ukrainian classics.

Mention should be made of Iurii Lypa, who really belongs to the Warsaw group of Ukrainian nationalist writers, but who made his mark on the outlook of the writers in Prague, as well. His first short story, published in *Studentskyi vistnyk* (in 1927), surprised Ukrainian readers in Czechoslovakia. Vasyl Koroliv, a writer of the older generation, who lived in Prague, commented in dismay: "Our editor-critics do not know their trade; they do not notice Lypa at all. But he is unusually versatile and expert in the Ukrainian folk-style narrative."[21] Lypa certainly proved that Koroliv was right, and he captured the imagination of readers with his incisive essays. True to his ideas, Lypa died in a fight against the Soviets, in the ranks of the Ukrainian Insurgent Army (UPA) in 1944. It may have been because of Lypa's influence that the Prague group, with the passing years, somewhat mollified its attitudes and grew critical of Dontsov's extremism and his "war of all against everybody."

To what degree the atmosphere of the only truly democratic country in central eastern Europe helped to modify the views of the group, and how much the sight of the freely flourishing literary life in Prague spurred on the young Ukrainian writers, it is difficult to tell now. There is not enough supporting material to risk any clear-cut statement. We do not really know whether the young emigres had any regular contacts with Czech literati, and there Ukrainians were emigres, first of all. They were firmly oriented toward the theme, "Ukraine and we,"[22] and were too involved in current Ukrainian events to be able either to follow the path of their Czech colleagues or to "open the window into Europe," as they had intended.

They formed a psychologically insulated group within the body of a foreign, though friendly, nation. They believed, with Malaniuk, that during those periods when a nation is deprived of a political leader, "the poets are her leaders," just as Mickiewicz and Pushkin had envisioned the futures of their respective nations.[23] These "tragic optimists" believed that the regeneration of their people depended on the abandonment of the quietist way of life and on acquiring the energetic approach of Western man. Above all, they believed that the artist should live within his own nationality, while he tried to transform it, and that he must give his life, if need be, for the ideals of his people. And they were true to their word; that cannot be said of some of their ideologist critics.

The most admirable thing about them was that they succeeded in attaining relatively high standards, in spite of, rather than as a result of, their ideology of integral nationalism. Their art grew through the tenets of the doctrine like green grass among forbidding rocks. Perhaps the Prague group was able to save their art from ideological corrosion by unconsciously embracing Malaniuk's view of art, expressed as early as 1923: "Dontsov speaks of literature as a consumer, an exploiter, while we speak of it as artists, as producers. . . ."[24] They contributed substantially to the growth of Ukrainian literature in the period when, as George Luckyj put it, "modern Ukrainian literature came of age."[25]

The Prague group of Ukrainian nationalist writers were little known in Czech society. In this respect, perhaps the group failed to grasp an opportunity—a failure we should not repeat here and now.

There is a long tradition of friendly Czech-Ukrainian relations. Even under communist oppression today, Czechoslovakia and Ukraine manage to find a common language. The Czechoslovak Republic is one of the two nations that have consulates in Kiev; nowadays, Czech translations of Ukrainian writing are the most numerous of all foreign translations.[26] There is also a genuine interest, among readers in Ukraine, in the cultural life of Czechoslovakia. Ukrainians and Czechs abroad should, perhaps, do even more: they could actually supplement the work carried on in their respective countries and, in a way, straighten what is being warped by the communists there.

As far as Ukrainians are concerned, their greatest need today is less "to know Europe and to be known in Europe" than to know their neighbors and be known by them. To know is to understand and appreciate. With this purpose in mind, the author has presented this sketch of the Prague group of Ukrainian nationalist writers as one of the aspects of life in the Czechoslovak Republic of the inter-war period.

REFERENCE NOTES

[1]*La République française,* 523 (April 16, 1873), p. 3. The comment referred to Mykhailo Drahomanov's article on contemporary Ukrainian literature under czarist Russian censorship; the article had appeared in *Revista Europea* earlier in the year.

[2]Mykola Khvylovyi, *Kamo hriadeshy* (Kharkiv, 1929), p. 42.

[3]Borys Krupnytskyi, "Istorychni osnovy evropeizmu Ukrainy,"

Literaturno-naukovyi vistnyk, I, (May, 1948), hereafter cited as *LNV.*

[4]C. A. Macartney, *Problems of the Danube Basin* (Cambridge, 1942), p. 120. Hans Kohn, "The Impact of Pan-Slavism on Central Europe," *Review of Politics,* XXIII, No. 3 (July, 1961), 323.

[5]*Z dejín československo-ukrainských vzťahov* (Bratislava, 1957). Cf. M. M. Mundiak, "František Řehoř i Ukraina," *Mizhslovianski literaturni vzaiemyny* (Kiev, 1958), pp. 279–87.

[6]V. E. Andic, "The Economic Aspects of Aid to Russian and Ukrainian Refugee Scholars in Czechoslovakia," *Journal of Central European Affairs,* XXI, No. 2 (July, 1961), 176–87.

[7]Symon Narizhnyi, *Ukrainska emigratsiia* (Prague, 1942). Cf. Roman S. Holiat, "Short History of the Ukrainian Free University," *Ukrainian Quarterly,* XIX, No. 3 (Autumn, 1963), 204–226.

[8]Narizhnyi, *op. cit.,* p. 72.

[9]M. M., "Pratsia ukrainskoho studentstva sered chuzhyntsiv," *Studentskyi vistnyk,* No. 12 (December, 1925), pp. 7–12.

[10]Narizhnyi, *op. cit.,* pp. 107–111.

[11]V. Doroshenko, "Literaturno-naukovyi vistnyk," *LNV,* Vol. 32, No. 1 (May, 1948), p. 48.

[12]*Ibid.,* pp. 52–53.

[13]D. Dontsov, "Agoniia odnoii doktryny," LNV, Vol. 82 (January, 1924), pp. 56–57.

[14]*LNV,* Vol. 82 (February, 1924), p. 177.

[15]D. Dontsov, *Natsionalism* (Lviv, 1924).

[16]See also a brief review of the writers of the Prague center in *Ukraine: A Concise Encyclopedia,* I (Toronto, 1963), pp. 1060–1063.

[17]E. Malaniuk, "Oksana Laturynska," *Kyiv,* VI, No. 3 (May-June, 1955), 118. For the translations of Javor's poems by Laturynska, see *Porohy,* No. 72–75 (December, 1956), p. 2.

[18]George S. N. Luckyi, "Ukrainian Literature: The Last Twenty-five Years," *Books Abroad,* No. 2 (1956), p. 139.

[19]E. M., "Z liryky J. S. Machara," *Studentskyi vistnyk,* No. 3–4 (1931), p. 2.

[20]Bohdan Kravtsiv, "Leonid Mosendz i ioho *Ostannii prorok,*" *Ostannii prorok* (Toronto, 1960), pp. xxix–xxxi.

[21]Quoted in M. Mukhyn, "Iasnozoryi Iurii," *Kyiv,* IV, No. 1

(Jan.-Feb., 1953), 44.

[22]Yurii Sherekh, "Styli suchasnoi literatury na emigratsii," *MUR* (1946), p. 72.

[23]E. Malaniuk, "Poslannia," *LNV,* Vol. 93 (1926), p. 302.

[24]E. Malaniuk, "Pro dynamizm," *Veselka,* No. 11-12 (1923), pp. 46-47.

[25]Luckyj, *op. cit.,* p. 134.

[26]Bohdan Osadczuk, "Wspólczesna Ukraina," *Kultura* (Paris), No. 5 (1964), p. 83. M. I. Molnar, "Ukrains'ka literatura v Chekhii i Slovachchyni," *Mizhslovians'ki literaturni vzaiemyny* (Kiev, 1958), p. 288; M. I. Molnar, "Ukrainistyka v Chekhoslovachchyni," *Literaturna Ukraina* (Kiev), August 18, 1964.

40

CANADIANS WITH A DIFFERENCE

If the romance between the immigrants from the Ukraine and the Canadian Prairies at the turn of this century has resulted in a reasonable harmonious marriage, it was due to the fact that—fortunately for Canada—the judgement of astute administrators prevailed against that of some opinionated but less-than-clairvoyant editors.

The wooing began with the arrival in Winnipeg of two West Ukrainian farmers, in 1891. Ivan Pylypiw and Vasyl Eleniak went to see first the lands around Yorkton, Saskatchewan, and Calgary, Alberta, before they became enchanted with the farming prospects in southern Manitoba where the Mennonites had made a striking success out of their 15-year-old agricultural venture.

Upon returning to the Austrian-held part of the Ukraine, Pylypiw was jailed for a month for "spreading tales" about the "free and fertile lands in Canada" among the Ukrainian peasants. But the "damage" had been done and nothing could have stopped the land-and-freedom-hungry farmers from going overseas.

The first Ukrainian-Canadian was born at Winnipeg in 1893. But the first Ukrainian rural settlement in Manitoba was founded August 11, 1896, when immigration from the Ukraine to Canada began in earnest. The first Ukrainian school district

Reprinted with permission from *The Montreal Star,* October 10, 1970.

was organized in the area of Dauphin, where now an annual Ukrainian Festival of Manitoba is held, usually in the first days of August. (Over 5,000 Ukrainian-Canadian youth swelled the ranks of the older generation there this year.)

Most of Manitoba

Thus, when Canada entered the First World War conflict, about 100,000 Ukrainians had already settled in the West, with Manitoba taking the bulk of the immigrant wave.

They came in a somewhat subdued mood as their hearts still remained with the people in their own country subjugated by Austria and Russia. And they never ceased thinking of returning, some day, to their Old Country because they saw themselves regarded as a less-than-desirable element in this part of North America. To quote one example of the then prevalent attempts at arousing public opinion against the settlers, here are two excerpts from a Winnipeg newspaper, *The Daily Nor'Wester*:

> The southern Slavs are probably the least promising of all the material that could be selected for nation building... (Dec. 23, 1896).
> By their unintelligent methods of farming they will lower the reputation of the products of the community...and their farms will be a centre from which weeds and animal disease will be disseminated in the fields and herds of their neighbours. (Aug. 3, 1897).

The *Toronto Mail* added much to the stir by spreading a canard story about some 50,000 undesirable Ukrainians coming to Manitoba via the United States.

But the sagacious Clifford Sifton, Minister of Immigration in Sir Wilfrid Laurier's government, held to his belief that the impoverished farmers from the Ukraine were indeed a "good quality." In this he was supported by the president of the Canadian Pacific Railway, Van Horne, and such immigration inspectors as Hugo Carstens who reported: "These people seem to me on the whole very frugal and industrious, and would get along well in this country, if they only had some means to start farming with."

Gradually, the attitude of the populace toward the newcomers began warming up, as they more than fulfilled the expectations of Canada's administrators. Indeed, they became modest but important co-builders of this nation — a fact recognized by one of the present government's spokesmen, Mitchell Sharp: "As a Westerner, born in Winnipeg, whenever I think of my Ukrainian friends I think of the great role (their) people played in opening and developing the West."

At first they received some of the poorest land, refused by the settlers from the British Isles as too uneconomic. But soon they would acquire better land from the discouraged settlers who moved to urban centers or to more profitable occupations. Eventually, the Manitoban Ukrainians, together with those of Alberta and Saskatchewan, came to share in the ownership of about 10 million acres of land.

The inter-war period saw more Ukrainians coming to Canada, and Manitoba absorbed most of these former soldiers, laborers and intelligentsia who vitally strengthened the Ukrainian community there.

Today, out of the half-a-million Ukrainian-Canadians about 115,000 call Manitoba their homeland, with Winnipeg harboring the largest concentration of them — 65,000. Being second only to the Manitobans of British stock as to the percentage (12 percent), the Ukrainians have made their presence felt in every field of that prairie community. Mind you, in 1951 there was only one judge of Ukrainian origin; today there are a number of them, including one woman — Judge Mary Wawrykiw. The first Ukrainian member of the Manitoba legislature was elected in 1913; today, there are seven — two of them cabinet ministers and one the Speaker.

Professional men — doctors, lawyers, pharmacists, engineers, ecologists and university professors — together with businessmen and thousands of highly trained persons in industry and commerce have changed the complexion of the Manitoba Ukrainian community once dominated by farmers. The community has been sending their representatives to the House of Commons and have their spokesman in the Senate — Dr. Paul Yuzyk, a man who was born in Manitoba and wrote a well-documented history of the Ukrainians in that province.

The post-war influx of about 40,000 Ukrainians transformed

Manitoba into a central Ukrainian region in Canada and Winnipeg into a virtual capital of this ethnic group.[1]

No wonder then that in that city a monument to Taras Shevchenko, the greatest Ukrainian poet-revolutionary, was erected on the grounds of the Provincial Legislature.

When the unveiling of the monument took place in July, 1961, (with Canada's Prime Minister John Diefenbaker taking part in this partly tri-lingual ceremony), I had an ample opportunity to observe the impact of the event on the Manitoba Ukrainians, old and young alike. A former rural school teacher told me: "This is the day that I have become a full-fledged citizen of Canada, in fact and not only in form, as one of our own people is being recognized as equal with the English and French men of culture."

And Capt. Stephen Pawluk expressed the feelings of the thousands of Manitoba Ukrainian war veterans at their convention held the day before: "This is our land and our country because we were born here, our ancestors rest in peace here, in the soil they had been toiling on and which we defended in two World Wars. And our cultural heritage is being respected by our fellow-citizens."

To be sure, in the First World War about 10,000 Ukrainian Canadians joined the Canadian force overseas. In the Second World War, the same number of Ukrainians from Manitoba alone fought under the Red Ensign for the cause of Canada, along with over 30,000 Ukrainians from other provinces. And they did this in spite of their aversion to the fact that one of Canada's allies was Soviet Russia, the oppressor of the Ukraine.

By sharing in the destinies of all Canadians, the Manitoba Ukrainians have found a good response among the multi-lingual citizens of the province. Often, there is a much better rapport between, let's say, the Polish-Canadians and Ukrainian-Canadians than there ever was between their grandparents when those lived side by side in East Europe. Inter-marriages with other ethnic groups are a common occurrence as well as the cases where members of such mixed families speak both their languages passably.

From my encounters with Manitobans of various ethnic extractions, I have got an impression that they feel first of all Canadian. Only then and there I understood the sentiments of a statement made by Senator Yuzyk last year in Winnipeg: he professed to never be able to accept that he be English or French but that he felt a Canadian first and above all. These sentiments are shared by most of the Manitobans, and they make them Canadians with a difference. Their Canadian patriotism is undiluted by the reminiscence of being the descendants of some great power; and it is devoid of the ridiculous anti-Americanism which spoils the stature of many a Canadian in the non-prairie provinces.

But what worries many a Manitoban of Ukrainian origin, is the question of the preservation of their culture to which their language is the essential key. Their hopes were raised in 1965, when the then Quebec Premier Jean Lesage made a sincere attempt at establishing French-Ukrainian cooperation in the field of teaching the two languages in the two provinces.

Now, the Manitoba Ukrainians are asking to have implemented the recommendations of the Fourth Report of the B and B Commission, no matter how limited these appear to them.[2] Fortunately, once again Canada seems to have astute administrators whose judgment may yet prevail against the opinionated editors of some Western Canadian newspapers.

Forum

The B and B Commission's recommendations were discussed at the forum of the Ukrainian Canadian Committee at Winnipeg last July, in the presence of Robert Stanbury, minister responsible for citizenship. The Ukrainian spokesmen stressed the point that they did not wish to become — as Dr. I. Hlynka put it — "pawns in the struggle between French and English Canadians."

But their approach to the issue is both constructive and optimistic as they put great store on the vitality of their own ethnic group as well as on the wisdom of Canada's leaders. "Professional and business people, and — what is more important, students — are joining our organized community in ever larger numbers. And no matter how assimilated they may be into the social fabric of Canadian life they still want to preserve and develop Ukrainian culture and language," said Dr. S. Kalba, executive director of the committee, while explaining to me the significance of the "Manitoba Cultural Mosaic Congress" to be convened at Winnipeg next week.

This congress, arranged by the federal and Manitoba governments, is promising to become the most effective in-depth study ever undertaken in Canada of the methods of promoting and preserving multi-cultural values. Manitoba Ukrainians are going to play an important part in this effort thus proving once again the sagacity of the builders of this nation who had envisaged the country as a free land of a free people for all the freedom-loving people of every cultural background sharing in its tremendous opportunities.

REFERENCE NOTES

[1]According to the 1971 census, there were in Canada 580,000 Canadians of Ukrainian origin, 114,000 of them living in Manitoba.

[2]In Volume IV of its report, the Royal Commission on Bilingualism and Biculturalism reported on the economic, social, and political position in the life of Canada of those groups other than of British or French origin and made recommendations for its strengthening.

41

A LIFE OF DISTINCTION

The Gazette Editor's Note: *How does a Ukrainian-Canadian feel about living and working in Quebec? What does he feel about bilingualism and biculturalism and the French fact? Most importantly, what does he feel about his own identity?*

Roman Rakhmanny is a Ukrainian-Canadian journalist who has lived in Quebec many years. His articles on East European subjects appear in Ukrainian, English and French-language publications in Canada.

There are more than 500,000 Ukrainian-Canadians in Canada, and 15,000 in Montreal.

We are Quebecers.

This is the prevalent mood among Ukrainian-Canadians living in this beautiful province and seems by no means unique. Other ethnic groups in Quebec take the same stance.

In the same manner, the Ukrainian-Canadians of Manitoba are Manitobans, those in Alberta or Ontario are first of all Albertans or Ontarians respectively.

What else could be expected in such a huge country as Canada with its different geographic and climatic regions, with a population of numerous cultural backgrounds, all subjected to different trends and pressures?

Reprinted with permission from *The Gazette* (Montreal), January 20, 1972, where it appeared under the title "Ukrainian-Canadians Pin Hopes on Life of Distinction, but Without Separatism."

To develop their own region into a better place to live is the desire closest to the hearts of the people in this province.

Without diminishing loyalty to Canada as a whole, any segment of the population in a given province can and should have a full life only by integrating into both provincial and municipal activities and by accepting sincerely the particular way of life of that region.

Participation

Thus, a Ukrainian-Canadian in Quebec will have a full life only through his participation in the affairs, events and interests of Quebec — be they economic, political or cultural. This includes also an intrinsic recognition of the aspirations of the Quebecois aimed at preserving and developing their language, their culture and their specific political identity as well.

But does a Ukrainian-Canadian have such an opportunity in a dignified manner? Does he feel really wanted and accepted by the French-speaking society here? And, for that matter, is he expected to take his rightful place in developing this particular province into a recognized unit with a special rights and a distinctive status within the Confederation?

Unfortunately, as of now, the answer to these important questions must be no.

As used to be the case in the English-speaking provinces up to the early 1950s, a Ukrainian-Canadian in Quebec still lives behind a "glass curtain of *desinteressement*."

All that is expected from him is (as it was in other provinces, 20 years ago) to work, to produce goods, to consume, and thus create more opportunities for the majority of the population.

Moreover, the more the fighting mood envelopes the younger generation of the French-language community, the more often one hears of old, familiar cry for assimilation of third-language groups.

Persecutions

Such a demand on the part of those who feel endangered by the 250-million strong English-speaking North Americans is more than strange to these small ethnic groups. Most of their members still remember cultural, religious, and political persecutions they or their kin suffered in Europe.

The calls for an outright assimilation of the third-language groups in this province puts before them a weird dilemma: either to become French-speaking or English-speaking persons without any right to preserve and develop individual characteristics of their own particular background.

Such a right means a great deal to any human being, even if the person may never exercise the right. It grants him a very intimate instrument of communication and self-expression as represented by the particular language and traditional customs of his original nationality. It was the very lack of such right in their own countries that prompted parents and grandparents of the third-language citizens of Canada to settle in this country.

What these settlers, and later on other immigrants, expected to find here was not merely a larger or tastier piece of their daily bread which could be consumed in more comfortable surroundings. A human being seldom wants to live by bread alone.

Consequently, the immigrants from Eastern Europe came here in search of equal opportunities both for themselves and their descendants, because these were denied to them in their own countries.

More than anything else, these immigrants to Canada desired a chance to develop themselves into complete human beings who, while being full-fledged citizens of this country, would preserve their own cultural heritage that would be respected and, perhaps, even utilized by their co-citizens for the common good.

No Separatism

No third-language group in Canada has ever aspired to establish here "a nation of its own." None ever aimed at taking over a slice of this country or developing it for its own exclusive use.

"You won't find another Ukraine in the whole world," Taras

Shevchenko, the great Ukrainian poet and patriot of 100 years ago warned his countrymen.

Every Ukrainian-Canadian believes this statement to be valid and applicable today. Thus, what the Ukrainian-Canadians desired here was a decent place to live in dignity and harmony with the people who pioneered this wilderness land.

The average Ukrainian-Canadian in Quebec is fully aware of, and has a great admiration for, the pioneer achievement of the Quebecois, for their development of their own way of life.

That they have achieved this on a continent dominated by the English has only strengthened our admiration.

But the admiration the Ukrainian-Canadians have for the Quebecois achievement results from a peculiar affinity they feel with the people of Quebec.

From the Plains of Abraham has arisen a distinctive Franco-Canadian people with specific culture and political identity of its own. This could have happened only within the peculiar English sphere of influence, in which fair play is practiced more often than in any other colonial empire.

It is worth noting, that in this context, the Ukraine lost its political autonomy and was deprived by Russia of its own legal institutions at about the same time as New France became a British dependency — in 1764. Yet, even today the Ukraine — formally a founding member of the United Nations — has not been able to regain as much of its autonomy in its internal affairs as Quebec had in 1867.

And the Ukrainians in the Ukrainian Soviet Socialist Republic, all appearances to the contrary, have much less freedom and fewer opportunities than the Ukrainian-Canadians in Quebec.

More French

While comparing the two unequal entities, and while observing the economic, cultural and psychological developments in Quebec today, the Ukrainians in this province are willing to say together with the rest of the population here: "We are Quebecers indeed."

More and more of them are becoming able to express themselves and work in French. More and more are acquiring a deeper insight into the aspirations of their French-Canadian co-citizens.

But does the French-Canadian society at large, comprehend this frame of mind of the people who never expected to face the present-day dilemma: either become English or French-speaking citizens of Canada with no chance to preserve your own cultural identity.

It seems that the average Quebecois, and the elite of this French speaking province as well, are too involved in their own affairs to notice this plight of a large segment of Canada's population.

But the fact is that the better the conditions for preservation of the so-called ethnic cultural heritage in Quebec, the stronger will be the bonds connecting these third-language groups to the destinies of the province.

42

THE CANADIAN OPTION FOR 1975

AND BEYOND:

UNITY THROUGH DIVERSITY

As we are about to enter the final quarter of the 20th century, two trends make themselves more and more evident in various parts of the world. Humane nationalism and socio-political diversity are replacing the great-state nationalism, and the imperial concepts of unity through uniformity, respectively. The cumulative result of these two inter-acting forces is reflected both in the rise of minorities and the emergence of hitherto "invisible nations."

Contrary to all the earlier predictions by publicists, politicians and scholars, almost every minority is holding its ground as tenaciously in the age of nuclear energy and space flights as it did in the earlier, less technological centuries. Nowadays, scholars at last concede that in spite of all the technology and rational organization modern states possess, conflicts in various parts of the world are still "tribal" rather than ideological. That is why world opinion is compelled to recognize, no matter how reluctantly, the existence of such "written off" minorities as the Crimean Tartars, the Soviet Jews, the Volga Germans, the

The keynote address delivered at the Montreal Conference on "The Future of Ukrainian-Canadians in Quebec," June 10, 1972.

people of Biafra and Bangladesh along with the more visible nationalities such as Belorussians and Ukrainians.

To be sure, forces of reaction are still waging a strong rear-guard action. They find their main support in the innate inertia which causes almost every society in any region and at any time to lean backwards and oppose the forward moving forces of the new age. That is why the idea that (to quote James A. Froude) "the superior part has a natural right to govern" and "the inferior part has a right to be governed",[1] still survives in most majority-societies. It is usually accompanied, and sustained, by a prevalent pseudo-scholarly practice of the majority ethnocultural groups to describe themselves in universalist terms while reducing "ethnicity" to a term descriptive of minorities and irregularities only — that is, of *deviations from the norm.*

(Whenever I use the term "ethnic" here, I refer to a nationality in the sense it is being more and more referred to by sociologists.)

Fortunately, new ideas (as that original economist Keynes found) have a strange and beneficial habit of spreading by osmosis — the tendency of fluids to pass through porous partitions and become diffused through each other; in our case, the two fluids are the two different streams of human thinking. If such ideas contain the stuff of life, they eventually inseminate the human mind and prompt a society to get rid of its outdated concepts.

We are witnessing such processes in many regions of the world where ethnic and other minorities become noticeable, respectable and acceptable; some of them are well on their way to reasserting themselves as equals among the majority-nationalities.

People of Ukrainian civilization are in the midst of that confrontation between the two camps — that of progress and that of reaction — both in Ukraine itself and in the countries of their settlement. Since they have been involved in their own struggle for identity for about two centuries, there would seem to be hardly anything new for them in the process.

But there is something essentially new and encouraging indeed. It is an unusually favorable situation for all the people interested in a more humane concept of inter-ethnic relations, which is evolving primarily here, in Canada. This confederate country composed of various ethnocultural entities is trying to attain two goals at the same time: to establish a harmonious all-Canada multicultural society which would be unified in spite of the diversity of its demography, and while doing so, to make its own imprint on the surrounding mankind within which the battle for human rights is far from having been won yet.

In that double-pronged effort, in which Ukrainian-Canadians are certainly more than mere spectators, many people are tempted by some pace-slowing desires. To quote Prime Minister Pierre Trudeau, there is this desire "either to abandon the past or to resist tenaciously anything unfamiliar."[2] While either course would be disastrous to opt for by any society, the third option is even more perilous because of its superficial acceptability: it is to remain comfortable without budging from the position the group of citizens had occupied long ago or which it acquired by the sheer inertia of negative traditionalism.

Well, none of us here wants to become as fossilized as those who simply have chosen to sit on their legacy. Neither do we intend to oppose new constructive trends or remain satisfied with the past which is still being presented to us as the only plausible solution of the life complexities on the North American continent.

What is then *the past* in this case of ours — that of Canadian citizens and residents of Quebec at the same time?

Essentially, this past is the old worn-out image of Canada as consisting of British institutions alone with the Anglo-Saxon element dominating the political, cultural and economic life of the population, with individualistic puritan-based approach to beliefs, and an immigration policy trimmed to the principle of "the natural selection of immigrants with the same qualities."

Such a concept of Canada, fortunately opposed by as many citizens of this country as it is cherished, still prompts Canadians of British background to view Canada's population as if it were composed of two unequal groups of citizens: the Canadians and the ethnics. By the same token, a Scandinavian immigrant regards himself and is tolerated by the majority group as a regular citizen without ethnic label. But a Ukrainian, Polish or Slovak Canadian remains an "ethnic" in spite of being a descendant of Canada-born parents.

It is obvious that any further continuation of the belief that ethnicity is descriptive of "deviation from the norm" rather than of distinctive nationality would only strengthen the psychological barriers dividing the two segments of Canadian citizens. These barriers are felt as visible signs of discrimination especially today when Ukrainian-Canadians, for one, are more than 80 percent Canada-born and are aware of the fact that thousands of their kinsmen fought in two world wars for the interests of Canada as their native country.

Thus, it is almost a truism to say that there has been an urgent need for a new concept of Canadianism, one that would manifest itself by a new sensitivity on the part of every Canadian as to his ethno-cultural background. Nevertheless, it is useful to reaffirm once again some obvious truths.

First, that all Canadians are immigrants or their descendants.

(While we accord the title of indigenous Canadians to Eskimos and Indians, this is only a recognition of these people being the original settlers on this continent. But to be a truly indigenous Canadian in the contemporary meaning of the term requires much more than nomadic or even settled residence on a given territory. It requires a conscious effort on a people's part to acquire and develop their own socio-political identity under the given name and within their own cultural and economic institutions. In that respect, only French-Canadians have a justified claim to call themselves a distinctive "nation," in the French or continental European meaning of the term.)

Second, most Canadians are descendants of immigrants who, at a certain point in their history, were either defeated or oppressed minorities.

Many Maritimers and Ontarians trace their origin to the United Empire Loyalists, the people who were expelled from the American colonies when these had chosen to secede from the British Kingdom. French-Canadians were conquered by the British and found themselves in the position of a minority. Ukrainians came to Canada to find freedom they did not have in their own country within the Austro-Hungarian and Russian empires. So did the Poles who also searched for more human conditions because of the same reasons. The German-speaking and Russian non-conformists were looking for a place where they could practice their own beliefs without any state interference.

Our conclusion then is as obvious as are the two premises.

There is hardly any good reason for clinging today to the old concept of Canada as it had been formed under the influence of the British political concept in which state and nation became interchangeable terms. One should not forget that the concept has been solidified here by the melting-pot ideas imported from the United States, the very country many a would-be Canadian shied away from because of its growing assimilatory practices.

But being realistic, as we are trying to be, we must also be aware of two important factors which continue to favor the retention of this concept in the minds of our majority co-citizens.

To begin with, there is geography.

Distances and climate create regions and regionally-minded people. The regionalism of the British Columbians is easily noticed and understood. But the existence of other regional enclaves — such as Anglo-Saxon Toronto or Southwest Ontario — may escape the attention of many a Canadian. Yet, the regional thinking is as much alive there as it used to be about 50 years ago in spite of the influx of European and other immigrants. Indeed, various groups of our population in one and the same province may, and often do, live separated from one another by the distances of race, origin, religion, cultural and political traditions or even socio-economic standing.

Consequently, Canada of the early 1970s still resembles a picturesque archipelago of human islands which exist in self-contained solitudes. Out of necessity, federal authorities seem to be cast more and more into the role of a sea captain who, by his regular visits to various islands, tries to keep communications open among them and encourages those who seem to be, or feel, neglected or discriminated against. It is only fair to admit that nowadays more and more ships of mutual contact and information reach the shores of these communities thanks to the modernized system of our government and the existence of developed mass media.

Nevertheless, these macro- and micro-societies retain a great deal of their insular character no matter what their designation is — be it British-Canadians, French-Canadians or any of the "others." Therefore, Mr. Trudeau hardly exaggerated when he said recently in Toronto:

"In this age of universal literacy, of professional communicators and electronic wizardry, a Canadian living in Nanaimo,

B.C., understands less of his fellow citizen in Sherbrooke, Que., than did a Spartan of events at Carthage."[3]

If this is true, as I believe it to be, then how much less by comparison does a Canadian of British or French stock know about his fellow citizens of Ukrainian, Polish, Czech, Greek, Italian or Serbian origin even though they may live in the same city or town?

But this regionalism — in geographic and psychological meanings — has been steadily intensified by the somewhat static constitution of Canada, the B.N.A. Act. It deals essentially with group rights rather than with individuals and their human rights.[4]

(By stating this, I do not mean we should blame the Fathers of Confederation for not having foreseen the complex demographic structure Canada would acquire a century later. And Ukrainian immigrants and their descendants in particular would refrain from raising such a charge, for the simple reason that it was under that "static constitution" that Canada gave them a better chance to live in freedom and dignity than they would have had on the Ukrainian territory under any of the foreign regimes).

But the fact remains that today's needs of Canada's population, as it developed over the last century, are essentially different from those in 1867. It is being widely felt that an important element is missing in our constitutional system and in our socio-political infrastructure because of that difference. What is needed is a deliberate stress on the rights of an individual citizen without regard to his ethnocultural background, with written-in guarantees for — and a practical acceptance by the majority — of a free use he can make of the total sum of his possibilities for becoming a complete person in a community of equal citizens.

Well, there is more practical sense to this statement than meets the eye. This postulate is deeply rooted in a fact of life fairly recently re-discovered by social sciences. It appears that "man has no other way to cope with the reality in which he finds himself, than by differentiating it." Thus, according to a sociologist, Professor Harold Isaacs, basic group identity "is not merely related to a need to be special, or unique, or different from others; but is fundamental to an individual's sense of *belongingness* and the level of his self-esteem." From works by such prominent linguists and anthropologists as Noam Chomsky and Claude Levi-Strauss respectively, one concludes that diversity is indeed "structured into the human experience itself."[5]

It is to be regretted then that the idea of "unity through uniformity" still finds a wide acceptance among Canadians. To an editorial writer on the west coast, "a pure, frank and unadulterated Canadianism" still seems to be superior to any multiculturalism even though the latter may grant a more dignified position to every individual citizen of any ethnocultural background.[6] Recently, the *Globe and Mail* editorialized on the protest by the vice-chairman of the Etobicoke Board of Education in Toronto against the Board's decision to permit a course in Ukrainian at Royal York Collegiate. That official argued: "If one ethnic group gets its language taught, there is no way we could say no to others."[7]

That educator still clings to the idea of compulsory uniformity in the same manner as his predecessors did in relation to the French language and culture in Canada a decade or so ago.

The two quoted instances from among many illustrate the ambivalence of the English-speaking majority of our citizens who extoll values of human rights on United Nations Day, demand granting unimpeded cultural development to any minority in other countries but themselves are torn by doubts and fears whenever similar rights are demanded by their own co-citizens.

Although enlightened in many other respects, Canadian English-language papers would not bother quoting from editorials in Ukrainian, Polish, German or Italian papers here though even these may comment reasonably on essential all-Canadian or provincial issues. The language is not the sole obstacle holding them back; it is rather the belief that the ethnic papers are "a deviation from the norm" and will soon disappear anyway. Perhaps they will cease to exist some day, as some English-language newspaper enterprises disappear from time to time; but as of now, the ethnic papers do represent a living, a numerous and an active part of the Canadian public opinion.

As to other mass media, these appear to be opposed to the B & B Commission's recommendation that the ethnic groups be given a chance to produce and receive programs in their own languages by means of modern technical arrangements.

In theory, thus, Canada has rejected the American melting

pot concept years ago. But in fact, pressure to conform is strong and the survival of other cultures is questionable.

Hence the growing craving for constitutional guarantees and public recognition felt so painfully by both the immigrants and their descendants. Hence the numerous cases of rejection of their ethnicity by immigrants' children while in their formative years. Hence the frustration they feel after having realized their own ambivalence in their adult age. Hence the striking cases of eventual returning to the "ethnic roots" by many of them in later years or by those in the second and third generations. All that combines to produce an unsteady citizenship, a kind of "dead souls" with the citizenship certificates in their pockets but ever ready to exchange these for another country's citizenship documents as soon as an opportunity knocks at their door.

Obviously, something had to be done, and quickly, if the erosion of Canadian citizenship was to be stopped. Listening to the voices of the young who had been clamoring for such a change, Parliament endorsed unanimously—in principle at least—the policy of multiculturalism proposed by the Trudeau Government of October 8, 1971.[8]

Since then we have heard and read a great deal about the policy, its benefits and shortcomings. The Ukrainian-Canadian point of view has been presented, in its natural variety, by a number of authors and organizations, including the students. For our purpose here, I must say briefly this:

In spite of all its shortcomings and temporary limitations, pointed out by our critics, the policy represents an important step forward on the road to Canadian citizenship with a more human face. For the first time in Canada's history, the non-English and non-French Canadians are being officially recognized as human beings whose cultural background is as valuable as that of the two "founding nations;" and because of that their cultural development deserves a legitimate support from this nation's treasury.

Modest as it is, the aid means much more than the actual amount of money assigned for ethnocultural projects. In fact, it is a recognition of the diversity itself which exists in our midst in spite of the pressure for conformity of modern technology and economy. It also helps re-vindicate the faith our ancestors had in this country in which they hoped to find personal freedom and prosperous life in dignity. Those hopes included, of course, the right to teach their children their language, with the given province concurring in the effort by administrative and financial measures, as was the case in Manitoba up to 1916.[9]

One might imagine the frustration felt by these people upon seeing their hopes turn into dust. That anticipation is behind the very acute sensitiveness of the "ethnics" to every sign of recognition or rejection of their cultural roots and achievements by the majority. The feeling of inferiority acquired in that painful process by the descendants of these immigrants is responsible for both the dejection felt by many among them and the demands, sometimes overstressed, to recognize them in words and deeds as fullfledged citizens; the feelings and the demands often puzzle the Anglo-Saxon majority as they would puzzle any dominant majority in any multinational country.

If only to free these people of their feeling of inferiority, as human beings, it would have been worthwhile to initiate a policy of multiculturalism; because such a policy is a manifest proof of the changing character of Canadian citizenship in step with the changing times. In this way, an end may be put to the division of Canada's citizens into two classes — the true Canadians and the ethnics. Provided, the words of the policy will be translated into action and find their reflection in Canada's citizenship requirements, the right to vote and stand for election, in census practices, in civil service employment, etc.

Seen in these terms, the policy of multiculturalism should be instrumental in changing the prevailing mood within the two majorities. As of now, however, both public opinions — English and French — look somewhat askance at the policy of multiculturalism, though for different reasons.

The English majority regards the multicultural policy as merely another maneuver of the party which wants to remain in power. In addition, there is a latent feeling of underestimation of the people of so-called foreign cultures. Thus, the majority simply refuses to discuss the issue of multiculturalism in a serious manner and treats the issue as non-existent or menial at best.

The French-speaking majority is concerned lest the Anglophone element in this dual confederation overwhelms, numerically and politically, the French element by means of the "bought off ethnics".

Neither objection should be underestimated by us because both rest on past experiences and on the ambivalence of Canadian politics. Ethnic voters had been placated in one way or another before every election, and not only in this country alone. The French-Canadians used to be balanced and contained with the help of immigrants — those "similar to the basic strain" and those from other nationalities. The newest figures on the 1971 census imply that the number of French-speaking persons has declined even in Quebec province. Small as it is, the decline intensifies the concern of the French-Canadian public as to its chance of surviving in the English-language ocean of North America.

These are the facts of life the Ukrainian-Canadians must be aware of in order to be able to act reasonably and practically toward the attainment of the objective which they have set before themselves, and which is envisioned as desirable by Canada's government as well.

Indeed, there exists a considerable amount of good will in the governmental circles towards finding a satisfactory solution to Canada's multi-ethnic problems. Some understanding is not lacking in the better informed segments of the two majorities either. But these segments are too weak yet to call the tune. That is why a great deal will depend on what use the third-language groups will make of the initial framework of the multicultural policy and to what degree they will be able to expand and upgrade it.

Numerous papers on multiculturalism by Ukrainian-Canadian authors — especially the elaborate essays by Senator Paul Yuzyk, Professor J. Rudnyckyj, Professor M. R. Lupul — have already contributed to the purpose.[10] Without prejudicing the rightful demands expressed in all these papers, I feel somewhat concerned with one feature latent in them: much too great a reliance on, and belief in, the change by a governmental decree. They seem to believe solely in the change from above. But our democratic system, and the age we are living in, calls for strong and sustained initiatives from below. What is needed, is an ever-growing awareness among the average Ukrainian-Canadians that the desired change would come first of all through their direct participation in every sector of this country's life, even in a direct competition with other co-citizens. No governmental decree, no parliamentary law and no constitutional guarantee will be enough to save our ethnocultural group from extinction if there won't be enough young people getting involved in the Ukrainian-Canadian cause and letting our presence felt in political parties, in economic and cultural enterprises, in federal and provincial fields of thought and action.

Herein lies the significance of such conferences as this one. They should help us in preparing ourselves for such an action from below without limiting ourselves to our rightful demands and proposals for action by federal and provincial authorities. But this means also a great deal of soul-searching and as much tearing down of our own outdated concepts and prejudices as concomitant acquisition of new ideas and new, positive approaches.

If so, then any concept of unity through uniformity (that is, through negative assimilation) is a costly proposition to any multi-ethnic society. All the attempts at destroying diversity lead to linguicide and often to genocide with a subsequent impoverishment of mankind itself. Thus, the well-known poetic words of John Donne from the 17th century acquire today a new and very modern meaning: "Any man's death diminishes me, because I am involved in Mankinde; And therefore never send to know for whom the bell tolls; It tolls for thee."

Of paramount importance is to realize the fact that our demands for recognition as a viable minority are based on the needs of human nature as understood and accepted by recent scholarly research. These demands are necessary, dignified and rightful because they are proof—often the only one possible—that a given ethnocultural group refuses to commit a voluntary mass suicide.

It means that our aspirations to be humanly different are not a sentiment cherished by old immigrants alone; neither is it the wishful thinking of a people who are not able to integrate themselves in the modern developed society, as it is often claimed by the spokesmen of the governments in various centralist states. No, we have been integrated in this country for over half-a-century, perhaps more sincerely than even some immigrants from the British Isles. Some of our predecessors built Canada in the regions where Canada had existed in name only.

Consequently, the Ukrainian-Canadians (individually and collectively) must recover their self-esteem by getting rid of their useless receptiveness to the ideas of negative assimilation. Many a good Ukrainian, Pole, Slovak or Italian went astray because he succumbed to the temptations of pseudo-universality and to the pressure from those who advocated a pseudo-scholarly argument that an immigrant is supposed to discard his own identity for the sake of a superior majority. Many a dead soul had been thus manufactured also in this country during the period of an official immigration policy based on negative assimilation. But neither Canada nor Quebec would profit from such dead-soul citizens, particularly in the epoch of the resurgence of minorities and invisible nationalities.

To achieve a higher standard of Canadian citizenship — the citizenship with a more human face — we ourselves must preserve and develop our ethnocultural educational facilities, our voluntary organizations, our churches, our traditional gatherings and customs, as well as our press. These institutions must regain their rightful place in our minds, as being useful and honorable instruments of human self-expression. Even the term "ethnic cultural ghetto" must be rehabilitated to mean what it truly is: a fertile ground for bringing up healthy individuals who, in their mature age, won't be chasing psychiatrists as do all the dead souls. It is regrettable that for too long they have been the butts of sarcastic remarks by those cynics among us who had been steeped in assimilatory practices. In that respect, our intellectuals must carry out a great deal of re-thinking.

To the timid ones who are staggering under the weight of the argument that such an approach would create a new Tower of Babel here, we must say the following:

On the contrary, by giving an individual citizen as much sovereignty in his cultural-linguistic development as he can reasonably manage, we would open up most of the enclosures which had been erected around each minority exactly because of the lack of true cultural equality among our citizens. In the new conditions which are being created now with the aid from our governments (federal and some provincial), an individual of each culture should feel safe to take a voluntary swim to another cultural island without any qualms that he would betray his own group; and he may return at any time to his group, for some constructive activities there, without being regarded by the majority as a person that is stepping down from a higher plateau.

There is also an economic aspect involved in the concept as this approach would create job opportunities for the young within their own open ethnocultural communities. These are, in fact, developed cultural and economic microcosms which are able to support a large number of talented and well-educated social workers, teachers, librarians, organizers, artists, editors, radio and TV specialists. As of now, the inferiority stigma, attached to every ethnic group by the majority-society as much as by the ethnic groups themselves, tends to keep quite a few young people from getting involved on a full-time basis in their ethnic institutions and ventures. The regained status by ethnicity itself should encourage the young people to engage themselves in the field they had always felt they could excell in and improve upon.

Canadian federal and some provincial leaders have already contributed to creating the preconditions conducive to such a full participation of all citizens in this nation's life as equals and mutually respected. The Report of the Special Joint Committee of the Senate and the House of Commons on the Constitution of Canada specifically recommends that "a new Constitution should recognize in the preamble that Canada is multicultural rather than bicultural or unicultural." The third languages of Canada ought to receive both provincial recognition and a federal guarantee in the form of "an umbrella provision in the Constitution to give them their due acknowledgement as one of the constituent elements of our country, ethnically and linguistically."[11]

These recommendations, combined with the official policy of multiculturalism which is based on the Report of the B & B Commission (Volume Four), ought to spur on the public opinion of the two majorities to re-thinking the desirability of uniformity. But the main burden of achieving that change will fall, I am afraid, again on the ethnocultural minorities themselves, especially on provincial levels. There, in each province, our interests are touched upon more directly and more regularly than in the federal scope of government; and there we must come out with some positive programs of action, we must make our presence felt.

This requires at least two basic ideas to direct our own thinking.

First, our own aspirations and demands must form part of

similar aspirations and demands of all other ethnocultural groups. They must be rooted in the principle of human rights for every group regardless of their size. Consequently, it would be advisable to refrain from making much ado about the number of Ukrainian-Canadians as a fact entitling them to some special consideration within the framework of multiculturalism. Even if there were 500 Ukrainian-Canadians, instead of 500 thousand, they would, and should have to, press for the same needs for human rights and constitutional guarantees and would have the same aspirations for equality with the majority-citizens as they do today as one of the larger ethnocultural groups.

This means that we must lend our unqualified support to the aspirations of every minority group in this country no matter what size the group is.

Second, we must acquire—and show—a sincere understanding of the situation our majority groups are in. And we should contribute to solving their problems or reaching their own goals because we are involved in their destinies as well.

This proposition brings us to the crucial, and somewhat neglected issue of the Ukrainian-Canadians vis-a-vis the French fact in Canada as a whole and in Quebec in particular. Within each of the two groups there do exist various preconceived ideas about one another, and some prejudices are not lacking either. Most of them are harmful to cooperation and hardly do any justice to the better qualities of each group and their individual members. Without going into details, which could and should be dealt with on another forum, I would rather confront you with a Kiplingian question. In his well-known poem "The English Flag", Rudyard Kipling wrote: "And what should they know of England who only England know?"

Applied to our own situation, that line may run like this: "And what should they know of Ukraine who only Ukraine know?"

If we continue to be preoccupied, as we are, with the Ukrainian issue alone, we won't be able to grasp the complexity of our neighbor's problem. And more often than not we *do* miss some essential points because our own issues loom so large in front of our eyes—often without any connection with the surrounding reality. While the majority society is a loser in this proposition, it is not the only one: the loss in good relations is ours as well because, for one, the Ukrainian-Canadian problem may have been taken out of the contemporary context by our isolationist attitudes and practices.

If we want to improve our own situation and put our relations with the French-Canadians on a practical level, we had better remind ourselves of some basic facts concerning the role of our French-speaking co-citizens.

To begin with, let's say to ourselves: Thank God there are the citizens who call themselves French-Canadians. Without them, and without their problem of preserving their linguistic and cultural identity, the Ukrainian or any other ethnocultural group in Canada would have faced almost insurmountable difficulties in surviving under the life conditions of English-speaking North America. Thanks to the successful self-assertion of the French-Canadians, this Confederation is on its way to becoming a bilingual country in practice, and it has begun evolving a concept of multicultural society as well.

Another fact, often forgotten by the French-Canadians themselves, is that it was the French who pioneered education in every province — from Newfoundland to British Columbia. Logically, one should expect from our contemporary French-speaking co-citizens a similar pioneer spirit in bridging all the different micro-worlds in this country by means of their language and educational facilities, and in a progressive manner corresponding to the new demographic face of the Confederation.

But above all, the Ukrainian-Canadians must recognize the fact that the French-Canadians are not as any other ethnocultural group of Canada's population, be it the English, the Scots, the Irish, the Ukrainians, the Italians or any other. Moreover, Quebec is not a province like any other province.

It means that we ought to recognize in practice now what we have known in our hearts all the time to be true—that this is a distinctive people with its own language and a viable culture practised in every day life and not in letters or for entertainment alone. This province is populated by over 80 percent French-speaking majority which elects its own legislators and administrators within its own constitutional and judicial systems; and it possesses an economic personality of its own. But what is more important, the French-Canadians living in Quebec possess that inner unity of purpose and that sense of their common past and present which are required for any people that desires to be called a distinct nation. So, while accepting bilingualism in federal affairs, we should support the demand that French be the working-language of Quebec.

Only by recognizing these facts, we may hope for a parallel recognition of a similar socio-political truth by the French-Canadians, and by the Quebecois in particular: that our or any other ethnocultural group which possesses a similar self-awareness is indeed a micro-nationality even if it does not have its own territory or legal institutions or both. As Professor Arthur Lermer of Sir George Williams University pointed out in his article, there is a world-wide need for accepting the definition of a nation as it had been formulated by East European sociologists almost 70 years ago rather than to continue using the definition of the sociologists of Anglo-Saxon origin.[12]

Relying on these facts and propositions, let's open up towards our French-speaking co-citizens and say:

We understand your struggle for the survival of your language and culture. We are able to grasp the nuances of that issue because our own people have been involved in a similar struggle for about two centuries. Different as they are, the Ukrainian and the Quebecois cases still bear enough resemblance to elicit from our people a sincere sympathy and active support for your cause.

By the same token, we expect the French-speaking co-citizens to understand and appreciate the motivations of the Ukrainian community here or elsewhere. The Ukrainian-speaking citizens of Canada are trying to preserve and develop their ethnocultural heritage without intending, or causing, any damage to a similar French heritage. There are other just and reasonable motives behind that effort. First, the Ukrainians are individuals, just like French-Canadians, who want to feel and be complete human beings; this aspiration could be achieved only with the help of their own ethnocultural traditions. Second, the Ukrainian-Canadians are preserving their language and culture also for the sake of Ukrainian civilization as such; they want to strengthen the Ukrainian fact in the collective mind of contemporary mankind.

In this respect, the Ukrainian case of ethnocultural identity is much tougher than that of the French-Canadians, difficult though theirs is too. The Ukrainians have been denied, for many decades, even the right to call themselves Ukrainians. Even in

Canada, the term was introduced officially (by Federal Minister of Immigration J. Pickersgill) as late as May 1955, and only after a protracted pressure from all the Ukrainian-Canadian organizations.

The official policy of Russification in the Soviet Union threatens even the 40-million strong Ukrainian nationality there with a linguicide and cultural genocide. Hundreds of Ukrainian intellectuals, professional people, peasants and workers have been recently put behind prison bars in the Soviet Union only because they stood up to the Kremlin which deprives the Ukrainian people of their human rights on their own soil. Unfortunately, many scholarly institutions and mass media in the West still tend to favor the policy of pressing the Ukrainians into the mould of Russian uniformity.

By standing up for the Ukrainian civilization, as a part of their own ethnocultural personality, the Ukrainian-Canadians are standing up for survival of one part of mankind in the same manner as do the French-speaking Canadians, in their own way and for their own kind.

Thus, it would be fair enough to address a Kiplingian question to our French-speaking co-citizens as well: "And what should they know of Quebec who only Quebec know?"

An absolute preoccupation with one's own cause may lead to losing perspective of things and neglecting both natural friends and potential allies. More understanding for the spiritual needs of other ethnocultural groups in Canada and Quebec by the French-speaking society would only help finding practical solution to our common problems, national and provincial. Any lack of such an understanding, and especially any attempt at negative assimilation of these minorities (as once the English majority tried unsuccessfully to impose upon the French here) would only increase the estrangement of these groups from the French fact. Both sides would be losers in the outcome.

Various proposals could be, and will be, forwarded for developing better French-Ukrainian relations here. I would suggest only the following:

— In the field of education, let's proceed from that practical starting point which had been agreed upon in 1965 by the then Quebec Premier Jean Lesage and Senator Paul Yuzyk, as the spokesman of the Ukrainian Canadian Committee, in Winnipeg:

Ukrainian language classes should be offered and financed by the Province of Quebec wherever there is a reasonable demand for them.[13]

—In the field of communication, Quebec French papers and other mass media should devote more space and time to informing the public about their Ukrainian-speaking co-citizens. A French-Ukrainian journal of a most modest size and circulation would be of tremendous importance in developing the mutual reconnaissance. Ukrainian-language papers and radio programs should pay more attention to the French-Canadian issues.

—Regular summer camps and youth exchange programs which would bring together young people of French and Ukrainian milieus both from Quebec and other provinces should be established as soon as possible.

—A Quebec Institute for French-Ukrainian Studies and Research is a must for students and scholars of the two nationalities. If lectures on Ukrainian civilization, literature and language were offered at lower university levels at least; if a scholarly publication were started, in the French language, for the discussion of French-Ukrainian subjects; if scholarships were awarded for those active in studies and research of the two cultures; if journalists and writers would acquire a more sophisticated knowledge of the two civilizations in relation to one another, then—a substantial number of Ukrainian students not only from the Quebec area but also from other provinces would be attracted here to get immersed in the atmosphere of the new inter-ethnic relations. In a few years' time, a number of bilingually-minded young people would be busy spreading the influence of French-Canadian culture across the whole country or even continent. Thus, the number of Quebec friends would be growing while the French-speaking society would acquire a substantial insight into the Ukrainian-speaking element and the Ukrainian civilization with its Canadian aspects.

Seen in this light, multiculturalism must not and need not become a tool for ancient designs aimed at limiting or subduing the French-speaking people on their own territory. On the contrary, this may become a potent instrument for mutually gaining friends. To those who advocate, for Canada or Quebec, a concept of dual uniformity by ordering every minority to select one of the two official melting pots—either English or French—we must address our reasonable appeal:

Only diversity opens up new prospects for all citizens to co-exist and co-operate in mutual respect. The French-speaking people on this continent may get a much better chance of preserving and developing their ethnocultural sovereignty within the concept of diversity than within a system of uniformity—acquired from outside or self-imposed.

Even the United States, for centuries the largest melting pot in the world, is slowly abandoning the concept of uniformity in favour of a dynamic citizenship of culturally different minorities. The Soviet Union is the only, and the last, multinational empire in which uniformity is being effected by coercive methods. The Kremlin leaders, doctrinaires as they are, still are clinging to the dialectical formula of Lenin who, before he knew better, wrote in 1913:

> A struggle against oppression of any nationality—unconditional yes. A struggle for every ethnic development, for any national culture—unconditional no. The proletariat refuses to defend the national development of every nation; on the contrary, the proletariat favors every kind of assimilation of nationalities excepting a forced one or which is rooted in a privilege.[14]

Out of this vicious formula, refuted by science and life itself, grew up the present Soviet system of cultural oppression within which the Ukrainians are carrying the heaviest burden. It would be a pity if in our Confederation, or in any single province, a similar idea of "unity through uniformity" took hold of the informed public opinion. This would lead only to dehumanization of, and subsequent conflicts in, our multicultural society which otherwise has an excellent opportunity to develop itself into a viable example of humane inter-ethnic relations.

Because of their unique experiences, the French-Canadians and Ukrainian-Canadians have a particular responsibility for achieving this desirable and dignified objective.

REFERENCE NOTES

[1]James A. Froude, *The English in Ireland in the Eighteenth Century,* 3 vols. (London: 1872–74), I, 2.

[2]*The Toronto Star,* April 10, 1972.

[3]*Ibid.*

[4]F. R. Scott, *The Canadian Constitutional and Human Rights* (Toronto: 1959).

[5]Cf. Andrew M. Greeley, "The Rediscovery of Diversity," *The Antioch Review,* XXI (Fall 1971), 343–65.

[6]Jack Clarke, "Careful We Don't Isolate Our Ethnic Groups," *The Province* (Vancouver), April 6, 1972.

[7]*The Globe and Mail* (Toronto), March 6, 1972.

[8]*House of Commons Debates,* Vol. II, No. 187, 3rd Sess., 28th Parliament of Canada, October 8, 1971.

[9]Cornelius J. Jaenen, "Canadian Education and Minority Rights," A Paper Presented to the Third National Conference on Canadian Slavs, Toronto, June 15, 1969.

[10]See bibliography in *The Brief* presented to the Ontario Heritage Congress by the Ukrainian Canadian Committee, Ontario Branches, June 2–4, 1972.

[11]*House of Commons Debates, op. cit.,* March 16, 1972.

[12]*The Gazette* (Montreal), April 22, 1972.

[13]See *Le Devoir* (Montreal), December 29, 1965.

[14]V. I. Lenin, "Critical Remarks on the National Question," *Collected Works* (4th ed.; Moscow: 1964), XX, 35.

43

THE INVISIBLE ETHNIC

During the past decade or so, I have sometimes stayed awake late thinking of Canada as a living concept. A growing anxiety would then envelop me — an anxiety I believed that millions of Canadians shared. They still do so, I think, even though I myself have somewhat subdued my own fearful worries.

Mind you, not that any of us ever felt nightmarishly afraid! We have encountered too many dangers in our earlier lives to be "scared." But, thinking about tomorrow's Canada (which must be an outcrop of today's Canada) our anxiety concerned our descendants in the maple-leafed country we had chosen as home.

We never wanted them (our children) to trudge the same path — the hard trail of uprooted persons — we had been obliged to follow. Nor did we wish them to be exposed to the undisguised and disguised discrimination and assimilatory patterns many of us had had to face in the not too distant past.

We sincerely and naturally hoped they would be treated as Canadian citizens without any kind of stigma attached to them because of their origin or variegated cultural background.

That's why we had been searching, as once our predecessors did, for a country where a man or a woman would

Reprinted with permission from *The Montreal Star*, May 12, 1973, where it appeared under the title "Uneasy Lies The 'Ethnic' As Founding Nations Stir Their Melting Pots."

feel a whole person—sovereign in thought and in legal act: Equals among equals pragmatically speaking.

As we looked for firm ground in which to plant our family roots, hopefully to flourish in a new climate, we were also deeply concerned about the constitutional guarantees that would preserve the rights which had been denied to many of us in our countries of birth. Above all, *the right to be one-self.*

For this reason so many "third-language" Canadians, impressed by John Diefenbaker's Canadian Bill of Human Rights in 1960, found the measure a hopeful vista.

From then on we were able to hope to become, and remain, loyal citizens of this country without losing, or having to mislay, our own identity.

Similarly, the policy of multiculturalism, announced by Prime Minister Pierre Trudeau in October 1971, found even stronger resonance in the hearts of about five million Canadians whose cultural background was other than British or French. In that policy, acclaimed by the leaders of the opposition parties in Parliament, we saw a step on the road towards what might be called human expression on its face.

The latter observation should not be taken as a dubious reflection on the quality of the citizenship about which many well-deserved praises have been sung by native and adopted citizens of this country.

In comparison with other countries, Canadian citizenship certainly ranks high in the minds of "ethnic" people.

Ukrainian immigrants, for one, have found here, more than anywhere else, the most favorable conditions for their survival, even compared with those in the United States.

But no eulogy should camouflage frailties. Even the most silvery cloud has its dark lining, they say.

And in this case *the dark lining* is that still far too many "third-language" Canadians feel rootless, appearances to the contrary.

Not that "ethnics" are visibly discriminated against, but rather because they are at worst ignored, or at best sedulously tolerated by what are called Canada's two founding nations.

This feeling of rejection is familiar to French-Canadians who, it is obvious, still nurse the wounds inflicted by centuries-long confrontation with Anglophones both in their own "pays" Quebec and in other provinces of a vast land they helped to discover, explore, and construct.

The "third-language" Canadians, to their own consternation, rarely realized the schizoid nature of the French-Canadian plight until the early 1960s: A neglect demonstrating how removed they had been from one of the realities of Canada's social structure.

Neither "founder" regarded their interest or sympathy worthwhile enough to be recruited.

As potential allies, as participants in debate, *we were paper puppies.*

British-oriented Canadians regarded it the only duty of any "third-language" Canadian—immigrants and their descendants—to merge with the Anglophone ranks, thus balancing the French-Canadian strategy based on high birth-rate and known as "revenge of the cradle"—their fecund means of gaining advantage over the British.

The French-Canadians on the whole detested the newcomers from Europe because they seemed much too eager to play the role of psychological mercenaries in that indigenous war of two cultures. The "neos" were too easily mustered to swell the opponents' ranks.

No wonder then that the powerful resurgence of the French-Canadian fact, and its subsequent meek acceptance (almost overnight) by the mighty "British-Canadians," took the non-English and non-French-Canadians by surprise. Soon, however, their amazement was replaced by the realization that there would be two melting pots to cope with instead of the previous single cauldron.

Now, how can we explain to "belligerent" French-Canadians that their claim to an equal share in the spoils of assimilation of the "other-language settlers," and their descendants, leaves the latter with the same spiritual trauma the French-Canadians themselves had suffered, and, as they claim, are still suffering from?

What is unpalatable sauce for the goose is equally unpalatable for the gander.

And how can we explain to English-Canadians—by now haunted by the specter of the growing French fact—the feeling of dejection felt by the "third-language" Canadians left in a pointed dilemma after decades of having been mobilized against a determined French resurgence of cultural identity?

As American sociologists begin discovering something of value in Canada's "cultural islands" and "Canadian cultural ghettos" (to quote Vance Packard among others), "third-language" Canadians find themselves abandoned in a no man's land between two opponents—by now formally raised to the status of two founding nations.

The "third-language" Canadians have no constitutional guarantees shoring up either their desire or their right to be themselves as sovereign human beings.

Yet, they do not wish to continue existing as "ethnics," especially in a world of the increasing visibility of once "invisible" nationalities, and hence "invisible" individuals who oppose any shattering of their cultural values.

To be regarded as an "ethnic" was, and still is, to be in an even harsher position than that occupied by the French-Canadians in the stone age of a complacent unilingual Canada.

It means—for a Pole, a Ukrainian, a Slovak, or any other non-British Canadian—the danger of being relegated to the bottom rung of the cultural, social, and political ladder.

Cultural treasures of these people have been treated as folklore oddities rather than as specific achievements rooted in the soul of a distinctive nationality with a centuries-long civilization of their own.

Thus, no one I know in Canada would disparage English square dances, kilts, or shamrock. No one would urge the abandonment of these stirring symbols of three different groups in the English-language segment of Canada's population.

But Ukrainian dances, embroideries, and artistic Easter eggs are still regarded by many as a sign of "old country" parochialism to be shed like dust from shoes as soon as one's foot touches the Canadian shore. The more sympathetic regard them as quaint whimsicalities.

Moreover, the prejudiced view that Ukrainians are an unhistoric nationality devoid of its own culture still prevails even in the enlightened circles here.

The decision of the secretary of state department to drop the term "ethnic" from all its documentation last year was, therefore, a milestone on the road to Canadian citizenship with a more human face. On that road, either no one or everybody should be regarded as "ethnic"—be they English, French, Welsh, Irish, Jewish, Polish, Slovak, Ukrainian, Italian, Greek, etc. No one should be put outside the pale of the Canadian cultural spectrum, bilingual yet multicultural, for the sole reason of not belonging to one of the founding nations.

The program of financial support for the preservation and development of all viable "third-language" cultures has a greater value than the actual money involved—that originally assigned early in 1972 and the increased sum granted by the reconstructed government of Pierre Trudeau.

It is a clear sign of an official recognition—to be eventually approved by the taxpayers at large—that being a Polish-Canadian (any hyphenated Canadian) is as dignified a status as that of being an English- or French-Canadian.

The psychological impact of such a notion (organized in a practical manner), on the minds of young Canadians of any language group can hardly be overestimated.

Bilingualism would get a boost because young people would start believing that the concept is not just another gimmick intended to keep together artificially something which could not have been preserved by a former imperial idea. Aiming at loyalty through personal dignity, one would say: Strengthen the individual citizen by recognizing and allowing him to express what is his cultural core, and you will strengthen the confederate state more successfully than by any other set of policies.

That is the thesis.

However, what worries "third-language" Canadians is the growing suspicion that the policy of multiculturalism may equally be viewed as just another stratagem for wooing the "ethnic" voters.

To be sure, no one doubts the sincerity of the architects of the policy; they did what they believed to be just and necessary for Canada. Nevertheless, there was no debate during the last election campaign, which would have clarified the primary issue of the problem: the need for constitutional guarantees for the "third-language" groups.

More specifically, neither the Progressive Conservative Party nor the New Democratic Party has included in its program any form of multicultural policy. The silence may be interpreted strategically as an attempt not to alienate French-Canadians in Quebec who had declared themselves against multi-culturalism.

Such an approach is mistaken and shows the inability of the two parties to fathom the mood of their French-Canadian co-citizens. The present-day government of Quebec, like any other future government there, would do a great deal — and does — for the "third language" groups of the province. What it opposes is the encroachment of the federal authorities in the field. And this means that the old fear of the "ethnics" of being used as a balancing factor against the French by the "centralists of Ottawa" is still very much alive in Quebec.

But even the English-language provinces which have put a great effort into the elucidation of a multicultural Canada are lagging.

The Ontario government supported a large Heritage Ontario Congress last June. A similar conference on multiculturalism was held in Alberta and its recommendations were upheld by the new Conservative administration. But, as Professor M. R. Lupul[1] of Alberta University remarked, neither has lifted a finger yet to put into practice the precepts they seemingly have embraced.

As to the enlightened Canadian public, the "dialogue" between the spokesmen of the two founding nations continues as a series of monologues. Almost without exception they talk over the heads of the "ethnics" as if no "third-language" groups really existed in Canada's population. They speak solely about and for their respective melting pots.

Thus, after a decade of searching for a workable formula of Canadianism, inspiring loyalty through personal dignity, millions of Canadians sit and think late into the night.

They know it to be true what Ortega y Gasset understood so well — *that language and culture are something more than just labels.*

Since they are not sure whether their legislators and public opinionmakers know this and hold it to be true, they are wondering: Must Canada become a nation of strangers. . . ?

That's what they are still afraid of.

Can you blame them?[2]

REFERENCE NOTES

[1]Professor M. R. Lupul, Director of the Canadian Institute of Ukrainian Studies established at Alberta University with a financial grant from the Alberta Provincial Government in 1975.

[2]This article was quoted extensively in the Canada's House of

Commons debates on May 30, 1973 by Dr. Stanley Haidasz, Minister of State for Multiculturalism, and Marcel Prudhomme, Parliamentary Secretary to Minister of Regional Economic Expansion. See, *House of Commons Debates,* Vol. 117, No. 92, 1st Sess., 29th Parliament of Canada, May 30, 1973.

44

TO UKRAINIANS, HE IS A MAN
FOR ALL SEASONS

The man who withstood Stalin's pressure and nowadays, like Samson pushing against two columns in a Philistines' temple, continues keeping the Vatican and the Kremlin apart, recently has visited his faithful in North America. And both the Canadian and the American Ukrainian Catholics, together almost 1,000,000 persons, are paying him the respect reserved only for a living martyr.

Well, His Beautitude Archbishop Major Cardinal Josyf Slipyj is indeed a martyr.

But meeting him face to face, as I did in early May in Toronto, you wouldn't even guess that the stately-looking 81-year-old prelate spent almost 18 years in the prisons and hard-labor camps of Soviet Russia. And, as he told me himself, at a crucial point during his imprisonment his life was saved by a Jewish camp doctor in the vicinity of the nefarious Vorkuta slave-camps center.

Written for and distributed by Southam News Services, this article appeared in several newspapers across Canada: *The Ottawa Citizen, The Windsor Star, The Edmonton Journal, The Calgary Herald,* and *The Gazette* (Montreal), July 2, 1973. Here, it is reprinted with permission of *The Gazette* and the Southam News Services.

Freed by John

Eventual release from the Soviet prison system was arranged for Cardinal Slipyj, then the Metropolitan of Lviv, by a man named John, better known as Pope John XXIII.[1]

To the spiritual princes of the Roman Catholic Church, gathered at their Second Vatican Council in 1963, it must have been quite an experience to see and hear the former Soviet prisoner pleading for the establishment of an autonomous Ukrainian Patriarchate within the framework of the Universal Church.

But unusual as it might have seemed to their legalistic minds, proposal was yet another proof of the man's steadfastness that makes him, perhaps, the strongest personality in the modern Catholic world.

Pope John XXIII was well aware of the fact. He appeared to favor the idea of a Ukrainian Patriarchate, which would unite all the bishoprics in Canada, the United States, Argentina, Brazil, Australia, France, Britain, and West Germany. Its autonomous existence would enhance the Vatican's credibility among the Eastern Christians, and particularly among the Ukrainians who persist in their fidelity to the Holy See even under the Soviet regime.

Altered Scene

That is why Metropolitan Josyf Slipyj was nominated Archbishop Major, a title close in authority to that of Patriarch.

But the untimely death of Pope John made way for a more conservative leadership in the Vatican. Under Pope Paul, it believes more in *Realpolitik* than in martyrdom. And ecumenism, being a form of rapprochement between various Christian denominations, favors the established churches, the Roman Catholic, the Anglican, and the Russian Orthodox rather than the Ukrainian Uniate Church, which has been living between the hammer of militant Polish Catholicism and the anvil of militant Russian Orthodoxy since its union with Rome in 1596.

Thus, while Archbishop Major Josyf Slipyj was made a

cardinal and was allowed to build the Ukrainian Church of St. Sophia as well as to organize a new Ukrainian Catholic University in Rome, mostly with funds sent by Ukrainians around the world, he has been hampered in his efforts to establish a working Ukrainian Catholic Patriarchate.

Duties Impeded

"We are impeded in our duties," Archbishop Slipyj told the Third International Synod of Bishops in 1971. "The Ukrainian Catholics who have suffered so much and for so long as martyrs and confessors are ignored by the Vatican as inconvenient witnesses of past evils."

True enough, the Ukrainian Catholic, or Uniate Church, was liquidated by the Kremlin in 1946. Five bishops and many of the higher clergy died in Soviet prisons and hard-labor camps. Its faithful and some priests were compelled to join the Russian Orthodox Church. Metropolitan Josyf Slipyj was the only senior member to survive the ordeal.

But the martyrdom of a whole church failed to carry the day for him in the Vatican. When the Ukrainian Catholic bishops from every country of Ukrainian settlement, at their own Synod of Rome in 1969, unanimously supported his demand for putting into practice what the Second Vatican Council decreed on the issue, the synod was declared "invalid" by the Vatican authorities. Yet, it continues to exist as a unit in spite of the invalidation.

Moscow's Price

The main reason for that somewhat strange behavior of the spokesmen of the Universal Church is the Vatican's desire to arrive at some *modus vivendi* both with the Moscow Patriarchate and the Kremlin.

And the two—"the most orthodox" Russian hierarchy and the "godless" Kremlin establishment—go hand in hand whenever the Ukrainian question of spiritual sovereignty is concerned.

Being centralist by its nature and mindful of its precarious symbiosis with the Soviet regime, the Moscow church hierarchy demands from the Vatican, as a price for the offered detente with Roman Catholicism, the abandoning of the Ukrainian Catholics in the Soviet Ukraine altogether and suppression of all the efforts of the emigre bishops at the unification of all Ukrainian Catholic bishoprics in the countries of the West.

Unconsulted

The Vatican has responded in kind. When the Russian Patriarch Pimen declared at Zagorsk, on June 2, 1971, that the Ukrainian Catholic Church had ceased to exist, Cardinal Willebrands, present at the gathering as a guest, remained silent. And there was no reaction of the Vatican authorities to Patriarch Pimen's unilateral declaration. Moreover, Pope Paul VI started nominating new Ukrainian bishops for Brazil and the United States without even consulting Archbishop Major Slipyj, the only one entitled to make such a decision for the Ukrainian Church.

I had known Archbishop Slipyj many years before his imprisonment as an eminent scholar, talented administrator, and a man of great integrity. Meeting him in Toronto again, I was impressed by his undiminished purposefulness.

As if honed by the martyrdom in Stalin's Russia, Archbishop Slipyj is more than ever bent on saving the Ukrainian Catholic Church from the two-pronged danger: from getting buried under the structure of the Russian Church in the Soviet Union and from being submerged under the assimilatory sea of Roman Catholicism in the West.

Nothing Illegal

"We are not doing anything revolutionary or illegal by demanding a patriarchate for our beleaguered church. On the contrary, we only demand what is due to the church according to the agreements made by our predecessors with the Apostolic See . . ., and what was acknowledged by the Second Vatican Council," said Archbishop Slipyj at a conference during his visit to Toronto.

In this resolve, he is enthusiastically supported by about two million Ukrainian Catholics residing in the coun·ries outside the Kremlin's immediate influence.

Meanwhile the Orthodox Ukrainians, whose autocephalous church was savagely destroyed by the Soviet regime in the early 1930s, are watching in disbelief the tribulations of their Catholic brethren caught between the Moscow hammer and the Vatican anvil.

REFERENCE NOTES

[1]Josyf Slipyj, Metropolitan of Lviv (Ukraine), arrested in 1944 and sentenced to 25 years of hard labor and incarceration; spent 18 years in Soviet prisons and labor camps before being freed in December 1962 by Khrushchev on the intervention of Pope John XXIII, and permitted to go abroad. For a description of the events and people surrounding his release, see Norman Cousins, "Notes on a 1963 Visit with Khrushchev," *Saturday Review,* XLVII (November 7, 1964), 16-21; and especially his "The Improbable Triumvirate: Khrushchev, Kennedy, and Pope John," *Saturday Review,* LIV (October 30, 1971), 24-35. Upon release from incarceration in the Soviet Union, Metropolitan Slipyj was elevated to Archbishop Major, a special position created for him by Pope John XXIII (1963), and to a Cardinal (1965) by Pope Paul VI.

INDEX

ABOUT THE AUTHOR

ROMAN RAKHMANNY is the pen-name of a Ukrainian journalist, broadcaster, and essayist. He was born in Western Ukraine where he received his secondary and university education; he did his graduate work in Canada, where he took his MA degree (University of Toronto) and a Ph.D. (University of Montreal) in Slavistics.

His early years were intimately connected with the Ukrainian liberation movement; during World War II, he took an active part in the Ukrainian anti-Nazi and anti-Soviet resistance. Immediately after the war, he directed a semi-legal news service, Ukrainian Press Service (UPS), providing news of military and political resistance in the Ukraine to West European publications, and edited two Ukrainian-language newspapers.

In 1949, Roman Rakhmanny settled in Canada, where he edited a newspaper and kept a weekly column in several Ukrainian-language papers. His commentaries and essays have appeared in major newspapers of Western Europe and North America in a number of languages (Dutch, English, French, German, and Norwegian). He is a recipient of the First Prize for political commentary from the American-Ukrainian Journalists Association (1973), and the Taras Shevchenko Medal for "outstanding contribution to the preservation of Ukrainian identity" from the Ukrainian Canadian Committee (1974). He is a member of the Ukrainian Free Academy of Sciences (UVAN-Canada), the Shevchenko Scientific Society, the Czechoslovak Society of Arts and Sciences in the USA, and the International PEN Club. *In Defense of the Ukrainian Cause* is a selection from his writings published over a period of thirty years.